DEFENDING THE DEVIL

My Story as
Ted Bundy's Last Lawyer

POLLY NELSON

WILLIAM MORROW AND COMPANY, INC.
New York

Transcripts of court proceedings and interviews reproduced herein have been edited for clarity. The names of minor children have been changed to protect their privacy.

Library of Congress Cataloging-in-Publication Data

Nelson, Polly, 1952–
    Defending the devil : my story as Ted Bundy's last lawyer / by Polly Nelson.
        p.   cm.
    ISBN 0-688-10823-7
    1. Bundy, Ted—Trials, litigation, etc.   2. Trials (Murder)—Florida.   3. Capital punishment—Florida.   4. Nelson, Polly, 1952– .
    5. Lawyers—United States—Biography.   I. Title.
    KF224.B86N45   1994
    345.759'02523—dc20
    [347.59052523]   93-23411
                                                                          CIP

Printed in the United States of America   345.759
                                               62523
First Edition   Nels

1 2 3 4 5 6 7 8 9 10

BOOK DESIGN BY PAUL CHEVANNES

DEFENDING THE DEVIL

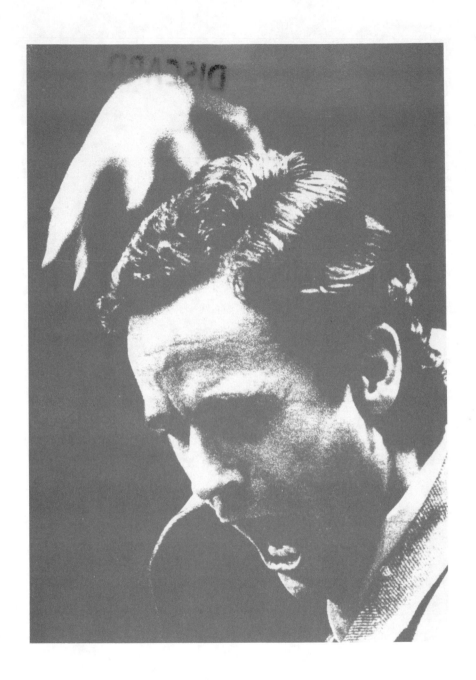

DEFENDING THE DEVIL

Bundy Executed

IÏ 3Ï

By Susan Lamb
Staff writer

The nation's most despised killer died in Florida's electric chair Tuesday morning for the brutal murder of a 12-year-old Lake City junior high school student.

The death of Ted Bundy came nearly 11 years after Kimberly Dianne Leach was kidnapped from Lake City Junior High School Feb. 9, 1978, strangled to death, and her body left in an abandoned shed near the Suwannee River State Park in Suwannee County.

In the most widely covered execution ever held in the nation, Bundy was taken to the chair just minutes before he was scheduled to die. A calm, resigned Bundy was strapped into the chair in front of 18 official state witnesses, including the men who prosecuted him for Leach's murder: Third Circuit State Attorney Jerry Blair, Assistant State Attorney Bob Dekle, and now Eighth Circuit State Attorney Len Register. About a dozen other witnesses crowded into the small, glassed in room to watch Bundy die.

Outside the high fence that surrounds Florida State Prison in Starke, a contingent of several hundred Columbia County residents and others from throughout Florida a-waited until word was received of Bundy's death before letting out a cheer. The moments after the execution was marked by fireworks, singing, and an atmosphere of thankfulness that Bundy was finally dead.

In contrast to previous executions, not one person against the death penalty was at the prison.

The 24 hours preceding Bundy's death were agonizing for the killer, his defense attorneys, James Coleman Jr. and Polly Nelson, of Washington D.C., who worked desperately to save their client, and the state, who worked equally as hard to see that the execution came off on time.

A last minute appeal was brought before Chief Third Circuit Judge John Peach at the Madison County Courthouse Monday morning but was denied. Blair said Coleman filed the appeal in Columbia County and didn't appear at the hearing, but rather was involved telephonically. Blair drove to Madison to attend the hearing in the judge's chambers where Coleman was hooked up via telephone. That motion was denied. The motion contended that former Circuit Judge Wallace Jopling, the trial judge in the Leach case, improperly considered a sentencing brief in the Chi Omega murder case in Tallahassee before he sentenced him for the Leach murder.

The Florida Supreme Court and the U.S. Supreme Court all failed to come through for the defense on the motion later Monday.

A last ditch effort that had been expected by Gov. Bob Martinez, Blair and Attorney General Bob Butterworth's office, never came as the hours ticked away. The state had expected defense attorneys to file a late motion Monday night saying Bundy was insane and could not be executed. Three psychiatrists were flown from Miami in the early afternoon Monday to the prison where they waited to examine Bundy if the motion came.

Before Bundy died, he reportedly talked with investigators from several northwestern states, detailing in the third person murders of at least 20 women. In all of the cases, Bundy withheld information in an effort to buy himself more time, Blair said. "Apparently he's back to playing games again," Blair said Monday afternoon.

The execution brings to a close a criminal career that may have started as a child exposed to alleged abuse and pornography, and certainly continued until Bundy's arrest in Pensacola in 1978.

"It looks like he was born to kill," said one investigator who talked with Bundy before he died.

PROLOGUE

Three weeks after Ted was executed, one of the managing partners of the law firm called me to his office. That was unusual in itself. When I arrived, he greeted me warmly, shook my hand, and invited me to sit down. From his corner office on the ninth floor, with a view beyond his balcony of the steeples and rooftops of Georgetown, the world looked very manageable.

He said that, first of all, he wanted to congratulate me on a job exceptionally well done on the Bundy case. Probably no other lawyer in the firm would have been able to handle a case like that, he said, or stick with it to the end. Then he passed an envelope to me and said that it contained my annual evaluation, and that he was glad to see the comments were all very favorable, a marked improvement over the previous evaluation. He hesitated before he went on.

One more thing, he said, finally. Now that the Bundy case is over, you should give some thought to what direction you'd like your career to go in from here. I said I would do that, having realized earlier that I had to develop a new specialty.

There was another telling moment of silence.

In fact, he began again, we should probably discuss some sort of time frame. Whatever seems fair—three months, six months. You should be able to find a job by then. You understand, he said, strictly from a practice-management point of view, you couldn't be allowed to stay at the firm indefinitely.

I went back to the few paying cases I had and tried to set about looking for a new job, but I hadn't been able to do much of anything since the execution. It had been bad enough before, but now I could barely lift a pen or compose a sentence. I was afraid to return phone calls. I kept expecting to feel better with time, now that the execution was behind me and I was finally relieved of the responsibility of saving Ted's life. Instead, I felt worse. When I could not work another day, I left. But that didn't solve my problem.

Representing Ted Bundy certainly was the case of a lifetime—just not exactly in the way I thought it would be.

PART I

CHAPTER 1

I was born to represent Ted Bundy.

From an early age, it was important to me to meet the needs of others, particularly those who seemed unhappy. I was the apple of my unhappy parents' eyes and I wanted to make them happy. When I was two years old, it is often told, my mother and father laughed so hard when I fell off the couch that I crawled back up and fell off again. And again and again.

When I was ten, I kept a "Home for Retired Worms" in the backyard. Not because I liked worms, but because I thought that it must be a terrible thing to be so ugly and despicable. My grandfather was a Lutheran pastor whose social ministry was informed by Christ's words: *Whatever you do for the least of them, you do for me.* Worms seemed to qualify. I watered a patch of ground, made a nice mud bath, and brought to it worms that had been stranded on the sidewalk after a rain. I wanted them not to feel so alone and ashamed to be worms, as they surely must. And, of course, if I was helping them, making them feel better about themselves, I had nothing to fear from them myself.

I grew up in central Minnesota, an oldest child with four younger siblings and two parents with problems of their own. Growing up, the needs of those six people seemed more important than my own. The benefit of my position as the competent person making other people feel better was obvious: I was a *very important person* in my family. The down side was harder for me to see. I had no clue as to my own feelings, needs, or wants, other than to be perfect and useful, a disappointment to no one. The absence of personal fulfillment or contentment didn't seem any reason to worry, however. I was sure it would come to me. One day I'd feel like myself, know what I liked, what I wanted for myself. Real Life would then begin.

It didn't begin in college. I floundered for six years while earning my undergraduate degree, unable to settle on a major. For one thing, it seemed to me morally wrong to seek a degree like everyone else. As I was already a *very* important person, it was untoward to accept such superfluous trappings. At first I was interested in statistics, then I dropped out to become a weaver, studying in Sweden and traveling the art fair circuit. When I returned to school, I began to work toward becoming an art teacher, but nobody would talk about the *why* of teaching art. What *problem* were we trying to solve? I couldn't get myself interested unless someone had a problem they needed me to solve. I switched to child psychology, where the problems were.

As graduation unavoidably approached, I still had not found anything inside of me to act as a guide. I had no desires of my own that I could discern. In lieu of a discernible career preference, I took all the civil service tests I qualified for; the first response came from the director of a small county welfare agency in northern Minnesota. I had no training in social work; my child psychology classes had been theoretical rather than clinical. But, as an oldest child, I was sure I knew everything and could do anything. Social work also was a family tradition among the clergy and laypeople on my mother's side of the family. The job offer had a certain ring of inevitability to it. At the Marshall County Welfare Department, in Warren, Minnesota, my moral responsibilities grew from my family of six to a hundred troubled strangers, and I seemed to see in all of them a hurt child longing to be acknowledged. I somehow couldn't detach appropriately. When I had to remove children from an abusive home, I felt the pain of the parents, the emptiness of their home, the longing of the children to return. I'd feel it all night and on the weekend. How could I be happy, enjoy myself in my off-time, if I was responsible for such unhappiness? I found temporary absolution in the rural taverns where farmers wait out the winter.

After two years of direct social work, I was beat. I had tormented my involuntary clients with unwanted home visits; I had felt totally responsible for their lives; and I had never felt I was doing enough. I couldn't be objective. I became too involved. I felt too inadequate when I found I really couldn't do anything to change someone's destiny. I moved back to St. Paul and to the Minnesota Department of Public Welfare (DPW) for the next three years, licensing day-care facilities. There I wasn't directly responsible for anyone. I should have been relieved, but instead the job felt empty and meaningless. I felt selfish, self-indulgent, enervated, and adrift. I continued to drink.

If I at least had a little wider range of influence, I thought, perhaps I'd feel fulfilled and life would begin for me. Since social work had fallen out of favor by then and DPW was top-heavy with masters of social work with no place to go, I decided to get a law degree to stand out in the pack, become a certified smart person. Maybe then I'd have a chance to be promoted to a policy position, and the power to make real changes in the welfare system would give me satisfaction at last.

I had one final social work hurrah, just before I left—a pure shot of caretaking adrenalin. The state hospital employees had gone on strike, and we bureaucrats at DPW were sent to watch over the patients. One nurse and I were in charge of forty or so severely disabled mentally ill patients, most of them lobotomized during the great psychiatric experiments of the 1950s and now brain-fried by the resulting seizures. I played the guitar for them, watched the royal wedding of Charles and Diana with them (some claimed to be related to the groom), and served doughnuts if they would sit down like ladies and gentlemen. At night I drank to oblivion with the other management temps. It was a perfect existence. I was needed, and I was stuck there. No need to figure out what I should do or what I was supposed to want to do day-to-day. I felt the nearest I had ever felt to being fully alive.

Law school was a little like that, too. I started at the University of Minnesota in the fall of 1981, when I was twenty-nine years old. I was still single. Although I'd tried, I hadn't found a man who was willing to solve the problem for me of who I was. Short of that, I could only try to mind read in a relationship—guess at how the other person thought I was supposed to act—which made everything very compli- cated for both of us. Law school was my refuge. Three years spoken for, no real decisions to make, no other responsibilities, not trying to change anyone; Real Life suspended until after graduation. I enjoyed it very much. And because I enjoyed it, because (unlike for most law students) law school represented not a burden but a freedom from obligation, I did pretty well.

I scrupulously avoided any subject having to do with direct service to people, courses like family law and criminal law. The one thing I knew for certain was that I would never again take on another individual's intractable personal problems. When I wrote for the law review, I chose the driest, most masculine subject I could find: the definition of buildings and structural components for purposes of the investment tax credit. The next year, as president of the review, I ushered into publication even more esoteric business articles—the more useless and distant from the lives of real human beings the better. By the time graduation neared, my horizons had expanded beyond my wildest dreams, certainly beyond DPW and home. I had no idea what else I might want to do with my law degree, but when the offers came in from big law firms in the big cities, I saw a ticket out of my old life and into *Real Life*. Surely this would all lead somewhere, somewhere I'd feel at home in my own skin.

After a year's judicial clerkship—which was boring and tedious and where real life definitely did not begin—I went on to Wilmer, Cutler & Pickering in Washington. I had worked there for a few weeks the summer after my second year of law school, and although I actually had a better time the next summer, which I had spent in New York at Cleary, Gottlieb, Steen & Hamilton, I was suspicious of that. Going back to Cleary, where I'd had so much fun and had felt so welcome, seemed, well, too obviously appealing to be the proper choice. Beware of pretty baubles, I thought. I guessed that the reason I'd been lonely and ignored at Wilmer was that the lawyers there had such rich personal lives that they couldn't be bothered entertaining summer associates. That was what I wanted for myself.

Wilmer, Cutler & Pickering is one of those Washington law firms that major corporations turn to when they are in really big trouble. The very name evokes sighs and reverential murmurs from knowledgeable lawyers of all types. A corporate firm of 150 stellar lawyers, Wilmer was renowned for taking on complicated, cutting-edge litigation usually involving pivotal matters of public policy. To support that kind of challenge, the firm had the policy and unquestioned ability to leave no stone unturned in pursuing the client's interest. No expense was spared either, and they charged accordingly. As a result, they were paying the top going rate that year for new law associates: forty thousand dollars a year—nearly three times my social work salary. On my way into town I bought my first brand-new, store-bought bed mattress in celebration of my luxurious new life to come, and moved right into an unbelievably good rental deal: I shared a fabulous six-bedroom townhouse with only one other woman for $450 a month. I wasted no time in fulfilling another fantasy by registering for regular facials at Tatyana's Skin Care Salon, whose hand-lettered sign in the second-story window above the health foods store on P Street attracted me immediately: It looked like a salon with integrity.

At Wilmer I was assigned to the PIER group: products liability, insurance, environmental, and other regulation. My first task was to research the rules and regulations for frozen dairy products; I told my mother that if I'd known I could be doing ice cream law, I might have gone to law school sooner. My other work involved exacting research on minute issues of obscure environmental law. It wasn't always as glamorous as it sounds.

Naturally, I took it upon myself immediately upon arrival at Wilmer to organize the other new associates. I naturally assumed they were unhappy and needed my attention. I got the firm to sponsor a Christmas party at my new home which easily held the hundred or so people who attended. Ordering enough liquor had been my first priority. At the party—at which I did feel as if Real Life had begun—a partner told me, without any particular judgment or emphasis, "You're drunk, and you were drunk the last time I saw you."

I had been waiting for someone to notice. I now could not go without a drink—without as many drinks as I could drink before passing out—after work. That part didn't feel like real life. Worse, sometimes "after work" was still *at* work, with the firm's frequent "happy hours." I was terrified of the impending consequences. I had managed to move forward in my life, jumping from ice floe to ice floe without seeming to fail, and I did not want to humiliate myself on this job. It seemed to be my last best chance to find—or at least invent—myself. I had no Plan B.

In early February 1986 I quit drinking with the firmest resolve ever, with the intention of drying out for six months and regaining some control. With that the last apparent barrier to real life eliminated, I expected great things.

Instead, I got Ted.

CHAPTER 2

Although eventually I realized I was born to represent Ted Bundy, when I first got the case it seemed quite accidental. It was sometime after eight o'clock on Tuesday evening, February 21, 1986. I'd come to that dreaded part of the now familiar pattern of working late at the office when I'd run out of delay tactics and would finally have to face the tedious task at hand. I'd already eaten my usual take-out Chinese dinner (Szechuan green beans, extra spicy, no meat) ordered through the firm's spectacularly helpful services department, and it was too soon to go stare at the snack machine. I didn't know anyone to call locally—I hadn't yet developed that rich personal life I'd expected. And I had already talked to my mother on her toll-free phone line at work. There was only one thing left to do: I turned to gaze out the window into the night.

I was facing a typical Wilmer brainteaser. It was a standard first-year-associate-size assignment: a single paragraph for a possible footnote to a draft comment on proposed agency rule-making. And, like most of what a first-year associate at a big law firm writes, it would probably be cut before the document made it to the client. This night I was supposed to compose a simple, matter-of-fact statement illuminating how one particularly explicit phrase in an especially tightly drawn environmental regulation did not mean what it so clearly said, but,

18

instead, meant the opposite. I was to show that it meant exactly what our corporate client needed it to mean in order to continue to dispose of its toxic waste in the usual manner: Into the public water supply. This was not supposed to be difficult to write. The partner who had assigned it to me could have drafted it while also filling out his time-sheet and barking orders to his secretary. But I was still new, still training to be a regulatory lawyer in the firm, and the task fell to me.

I'd kept my office purposely dark that night, except for my desk lamp. I thought the blanket of darkness, with only a pinpoint of light, would focus my mind by spotlighting my pile of cases and every legislative burp interpreting every law and regulation with similar lan-guage or intent. Practicing law the Wilmer way. But here I was staring out the window, commiserating with my own image in an eerie chiar-oscuro, my face and hair rendered a garish yellow by the desk lamp, my shaded eyes looking back at me. Accusingly. When I turned around to face my desk, a strange figure loomed in the doorway.

It took me a second to make out who it was, standing there backlit by the hall light.

"Working late?" the bulky form said. It was Jeff Robinson, the associate from two doors down. Jeff had never stopped by before; he'd apparently not felt obliged to make a fuss over or even greet a new associate, as was the custom. He was a black man and quiet, and I knew he had done some civil rights work. I'd figured he'd had weightier things on his mind than making small talk with me. I was pleased, then, that he'd stopped by to say hello tonight.

It turned out he had a purpose.

"Wanna little pro bono project?" he asked.

Hallelujah! Another diversion from the work at hand, like manna from heaven. "Sure," I answered, without hesitation.

That's it. That's how simply I was ambushed by Destiny.

I was surprised Jeff had thought to ask me. I was extremely flattered he believed I could handle something on my own already. Jeff knew exactly what a new lawyer on the law-review-clerkship-big-law-firm track typically knows about the law: everything in the abstract and nothing in particular. So I assumed it must have been some personal characteristic in me he'd noticed from afar that made him think I was equipped to handle a pro bono matter.

Not so.

As Jeff explained when he'd settled with a sigh of relief in the chair by my door, he had made a list of all the new associates and was going to approach them one by one until he found a taker. Since I was situated closest to his office, he came to me first. It wasn't until much later I understood why Jeff was only going to approach the *new* associates, and why he thought this pro bono case would be such a hard sell. The case was not going to be partnership-track material. But I didn't know that. In fact, when Jeff went on to explain what type of case it was, I thought it was *exactly* what law is for.

"It's a death penalty case," he said. "A guy down in Florida is scheduled to be executed on March fourth and needs a stay in the Supreme Court."

I bonded instantly to this endangered stranger, whoever he was. I pictured him alone in a dark cell, looking death in the face, as frightened as imaginable, his inner child trembling in complete terror.

"You remember Ted Bundy?" Jeff asked.

"Sort of. Which one was he, the guy who killed the nurses in Chicago?"

"No, that was someone else, Richard Speck, maybe. Bundy was the one with the coeds in Florida."

"Oh, uh huh."

I didn't have a firm recollection, but it didn't matter. Jeff said more about the case, but most of it slipped past me. I really didn't care who the client was or what the case would entail, as long as it was different from what I was doing right now, something that would be real and active and wouldn't feel like a mental grindstone. A fresh problem to tackle, one I could really get involved with. I believed in this cause— saving a life. It would energize me. Real Life Would Begin.

Obviously, accepting such a case was enough work for one night. As soon as Jeff left, I turned off the light on the precarious heap of untouched regulatory materials on my desk and went home.

One might think I would have paused here to consider if I were qualified to take this case; to ask how much work it would be; to think about whether I might have a tendency to get overly involved in a case like this—that it might drag me down like my attempts at social work had. But I didn't. Being a lawyer, armed with the useful and dependable framework of rules that is the law, would make all the difference, I thought. My job would be technical, not psychological; I'd have concrete tools to work with. And unlike my past attempts to help others, the client would do as I say and be glad for the advice.

Just as I assumed Jeff knew my limitations as a new lawyer (he did) and believed this critical work well within my reach (he figured that would come with time), I assumed without doubt that Jeff was a messenger for the powers that be at Wilmer (he was not), who were hoping someone would volunteer (they didn't even know the case existed). This was a very basic misunderstanding. I thought I was doing what the firm wanted me to do by taking the case. I didn't realize Jeff was acting on his own, at the request of a friend in Florida, and that by volunteering *I* was accepting the case for the firm. I didn't realize then that the firm would come to think that *I* had saddled them with this unsavory million-dollar case. I didn't figure that out for a very long time. No wonder Jeff had thought it would be a hard sell.

When I woke up the next morning, with the sun shining through the shutters, I felt an uncustomary thrill of anticipation at the thought of going to work. I walked down to the office with renewed enthusiasm for the law. When I got to work, Jeff filled me in more fully about this case I had accepted, probably repeating everything he'd told me the night before. The case had come to Jeff through Mike Mello, a lawyer in the office of the Capital Collateral Representative (CCR), the Florida state agency charged with representing death row inmates. Technically, CCR couldn't handle Bundy's case at this point because his petition to the U.S. Supreme Court was still in the "direct" line of appeal, not in the "collateral" stage that can follow.

Direct Appeal Process

(1) criminal charge in state trial court
↓
   (2) highest state court
↓
     (3) U.S. Supreme Court

After the direct appeals process proves fruitless, then the collateral appeals process begins. Only then can CCR become involved.

Collateral Proceedings

(1) motion to set aside conviction in state trial court
↓
   (2) highest state court
↓
     (3) habeas corpus petition in U.S. District Court

↓

(4) U.S. Circuit Court of Appeals

↓

(5) U.S. Supreme Court

So far this case had completed only two of the first three steps in direct appeals: the trial and the appeal to the Florida Supreme Court. Asking the U.S. Supreme Court to review the decision of the Florida Supreme Court would be the last step in the direct appeal.

A year earlier, also at his friend's request, Jeff had taken the case of Stephen Todd Booker, another Florida death row inmate. At the time, Booker's third scheduled execution was only ten days away. No one in Florida thought he could be saved. While in Bundy's case we could be reasonably confident we'd receive a stay, because prisoners were never actually executed on their first warrant, a third warrant was presumed to be fatal. Booker was a marked man. Immediately marshalling Wilmer's considerable resources, Jeff, along with Jim Coleman, a partner in the firm, stopped the execution in its tracks and now were continuing on with the appeal. The two had been so accommodating in taking on the case at the last minute and so spectacularly resourceful in successfully litigating it, CCR wanted Wilmer to take another death case off its hands.

Jeff gave me the phone number of Mark Olive, CCR's chief litigator, for specific instructions on what to do next. Mark Olive was a longtime recruiter of volunteer lawyers for death row inmates—even before CCR was formed—and he had perfected the art of the soft hard sell. With his deep, velvety Southern drawl, Mark Olive put the purr in persuasion. Not that I offered resistance.

I was surprised when, after I'd introduced myself, Mark launched into a sales pitch on why I should take the case, and on why I should take it seriously: a man's life was at stake, a man on death row was a human being like everyone else, the state of Florida was trampling on inmates' rights and they needed advocates desperately. I thought, wasn't that all immediately obvious? How else would anyone see the situation? Death row inmates were human beings in the worst trouble imaginable. I had long since stopped thinking of myself as a Christian, but it still rang true that these were "the least of them," most needy of compassion.

I chose to ignore Mark's apparent assumption that corporate lawyers such as myself were cold, heartless sellouts, nearly impossible to motivate if a client could not pay. He seemed to assume he had to build up the "public duty," "constitutional rights" guilt aspects or I wouldn't follow through with the case, since the client was so hideous. But it seemed clear to me. A man on death row needed a lawyer; time was running out. What else would anyone, any lawyer in a position to help at least, possibly need to know, take time to consider? I enjoyed the pitch, though, allowing Mark Olive's smooth, insinuating voice to slither over me like a warm snake.

When the sales talk was over, Mark gave me an overview of what needed to be done. It seemed pretty simple, as I'd assumed. In January this inmate, this Ted Bundy, my new client, my first client as a lawyer, had asked the U.S. Supreme Court to review his conviction and death sentence. The state of Florida had responded by setting his execution for March 4. He had then asked the U.S. Supreme Court for a stay, but had been turned down, with the suggestion that he get counsel. One reason his stay had been turned down was that he had not followed the correct procedure. Because it was the Florida Supreme Court's order affirming his conviction and death sentence that had allowed the governor to sign a death warrant, a stay of execution had to be requested first from the Florida Supreme Court.

Of course, presenting a motion to the Florida Supreme Court for a stay of execution would be useless—there was no chance of success. Florida in those days was vying with Texas to be the state with the most executions. Nonetheless, that would be my job: file a motion for a stay of execution in the Florida Supreme Court, wait for its inevitable denial, then apply again to the U.S. Supreme Court for a stay, where all concerned expected it to be granted. The whole process seemed simple and straightforward. And it was. What I didn't know was that this was only the beginning of a long journey, the bait. A quick and easy first stay of execution.

I understood the procedural posture of the case, but I had no idea what specific legal arguments usually were made to stop an execution. I hadn't given it much thought before, but it had always seemed to me that executions never went through. Some lawyer always ran up some courthouse steps with a motion for a stay and some judge always granted it. Now I had to understand that process in a little more detail. By the end of Mark's speech I had picked up a few salient points about the necessary legal language, and I snapped fully alert with his last words:

"Call your client."

That had more of a sound of hard reality to it. The way he said it sounded like, *Talk to the man whose life you've taken into your hands, you vile corporate scum*. And facing that phone call was the first time I considered how scant my qualifications were. A real person had to *really* depend on me. For his very life.

"Flar'da State Prison."

I called FSP a lot over the next three years. The staff there had an emotionless, military style of speaking, a Joe Friday lack of small talk. Not a single word volunteered. Even in the twenty or so visits I made there, I never did have what you would call a conversation with anyone at the institution. As a death row inmate's out-of-state defense lawyer, I was clearly an unwelcome presence in a place duty-bound to put people to death. I think it would have been different, the coldness with which I was treated at FSP, if my client had not been an inmate with a sentence of death. With other prisoners, correctional personnel can indulge in a more natural, ambivalent attitude. In fact, for most prisoners, their jailers have to be prepared to let them out one day. They have reason, then, to hope for their rehabilitation and to see them leave with their humanity restored. But with death row prisoners the prison personnel have to prepare to set them in the electric chair; to assist in their extinction. It requires a whole different mind-set.

Placing a call into Florida's death row had the same feeling as walking in. It was like going through a series of locked doors, being transferred from one guard to the next, to places deeper and deeper within the prison. Prison procedure had a kind of beat to it, a dead serious cadence that never ceased to intimidate me.

"Flar'da State Prison." The second guard said.

"Superintendent's office," said the third one.

"Ham Mathis." This was the man I needed to talk to.

Superintendent Hamilton Mathis had two concerns when I told him who I was and that I needed to speak with Bundy. First, he wanted to make sure that I was indeed Ted Bundy's new lawyer, so he asked for the law firm's telephone number. I supposed he wanted to make sure I was not some groupie or sneaky reporter, but I was a little surprised I had to prove anything to get through to my new client. I was, after all, the man's lawyer. We hung up and Superintendent Mathis called back a few minutes later, clearly amazed that when he had asked the receptionist if I was a lawyer in the firm, she had referred him to Wilmer's personnel department for the answer. I was part of a pretty formidable institution myself.

Superintendent Mathis also wanted to make sure I understood that phone contact with an inmate was a rare, and revocable, privilege that was a tremendous burden on the system. A guard had to be taken off duty elsewhere just to supervise that one inmate. Phone calls were appropriate only when there was a legal development that required immediate consultation with the inmate or when, as now, the inmate was on "death watch," the cells near the death chamber reserved for inmates whose execution dates have been set. Otherwise, he said, I could just write or "your law firm can fly you down." I heard that as *Your great big fancy Washington law firm can just sacrifice some of its dough if it's going to put its muscle behind depriving Floridians of their right to execute whom they please.* Mr. Mathis said he'd arrange for Bundy to call me back, collect. I had expected to be put right through, but what was I thinking? It wasn't as if my client was in a hotel.

I pushed my chair back and waited. Outside my office secretaries in their cubicles kept on typing and answering phones. Lawyers in shirtsleeves strolled past, talking to each other, carrying cups of coffee back to their offices. Services came around with the mail cart. Any time now, the phone was going to ring and on the other end of the line would be a person, my client, calling from death row. And yet, all around me it was business as usual. It was like the time when I was a social worker making home visits on a cold winter day; my car hit a slick patch of ice on a long, empty highway, and there was nothing I could do but lift my feet from the pedals and wait for the impact. What had seemed so strange then was that, as the car spun out of control, the radio kept on playing, same as before, the windshield wipers kept sweeping back and forth, the heater kept on blowing out warm air— all as if nothing at all were about to happen.

I was so carried away in the feeling that I was startled when the phone rang.

"Collect call for Polly Nelson from Ted Bundy. Will you accept the charges?"

At least the long-distance operator was in on my reality. I wondered if she recognized my caller's name.

"Yes," I said.

This was it, the real thing. I realized suddenly I had no idea what he would be like, this death row inmate. He could be openly hostile, demanding to know my qualifications to take his case. He could be scared out of his wits. He could very well be psychotic, unintelligible, delusional. Suddenly, I didn't feel ready for this.

"Go ahead," the operator said.

Dead silence. Then I realized she meant me.

"Hello?" I said.

A gruff voice responded.

"Is this Polly Nelson?"

Oh, no—he's hostile. This is going to be awful. "Yes, hello," I said.

"Just a minute, Ma'am, I'll put Bundy on the line." Whew, only a guard.

Then another voice.

"Uh . . . uh . . . hello?"

This voice was tentative; this man sounded insecure. I could handle that. I relaxed. I could deal with this man with a hesitant, deep, gravelly stammer. I could help him.

But there was one more thing I hadn't thought of. How was I going to address him, what name should I call him by? Not just "Bundy," of course, as Jeff and Mark had been referring to him. That was too disrespectful for this, my new legal client. But "Mr. Bundy" didn't seem quite right either—too cold under his scary circumstances, I thought, too distancing. I wanted this man on death row to feel safe and secure. But "Ted" seemed too condescending to start out with. So I avoided calling him anything at all.

"Hello. This is Polly Nelson. I think Mark Olive told you I would be representing you on the motions for a stay?"

"So you're . . . you're . . . taking the case then?" he stuttered.

What a question! It had never occurred to me that he, too, would think he'd have to make a pitch for his own case. A death warrant was pending, an execution was scheduled in three weeks—of course I was taking the case. I was shocked that he thought he might have to pass some sort of inspection first. I imagined him standing outside a prison cell on death watch, dropping dimes into a pay phone, calling law firm after law firm, trying to talk someone into taking his case as the execution grew closer and closer. What a grisly prospect. There arose in me a fierce protectiveness toward this man I'd never seen and knew nothing about. Except that they were trying to kill him.

From that moment on, until the very last day, I felt 100 percent responsible for saving Ted Bundy's life. As if Ted bore no responsibility at all. After a while, after a year or two, even I knew I was wrong to feel that so strongly—for my own sanity if for nothing else. But I couldn't change it. I'd try to talk sense to myself, tell myself that I hadn't gotten Ted into this mess in the first place, that the impossibility of the case was due primarily to forces beyond my control, beginning in no small part with Ted's own conduct in committing brutal murders over and over again. But it never sank in, it never rang true. I was the responsible one; if I lost the case it would be my fault he died.

Ted was not similarly deluded and he knew of no reason to take my representation for granted. It was going to be a very demanding and expensive matter. Ted couldn't be sure of the firm's commitment to pro bono work, and he knew much better than I the facts about his case that should have given me pause, the same facts that probably led CCR to seek a law firm outside of Florida for him. Such as his notoriety, and the consequent ferocity with which the state of Florida would seek his execution—I didn't know that. Such as the horrible magnitude of his crimes and his demonstrated inability to cooperate with his attorneys—I didn't know that fully, either. I had barely recognized his name. To me he was just a human being who was about to be killed. Anybody, I thought, would help such a person.

I strained to remember what Mark had told me I was supposed to do, so I could sound semi-intelligent. I managed a sketchy description, and Ted did not press for details. He didn't ask me about my qualifications either. He just seemed relieved that he had someone to represent him, particularly someone with the backing of a law firm like Wilmer—Mark Olive no doubt, had emphasized to him the advantages of that. We did not linger on the phone long. In signing off, now that we'd met, now that I'd heard his voice and felt his apprehension, I had no trouble calling him by his first name.

"Good-bye, Ted."

He was my baby now.

That day and the next, as I struggled with my three-page motion for a stay in the Florida Supreme Court, I got my first glimpse of the bitter tone of death penalty litigation. I called Jeff at his home on Wednesday night to read him my first draft, which I'd based on a standard pleading form.

"How's this, Jeff? 'Defendant Theodore Robert Bundy respectfully requests this Honorable Court to . . .' "

Jeff stopped me there.

"Strike 'Honorable.' " He fairly hissed. I eventually came to understand why he thought the courts in these cases were something less than honorable, but I was still wet behind the ears as a lawyer and I was shocked.

By Thursday, only my second day on the case, CCR had already grown impatient with my efforts. Because CCR had all of Ted's records and had recruited me only to take on the final step in the direct appeal, they still bore the responsibility of preparing to initiate collateral proceedings in the event that I was unsuccessful. When an execution is pending, a stay of execution can never be taken for granted; all contingencies have to be covered. But every day CCR continued to work on Ted's case was time stolen from the inmate who was already scheduled to be next in line to be killed. Governor Bob Graham did his best never to allow one of those four special cells near the death chamber to stand empty. Mark wanted Ted's stay by Friday so he could spend the weekend on the next man's case; he pressed me to just fax him my law firm's stationery and let him make the Florida Supreme Court filing himself, under my name. Despite my enthrallment with his velvety voice, that unfamiliar Southern drawl, I did not feel comfortable with his request. There was no point in being just a puppet in this case, and I was concerned about turning over the firm's stationery to an outside lawyer—Wilmer might consider that a breach of trust. When I brought this problem to Jeff, he took me to see Jim Coleman, the partner who, apparently, was supervising me.

I had never met Jim before, but I was certainly aware of him. A tall man in his late thirties with horn-rim glasses and an athletic build, one of two black partners in the firm, Jim had often bounded past my office on his way to see Jeff. He'd always stop first and win a smile from Jeff's otherwise dour veteran secretary. At the firm's social events he inevitably could be found regaling a cluster of spellbound associates with some tale of misadventure on the litigation trail. Among the generally reserved lawyers of this very serious-minded law firm, Jim Coleman's irrepressible exuberance was definitely unique.

Our first meeting was brief. After a little light banter with Jeff, Jim swiftly dealt with my dilemma. He told me what I wanted to hear this time, but it would not always be the reply I was hoping for from him. "Do whatever you think is best," he said. "It's your case. You're Bundy's lawyer."

*   *   *

Tallahassee is the capital of Florida, but it is not exactly the kind of place you imagine when you think of the Sunshine State. I was surprised, at least. Never having been to Florida before, I thought of the whole state as a pink-and-blue vacation paradise; one big picture postcard. Instead, emerging onto the tarmac of the Tallahassee airport from the prop plane from Atlanta, I found myself in Alligator Country. I was hit by a blast of hot humidity that made it hard to breathe; as if I'd been punched in the stomach. The small terminal building was surrounded by spiky, spindly palm trees set against a gray sky. In fact, the sun rarely seemed to be shining when I was in Tallahassee.

I walked all the way through the cool terminal building without anyone claiming me. I assumed CCR had become too busy to spare someone to pick me up and that I was supposed to take a cab instead. Just then, though, when we were practically the only two people left in the lobby, I realized that the man I had just passed was probably Mark Olive. He hadn't recognized me either. Both of us, I suspect, were looking for someone who looked like a lawyer.

Perhaps I'd gotten a little carried away with the idea that I was traveling to sunny, vacation paradise Florida, all expenses paid by Wilmer, Cutler & Pickering. As an associate I had my own corporate credit card and needed no particular authorization for travel. Uncharacteristically, even for me, I was wearing a snug pink suit and tottering on heels. I never did get the lady lawyer look I'd imagined I would as part of my brand-new life—I continued to intimidate myself in a dark suit. But still, I didn't usually wear pink, and certainly not high heels. I can understand that "Washington lawyer" would not have been an observer's first guess, and "death penalty lawyer" would have seemed even more improbable.

Mark Olive did not look like the lawyers at Wilmer either. His appearance, though, was anything but a disappointment. The whole situation was pretty intoxicating: a ticking time clock, a man's life on the line, my complete inexperience and naïveté, a free flight to Florida for the first time. Now add, in person, the wise teacher with a voice like simmering molasses, brown hair that fell to his shoulders, wire-rim eyeglasses, and beat-up blue jeans. For someone like me, who had been sexually imprinted in the 1960s, this was a powerful combination. When he spoke my name, my knees nearly buckled beneath me.

CCR's humble offices tugged my '60s heartstrings as well. I imagined that this must have been what the beleaguered storefront civil rights offices had been like; unpretentious in the extreme. Boxes of files were strewn everywhere, everyone was dressed in either old jeans or long cotton skirts, there were no obvious hierarchical or professional class distinctions. It couldn't have been more unlike Wilmer, Cutler & Pickering.

Following introductions all around, Mark took me to that portion of the clutter serving as his office. He read the motions that had taken me two long days to draft, pronounced them "pretty," and started over from scratch. I had thought they were ready to file. But CCR did dozens of death penalty cases every year, and they had their own way of doing things. Where Jeff had been bitter about the dishonesty of the courts in dealing with these cases, CCR was venomous. My motions were far too polite and dispassionate for them. I lost all hope of making a favorable impression on these inestimable people.

I had learned a little about my case in these first couple days on the job, although, with a death warrant pending, the main emphasis is on *doing*, on getting the paperwork done. Ted, it turned out, was under two separate death sentences in Florida. He had received the first for the January 23, 1978, murder of two college students in the Chi Omega sorority house at Florida State University. The second was for the kidnapping and murder a few weeks later of a twelve-year-old girl who had been walking between two classroom buildings at Lake City Junior High School when last seen alive. It was the Chi Omega death sentence for which Ted was to be executed at this time. I didn't even wonder about the status of the Lake City case. No one mentioned it.

The basis of the stay motion in the Florida Supreme Court was that, given the undeniable seriousness of at least some of the twenty-two issues they themselves had taken over two years to decide, a petition to the U.S. Supreme Court certainly would not be frivolous. Those issues ranged from the simple claim that a mistrial should have been declared when the judge repeatedly acknowledged a sleeping juror, to such complex issues as the scientific validity of positively identifying a perpetrator through a photograph of a bite mark on the victim's body. Under the law, if we had at least one arguable claim we had a right to a stay to pursue it. An execution, of course, would moot all review.

While Mark Olive rewrote my motion to include many more details and much more strident language than I had, I was relegated to a spot on one of CCR's dilapidated couches, where I sat sunken with my knees nearly up to my chest. I felt uselessly "pretty" myself, in my pink suit and high heels, while the CCR litigation machine did what it does best. In addition to the stay motion, CCR lawyers redid to their own style the tedious half dozen other documents that always needed to accompany every filing: an in forma pauperis motion to waive filing fees because of the indigency of the petitioner (including notarized documentation, although any money a death row inmate may have had is certainly gone by the time review is sought in the U.S. Supreme Court); a routine and rarely denied (one of those rare exceptions being Ted's first choice of counsel at trial) motion for admission *pro hac vice*, that is, for me to be allowed to make this filing "as if" I were licensed to practice law in Florida; along with a lengthy memorandum in support of the stay motion, detailing the applicable law, facts, and arguments. All this, mind you, for an utterly hopeless stay motion that I was filing only to get the requisite denial so I could file the real stay motion in the U.S. Supreme Court.

Combine all the different (and critical—forget even one of them and the whole process comes to a halt) pleadings with the necessity of raising every available legal issue, no matter how small or hopeless in order to "preserve the record for appeal" (the law may change and its prospects improve), and you can see why litigators are so unpleasant.

Submerged in the couch, a practically irrelevant figurehead in the process, I was not at all resentful that CCR took over—they were the experts. Once in a great while my presence was acknowledged. A staff lawyer pulled up a chair abruptly, straddled it backward, and ran through the issues he and Mark Olive had already identified in the few days they'd had the case before I took it. Occasionally a paper would be stuck under my nose with the command "Sign here!" The rest of the time, however, I was the still center in an incomprehensible whirlwind of activity. I was as grateful as I was humbled.

When the documents were in order, Mark told Mike Mello, Jeff Robinson's friend, to dig up the communal court appearance suit jacket that lay crumpled in a corner and accompany me to the Florida Supreme Court clerk's office to make the filing. This was usually done by a staff person, I suppose, but Mark must have thought I should be allowed to do *something*, since I'd come all the way down from Washington. Mike carried the hefty box of the required twenty copies of each document. I trotted alongside. There wasn't a whole lot of fanfare in the old-fashioned courthouse. It was late in the day, the clerk's office was quiet; only a couple of employees were still at their desks behind the counter. Without a glance or greeting, the clerk of the court stamped the motions RECEIVED, and my masterful lawyerly duties were done for the day. I flew back to Washington, my head still reeling.

I spent the weekend preparing the secondary documents all over again in the form required by the next court down the line, the U.S. Supreme Court. Mark dictated the bulk of the memorandum in support of the application for that stay to Wilmer's word-processing center, and I belabored the few substantive paragraphs that were my responsibility. I felt very productive. I was starting to catch on to which end was up, at least.

On Monday morning at ten CCR faxed me the Florida Supreme Court's decision: DENIED. I'd expected that, of course, but it was still a blow to lose my first legal motion. The U.S. Supreme Court papers were lying in wait, and they were filed by a messenger as soon as the news of the lower court decision arrived. Then there was nothing to do but wait for their decision—and answer the phones.

With the announcement that the Florida Supreme Court had denied Ted Bundy's motion for a stay of execution, the press learned he had a new lawyer. Me. What followed came as a complete surprise. I thought the first reporter who called was kidding when he asked me if I was going to establish a press office to answer inquiries. It was no joke, and I was inundated with calls. The Associated Press, the *Tallahassee Democrat*, the *Miami Herald*, newspapers in Seattle and Salt Lake City, a scattering from elsewhere. CCR later told me a Swedish newspaper had called them that day to ask if I were a famous American death penalty lawyer. (I can only imagine CCR's reaction.) What a change of pace from six days before—from faceless associate drafting fruitless footnotes to feted "Bundy's lawyer," the toast of the town! At least it felt that way. I didn't bother to make the distinction between fame and infamy. I felt sure that the reporters saw the situation as I did, they were so solicitous and agreeable. Clearly I was an avenging angel saving a human life from the universally despised death penalty. I couldn't imagine anyone seeing it any other way.

One effect of publicity in this case was to spur each time a small rash of letters purporting to offer fresh evidence, always exonerating my client. In this first batch one writer claimed to have seen the murders committed, and they were not committed by Ted Bundy but by "George Peppard and his wife Elizabeth Ashley, along with their son Dirk Benedict." Another writer claimed it was his brother who had committed the murders; apparently it was a problem generally among his family and friends, and it was getting on his nerves: "Also, I believe that my parents and neighbor are continuing their attempts to murder me. I cant let that continue forever."

My new circumstances were easy to get used to. I spent the rest of that first full week on the case talking on the phone with reporters all day, and catching up on my nose-grinding regulatory work at night. Heroine/celebrity by day; scholar/corporate lawyer at night. I had arrived. Now this was practicing law! I loved answering press calls. It was such a luxury: Reporters were anxious to keep me talking, drawing me out. They never disagreed with me, and their questions were simple compared to the real issues in the case—I had the answers at my fingertips, and I was never interrupted. I told one after another what had been filed, what the Florida Supreme Court's denial meant, what the legal basis was for a stay at this time. And, since they were reporters, not judges or prosecutors or senior partners, I didn't have to respond to any question I didn't have an answer for. Such as how I was going to stop the execution if the Supreme Court denied the stay. Such as what if I were so successful that Bundy actually was set free in the end. Such as, "What about the victims?" Reporters usually knew better than to ask.

On Wednesday, February 26, two days after the Florida Supreme Court denial, the designated death penalty clerk for the U.S. Supreme Court called me to say the Court had granted the stay. I had been so naïvely confident about obtaining a stay—if the Supreme Court wasn't there to prevent people from being killed at the hands of the government, what *was* it there for?—I was not at all grateful for the decision, though I was glad it had come down so fast. The waiting was over. Ted would not be killed March 4. The Court had stayed the execution till March 29 to allow me to prepare a supplement to Ted's petition. Another rush of press calls came in. Again it seemed all the reporters shared my joy at justice triumphant and the sanctity of human life affirmed. It would be a few days before I saw the finished news articles. The story was more like BUNDY ESCAPES DEATH and KILLER'S EXECUTION DELAYED.

Now I know I'm prejudiced, and that hard cases probably make for bad journalism—as they make for bad law—but I was surprised throughout at the uniformity of press reports on the case. Dozens of reporters calling, ten or twelve attending our court appearances, and still the exact same news copy every time. There was one official view of the Bundy case, legal intricacies and all, and that's all I ever saw publicized. A single news service could have served them all.

I received a variety of reactions from people in the firm. At one point in the day, I burst into Jeff's office, crowing, "It may be only temporary, but even doctors only prolong life!" Jeff and the person with him, a physician as it turned out, laughed out loud. Another associate came by to say that he had heard my name on the radio that morning, did I know about that? I brushed his enthusiasm aside with a wave of the hand. "Oh, I'm all over the news now." He turned heel without saying anything and walked away. I had meant it to be celebratory, not bragging. Most surprising, I noticed that the secretaries on my floor stared at me when I walked by. And I noticed they weren't smiling. Their eyes said, *How could you represent someone like that?* I dismissed their reaction as lacking a lawyer's perspective on defending the indefensible.

As soon as I received the news of the stay, I put a call in to Ted. When I told him he was silent for a moment, and then he managed a hoarse and quavering whisper,

"Thank you, Polly."

I could just imagine him there—bent, frightened, standing by the phone, hearing he would not be killed in twelve days after all. I could just imagine his unimaginable relief. I felt good that I could do that for him.

It was hard to maintain that feeling, though, because Ted wouldn't stick to the role I had assigned to him in my mind. When I talked to him again a few hours later, he repeated his thanks, but also expressed annoyance that he was still being held on death watch and had not been moved back to his regular cell yet. I called Superintendent Mathis, who said Ted would be moved soon. By the third call Ted was steaming mad. He was very grateful for the legal work I was doing for him, he said, but getting back to his cell immediately was important too, because this was his life after all, and there were no exercise privileges on death watch, and they had better not search his property again when he got back because they had already searched him on the way out, and I should call Mathis again and demand that he be moved back to Q Wing *today*, and if Mathis gave me any trouble, to call the governor's office, because they know what the standard procedure is when a warrant's been called off, and every other guy who'd ever gotten a stay had been returned to his former cell right away, and "I will not be treated differently because I'm Ted Bundy!"

I could see that Ted's perspective on all this was a little different from mine. But then, after all, he was a murderer, apparently; he had to be nuts.

To me it should have been enough for Ted, at least for that day, that his imminent execution had been canceled. I halfheartedly cooperated with his requests, but I really thought his attitude was inappropriate. For the most part, though, I put it out of my mind. This was *my* victory, after all, my coming out into real life, which, in contrast, was *just* as I had imagined it would be—a continuous high, a feeling of being powerful and effective. As I saw it, Ted was virtually irrelevant to this case. It was strictly a legal matter, albeit to his benefit, of course. I was going to save him and make him feel cared for in his heart of hearts, but not in his day-to-day life.

PART II

CHAPTER 3

"Very happy news." It was a little startling to see my words in print. I had to learn not to say chirpy things like that to reporters. I could see that, when presented in the context of the crimes, in the context of *grisly slayings*, "very happy news" looked somehow inappropriate— bizarre, even. But I was honestly surprised to see the murders mentioned so prominently. For me the whole issue was the death penalty and, legally, the crimes were irrelevant now. I was appealing only errors in the trial, not the specific finding of guilt. I hadn't expected Ted's name to be placed so close to the murders, either. I wasn't assuming he was proven guilty, and I had expected the newspapers wouldn't either. I chose to ignore the fact that a conviction overcomes any presumption of innocence. Besides, saving lives was of the highest good, and the only life that could be saved at this point was Ted's. Why were they sensationalizing this?

After another day or two of frenzied press calls, my phone fell utterly silent. Ted was no longer news. I felt somewhat abandoned by my new suitors, those attentive reporters. Ordinary life seemed so quiet. I reluctantly returned to my tedious paying work and to the supplement to Ted's petition. I didn't know exactly where to begin with the supplement, though.

I knew the basic facts of the case. Ted had been convicted and sentenced to death in 1979 for a 3:00 A.M. attack in 1978 on residents of the Chi Omega sorority house at Florida State University in Tallahassee. Five women had been attacked while they slept, bludgeoned ferociously with a club, and sexually assaulted with ordinary objects in their own rooms. Two women were left dead, and three more had been seriously injured. At the time, Ted had been on the run from Colorado Springs, Colorado, where he had been on trial for the murder of another young woman. He had been extradited to Colorado from Utah, where he had begun serving a fourteen-year sentence for the attempted abduction of a nineteen-year-old woman in 1976.

My job now was to select and develop the two or three issues in the Chi Omega case strong enough to justify U.S. Supreme Court review on "cert." A "cert" petition asks the Court to issue a *writ of certiorari* to the court that last considered the case, requesting that the record be certified for review. The U.S. Supreme Court receives more than five thousand cert. petitions each year and grants review to less than 170. The Court has complete discretion over which cases to accept for cert. review and accepts only those few that raise a substantial constitutional issue on which the Court wishes to be heard. Death penalty cases are no more likely to be accepted for review than other cases, and even where cert. is granted, the Court generally will only look at one of the many legal questions a case raises.

When Ted had filed his own cert. petition with the U.S. Supreme Court in January, he had made a telling selection of issues he had thought were most "certworthy." He chose none of the dozens of important legal issues his public defenders had raised on his behalf at his trial. He chose none of the issues that related to his factual guilt or innocence. Nor had he chosen any of the other issues that reflected on him personally, such as those questioning his mental state or ability to act as his own attorney or co-counsel. In fact, he had chosen instead those few technical legal issues he himself had argued without benefit of counsel. Egocentricity, even at the cost of his own best interests, was typical of Ted.

According to the cert. petition Ted had filed, then, the three most important, most pivotal, most certworthy issues in the Chi Omega case were that he had been denied the lawyer of his choice (Millard Farmer, an expert death penalty lawyer from Atlanta, had offered to represent Ted without charge, but was denied permission to appear *pro hac vice* by the Florida courts); he hadn't been allowed a hearing on the effectiveness of his public defenders immediately after the trial (such a hearing is not appropriate until collateral proceedings, after completion of the direct appeal, but the trial judge had misled Ted into believing he had to raise the issue immediately or lose all right to raise it later); and he had not been given a fair opportunity to challenge the grand jury that had charged him with the Chi Omega murders in the first place. Ted was blind to the fact that the overall implication of his petition was that he was claiming to have been convicted and sentenced to death only because he had the wrong lawyers and a flawed indictment. That was not going to be convincing. In fact, there were many more substantial, more compelling, and more believable grounds for cert. in the Chi Omega case.

The very best legal issue in the case was not yet "ripe" for review. The U.S. Supreme Court—or any appeals court, for that matter—doesn't take evidence or hear testimony or consider legal issues that have not been decided already by a lower court. Ted himself (with the eager consent of the trial judge) had prevented any evidence being taken on the best issue: his mental competence to assist his lawyers in defending him. His trial lawyers had tried to raise this issue several times, as Ted's irrational conduct both in court and behind the scenes ruined their legal strategies and attempts to save his life. When Ted objected to having these issues aired in a competency hearing, the judge went along with him. Because the evidence of Ted's incompetence had not been allowed on the record, then, appellate consideration of it would have to wait for the collateral challenges, when an attempt could be made to fully explore it in an evidentiary hearing.

Similarly, Ted's claims regarding choice of counsel and effectiveness of appointed counsel needed further factual development in collateral proceeding. The grand jury issue, while not a great issue, was ripe for review. I was sensitive enough to Ted's feelings to hesitate throwing his entire cert. petition out the window, so, in my supplement to his petition, I included it. It did seem to present an unfair catch-22. In Florida, a grand jury decides whether enough evidence exists to indict a person for the crimes alleged by the police. In neither of Ted's two Florida cases was the evidence against him very strong, but he had already received a great deal of publicity by the time the grand jury convened, in secret, to consider his indictment. Florida law gives a defendant the right to challenge the impartiality of a grand jury considering evidence against him, but only *before* it issues an indictment and is dissolved. The catch is that grand jury proceedings are kept secret until *after* an indictment is issued. When Ted sought to have his indictment quashed on the ground the grand jurors were prejudiced by the extensive pretrial publicity, his motion was denied as untimely— the court ruled he should have filed it while the grand jury was still considering the indictment. In secret. Ted became very hot about technical injustices like that.

It was a valid issue, but not likely to influence the U.S. Supreme Court to grant cert. Not only did it not go to the essence of Ted's conviction in a way that would make a Supreme Court justice take an interest, it was not going to clear the hurdle of "harmless error." Even a clearly unconstitutional ruling at trial won't result in the conviction being overturned unless it is reasonably possible that "but for" the error the outcome of the trial would have been different. In this case, any prejudice on the part of the grand jury was probably rendered constitutionally "harmless" by the separate and independent judgment of the trial jury that ultimately heard his case.

The other two issues I chose for the cert. supplement did not have a "harmless error" problem. The outcome of Ted's trial may well have been different "but for" the state's use of hypnosis or the trial court's coercive "death qualification" of the trial jury.

Nita Neary, the principal eyewitness in the Chi Omega case, had been hypnotized at the direction of the prosecutor and the police in order to fill out her description of the man she saw leaving the sorority house with a club just before the bodies were discovered. But when testimony has been enhanced by hypnosis, the witness often cannot distinguish between what he or she actually saw and what might have been suggested during the hypnotic session. This can make the witness nearly impossible to cross-examine—in violation of the defendant's constitutional right to confront his accusers. There was a great deal of disagreement among courts around the country as to how to handle such testimony—which itself is an excellent argument for cert.

The third issue, "death qualification," concerned the exclusion of potential jurors based on their feelings about the death penalty. In a 1968 case, *Witherspoon* v. *Wainwright*, the Supreme Court decided that courts cannot automatically exclude potential jurors who oppose the death penalty, as long as they can still be impartial as to the question of guilt or innocence. The reasoning of the Court was that automatically excluding such jurors would deprive the defendant of his or her right to a jury that was representative of the community. There is also evidence that a jury composed only of death penalty supporters might be more supportive of the prosecution, more "conviction prone," than a balanced jury would be. The Court's solution was that capital trials would be conducted in two phases. In the guilt phase, any juror who could be impartial about guilt or innocence, regardless of their views on the death penalty, could participate. If the defendant were found guilty, the trial would proceed to the penalty phase, where only those jurors who were willing to consider imposing the death penalty would determine the defendant's punishment.

After *Witherspoon* courts did conduct capital trials in two phases, but many, on the urging of prosecutors, continued (and still continue) to exclude all death penalty opponents from serving as jurors. In the Chi Omega case the judge and prosecutor badgered and confused every potential juror who expressed reservations about the death penalty until he or she said something that appeared to disqualify them. Not once was allowed to sit on the jury.

I had my three issues: inability to challenge the grand jury; hypnosis of the state's witness; and improper exclusion of jurors opposed to the death penalty. I also had the entire transcript of the trial, sent up by CCR, which was more than fifteen thousand pages long. Its fifty volumes were in boxes piled up behind me. Jim and Jeff were strictly hands-off and provided no more guidance than a smile and a shrug. They knew a postconviction death case was a sticky tar baby, and they wanted to make sure responsibility for the case remained with me. I was on my own in deciding how to proceed.

I took my cue from the little legal experience I did have. Based on my year as a law clerk, I could well imagine some judge glaring down at me from a high bench and scowling, "You mean you haven't even read the record in this case, Counselor?!" So I began doing just that, beginning at page one. This was not a good idea, of course, the sheer volume of material made it impossible. I couldn't have even speed-read the whole thing by the March 28 deadline for the supplement and, worse, the first few volumes of the record were so fascinating I found myself reading every word as if it were a novel.

Told entirely in dialogue like the script of a play, the individual life stories of each of these ordinary citizens called to jury duty came vividly alive through their candid answers to routine questions. As a group they'd be asked what their job was, their leisure activities, what newspapers and magazines they read. One picture would emerge of a juror whose answer on the first round was "hairstylist;" on the second round, "going to the beach;" and on the third round, *Mademoiselle, Glamour.*" Another picture entirely would be evoked by the answers "truck driver," "hunting sometimes, fishing," and *"Rod and Gun."* Each was unique, distinctive, defining an irreproducible human being. Each life seemed to be driven by its own inevitable internal logic. I envied them their ordinary lives, unencumbered by the responsibility of saving a man from the electric chair. After a week of this I knew I was in trouble.

I was rescued one day by a senior associate, Pat Douglass, who happened to peek in my office. I knew Pat little more than I had known Jeff Robinson when he first stuck his head in. Apparently, though, I had such a terrified look on my face when Pat casually asked how things were going that she came in and sat down.

"Isn't anyone helping you with this?" she asked.

I could only stare at her with wide-open eyes. Taking pity on me, Pat gave me direction. For one thing, she pointed out that the entire transcript could be summarized for me by legal assistants practically overnight—I still hadn't comprehended the extent of the firm's resources. She gave me some sample cert. petitions to use as models. Best of all, she took over writing the hypnosis section herself.

It was pure coincidence that the issue Pat took over was the only one of the three that touched on the crimes themselves. Nita Neary had testified she'd seen a man with a club leaving the sorority house as she came in the back door at three o'clock the morning of the crime. Writing the hypnosis argument meant comparing every detail of Nita Neary's description before, during, and after hypnosis; going over those few horrible minutes over and over again. By Pat taking the hypnosis issue, I could continue to ignore all that. It just happened to work out that way. My own two issues were strictly procedural, having nothing to do with the crimes themselves. Just like the issues Ted had picked out for himself. With Pat's help, I met the Supreme Court's deadline of March 28.

Meanwhile, back at the fabulous townhouse. I was not being a very good roommate. When I first moved in, I'd been home a lot, available to chat, to help out. I hadn't known anyone in Washington, and I had been glued to the kitchen by my nightly drinking habit—I hadn't dared go out in public and end up dancing on tables. But now I was sober, gone from home all the time, not available for communication with my roommate, who held the lease. I was in the office busy being "Bundy's Lawyer" at all hours. How could I take time for anything else? A *life was at stake!* What could possibly be more important at any given moment? My roommate's dog, whom I'd cared for over the holidays, now barked at my unpredictable comings and goings as if I were an intruder. By mid-March my roommate had had it and told me I'd have to move out in a month. I proceeded to avoid making plans. I couldn't possibly spend time at the frivolous task of finding an apartment for myself; I was engaged in a profound mission.

Ted was safe from execution in the Chi Omega case while the Supreme Court decided whether they would grant cert. If they denied cert., their stay would expire and Ted would be vulnerable to a death warrant again. It was my fervent hope the Court would hold the petition past its June recess and not issue a decision until it reconvened on the first Monday in October. I wanted time to clear my head and do some regular work for the partners. I still needed to learn how to be a real lawyer. The problem was, even if the Supreme Court held onto the Chi Omega case for the summer, Ted had another death sentence out there.

The Florida Supreme Court had taken four years to uphold Ted's conviction and death sentence for the murder of Kimberly Leach in Lake City, Florida. Although his two cases were completely separate, they presented many of the same general issues. The competency issue was going to be very strong in the Chi Omega case because Ted's lawyers had tried so hard to raise it on the record and the judge had so clearly erred in letting Ted overrule them. It was an element in the Lake City case, too, because Ted presumably had the same mental condition he did six months earlier at the Chi Omega trial and similarly bizarre things happened in both cases. However, Ted's lawyer in that case had never raised it at all.

Both cases presented the issue of hypnosis, but then the Lake City case was the stronger. While Nita Neary's recollection of events at the Chi Omega house had not really changed much with hypnosis, the recollection of the alleged eyewitness in the Lake City case was virtually *created* during hypnosis sessions. The issue was ripe for U.S. Supreme Court review, having been thoroughly explored at trial and on appeal. All the necessary facts were on the record.

The crimes, the suspicions, and the history of Ted Bundy were widely publicized in Florida from the time he was arrested in February 1978. So much so that, in May 1978, Ted tried to get permission to hold a press conference so he could refute the reports in the newspapers and on television. The judge denied this foolhardy request, noting that he felt compelled to "save Bundy from Bundy." His opinion described the publicity that had built up in the three months since his arrest:

> Virtually no aspect of Bundy's past or present life, real or imagined, has evaded media discovery, analysis and comment. Fact, speculations, characterization and impression have combined to give Theodore Bundy, wanted or not, a mystique of sorts. He enjoys (or tolerates, as the case may be) a name identification in this area of Florida at least equal to that of Florida's most notable personages.

In particular, the monthlong search for Kimberly Leach following her disappearance in February 1978 had prompted frequent news reports asking for information and giving a detailed description of the victim and what she was wearing when last seen. Kimberly Leach had been reported missing by junior high authorities when she failed to return to class after leaving to retrieve her purse from another school building. It wasn't until July 21 that the grand jury formally charged Ted with the murder of Kimberly Leach, and it wasn't until a week after that that the state obtained the evidence that would convict him: the alleged eyewitness testimony of Clarence "Andy" Anderson.

Andy Anderson was watching television at the Lake City Fire Department where he worked, when he saw a news broadcast showing Ted being led from the courthouse after his indictment for the Leach murder. In fact, someone called his attention to it, saying, "There's Bundy, the guy accused of killing the coeds—and the Leach girl." Anderson, like all of Lake City, had been following the case since its inception and had seen the frequent news photographs of both the victim and Ted, the number one suspect. He already knew that Ted had been identified by two teenagers as the man driving the stolen white university van in Lake City the day Kimberly Leach disappeared. In addition, the fire station was in the same building as the police department, and Anderson knew the detective on the case. Nonetheless, it wasn't until July 28 of 1978, when he saw the news of Ted's indictment, that Anderson told his boss, the detective, and the prosecutor that he thought he remembered seeing a girl some months back fitting the description of Kimberly Leach being led from the junior high by a man who looked like Ted Bundy. He had not come forward before, he said, despite five months of public appeals for information about the crime, because he hadn't been sure until just now.

The prosecutor had leapt at the chance to present an eyewitness at trial. The only other evidence linking Ted to the crime was the testimony of a fiber analyst that it was "extremely probable" that some of the fibers found on the floor of the stolen university van came from Ted's clothing and some others came from the clothing of Kimberly Leach. Not much for a jury to go on, particularly to find beyond a reasonable doubt that the clothing from those two people had been in the van *at the same time*. But an actual eyewitness to the abduction would tie it up. Unfortunately for the prosecution, however, Anderson's recollections turned out to be sketchy, and worse, contradicted known facts. Most problematically, he said he remembered seeing this man pick up a girl at the junior high in April, while Kimberly Leach had disappeared at the beginning of February. He also said that the rear windows of the van were covered up, so that he could not see the man and the girl after they got in.

In order to improve his recollection, the prosecutor and the detective had Anderson hypnotized in their presence. Under hypnosis, he still said it had happened in April, but he also said that even though he was four cars behind the van, he could see that the girl was crying *after she got in*. He said that he was coming off the night shift at the time, and that afterward he went home, took a shower, and went to bed. That, too, did not fit the facts. The prosecutor checked and found that Anderson had worked the *day* shift the day of the crime, so he was wrong again. Anderson was sent home with instructions to think about it. He talked it over with his wife who told him that Kimberly Leach had disappeared on February 9, the day of their daughter's birthday.

Three days later Anderson was hypnotized by the police again. This time he explained that, yes, he did work the day shift that day, but had run home for a shower, and to "eat a piece of my baby girl's birthday cake." He also gave a much more detailed description of the man and the girl than he'd given before—although nothing he said hadn't been printed in the newspaper dozens of times before. He said he remembered now that the van had a green and white license plate (which, as was proven at trial, it did not). While he was still under, the hypnotist told him, "You will remember all the details that you discussed with me." Indeed, at trial, Andy Anderson testified to the facts as he "recalled" them during the second hypnosis session, but told the judge he'd remembered all of it from the very beginning. The trial court took his word for that and denied Ted's attorney's motion to have Anderson's testimony thrown out for being hypnotically altered.

The Florida Supreme Court had a *very* difficult time with Anderson's testimony and hypnosis, a majority finally deciding Anderson's testimony had indeed been altered by the hypnosis to the point of unreliability, but that its admission had been "harmless error." The chief judge of the Florida Supreme Court disagreed vehemently, writing that Anderson's testimony had been "the crucial link in the chain of circumstantial evidence" and that had Anderson's testimony been altered by hypnosis, the conviction would have to be overturned. But since, in his view, Anderson's testimony had not been altered by the hypnosis, he voted to affirm Ted's conviction as well.

Given the similarity of the issues in the two cases—not to mention that it would make no sense to try so hard to save Ted in one case only to have him executed in another—it was clearly necessary to file a cert. petition in the U.S. Supreme Court for the Lake City case. It was already past due. The Chi Omega cert. petition had been late as well, but the Court accepted it on the ground that Ted had just obtained counsel. Now Ted had the backing of a law firm that was eminently capable of representing him in both cases and that excuse was not going to fly twice. I wrote to Ted, telling him I thought we should file a Lake City cert. petition as soon as possible. To my astonishment, Ted respectfully declined, writing, "I certainly didn't intend that you and your firm would be pulled into the Lake City case. The Chi O case by itself is enough of a burden I'm sure, and I feel fortunate to have your help on it alone."

I wondered what gave him the idea he had a choice in the matter? It was definitely time to meet my client face to face.

CHAPTER 4

Although I had been representing him for nearly two months, the first time I met Ted Bundy in person was on April 6, 1986. I felt silly driving the big white Oldsmobile I rented that day, but I just had to do it. They were on special, I was alone, and the law firm was picking up the tab. Besides, I was in Florida now, the land of excess. Excess sunshine, excess leisure, excess heat. Somehow, renting an excessive luxury car seemed like the thing to do.

I didn't have a car of my own back in Washington. When I'd left Minnesota I'd ceremoniously transferred the title to my trusty Pinto station wagon to my sister and her husband, and they'd unceremoniously driven it straight to the dump. It had done good duty, though, when I was a social worker. It transported the eight Ignacziewski kids back and forth to the nun-dentist, their faces pressed against the windows like goldfish in a compact fishbowl. It raced down rutted country lanes from Grygla to Gatsby to Gonvich on the far eastern end of Marshall County, becoming airborne over railroad crossings. But oh, those landings! The Pinto definitely communicated the feeling of the road. In contrast, the shiny white Oldsmobile I rented at the Gainesville airport felt like an overstuffed davenport on an unfettered waterbed. It virtually sloshed from side to side around the sharp speed curves on the way to the main road.

March 6, 1986

Dear Polly,

Again, I want to thank you
and Jeff and Jim for your
exceptional effort in my behalf. I am very grateful for
your involvement.

You deserve special praise.
You were introduced to my case
under some very difficult
circumstances and you were
just outstanding.

My wife, Carole, and I and
our family are deeply appreciative of your help.

I am looking forward to
meeting you.

Peace
ted

Thank-you card from Ted

Once on the highway, I set the cruise control, electronically glided
the deep driver's seat way down and way back, and turned the stereo
on loud. A lowrider in a big car, I floated through the bleak, scruffy
countryside of middle Florida like an alien in a space bubble. I felt
estranged from the world outside, conspicuous in my big white car.
Stands of tall trees flanked the road, occasionally revealing a ram-
shackle beer tavern or hot-peanut stand. I thought of how unwelcome

I'd be if the people who lived among those trees knew my destination, my mission.

My reverie ended abruptly at Starke.

Starke is a no-frills prison town six miles south of Florida State Prison, midway between Gainesville and Jacksonville. Although the prison is officially identified with the town of Raiford—which is actually closer, but so small it's easy to miss—most people refer to FSP simply as "Starke." Certainly the townspeople felt that affinity in a big way. When an execution was imminent, the people of Starke would cheer on the home team. Portable flashing signboards that usually advertise LIVE BAIT or MOWERS ON SALE would read BURN BUNDY BURN and FRY TED.

The approach to Starke from the west began with a few large discount stores, a phalanx of fast-food places, then a sharp left turn over crisscrossing railway tracks with a jumble of dangling utility lines swinging overhead. I always found it disconcerting. After a few blocks of single-story storefronts, the town petered back out. At the Stop-Shop gas station at the far end of town, a sign pointed north: FLORIDA STATE DEPARTMENT OF CORRECTIONS. There I'd turn left and start down the last six miles to the prison. The final stretch would always affect me the same way it did that first time. My head would begin to hum. I'd feel compelled to snap off the radio. A certain dread would descend and I'd get the distinct impression that there was no turning back. It was as if the prison broadcast some sort of psychic radar that had captured me and pulled me toward it. The tall trees stepped in closer and cast long shadows across the road. My car-boat, silent and cool on the inside, was taking me somewhere I was no longer certain I wanted to go.

Abruptly, the dark tunnel of trees ended at two man-size stone booths with long, narrow, vertical peepholes, linked together by a wrought-iron sign that arched over the road: FLORIDA STATE PRISON. Beyond that there were no more trees. Only a big expanse of field on either side of the road—and my first sight of men in captivity. Spaced evenly along the ditch, a dozen men—all black, all dressed in thin, blue coveralls—moved slowly, heavily, at their work. They kept their heads bowed even while turning to gaze disinterestedly as I passed by. I felt ashamed. Even though I was representing one of them, a fellow inmate, with my big white car and my freedom to come and go I was just another part of the system that kept them there.

At the manned guard towers I obediently slowed to the posted five miles an hour and rolled cautiously over the speed bumps. I imagined the pinpoint sight of a rifle trained on the back of my neck, the atmosphere of control was so strong. More prisoners were working the grounds, trimming the hedges. They were all in blue. All captives. In my chest, a gasp collided with a sigh, and I felt filled to bursting with a dreadful feeling I could not identify.

Scrupulously avoiding the spaces marked for official vehicles, I parked the car in the lot and sat for a moment before surrendering myself to this institution. When I stepped out into the parking lot I was nearly blinded by the light. Although it was still early spring and the air was still cool, the brilliant Florida sun sent searing rays of heat to the earth. Gleaming coils of razor wire sparkled like a fountain between the two tall fences surrounding the prison. Beyond the fences, limp T-shirts and flat, wet blue jeans hung drying from the dark windows of four or five large cement buildings. The air was filled with the muffled roar of a thousand human voices made wild by confinement and uselessness. It was the sound of an animal house. I felt I was entering a prohibited dimension of human experience.

"Hey, darlin'!" I'd heard that voice on the phone several times already. I knew it could only be one man, although it took a while before my eyes could see him in the relative darkness of the entryway. J. Victor "Bud" Africano had been Ted's trial lawyer in the Lake City case and had handled his appeal to the Florida Supreme Court as well. He had a private law practice in Live Oak, a town about an hour north of the prison. He was at the prison today to introduce me to Ted, and it was a comfort to have him there. Vic was a big-hearted good ol' boy and an unrepentant ladies' gentleman. For the entire time I represented Ted, even when I had to prepare to discredit him if necessary, Vic was as gentle and solicitous of me as if I were the one in danger here.

Vic cared about Ted. Although he had long since stopped being paid for it, Vic still made himself available to Ted whenever he was needed. Their association was more than six years long, and Vic's fondness for him was evident. But Vic just as truly believed Ted killed Kimberly Leach and deserved to die for it. Vic did not seem to have to reconcile his conflicting feelings—he somehow managed to simultaneously love Ted like a nephew and unabashedly believe he should be executed.

Even with Vic's reassuring presence, I felt a little shaky and overwhelmed by the meticulous security protocol at the third of the five iron gates that are never open at the same time. The first time through the metal detector I set off the alarm and had to slip my shoes off to pass through—even the tiny nails that held my shoes together registered on the sensor. The captain in charge asked for my bar certificate to prove I was an attorney and kept my driver's license for a positive ID on the way out. He stamped my hand with invisible ink so that no inmate could escape by disguising himself as me. Vic took it all in stride, amiably addressing the guards by their first names. He was a regular around there—and a local guy. He got to keep his shoes on through the inspection process.

We were escorted through the long, empty hallway that preceded the final gate. The sound of my clicking heels bounced off the high walls that, like everything else in the prison, were painted a dull industrial yellow. No one spoke. When we reached the end our escort signaled to the guard in the next booth, who nodded back, and the gate slid open to let us pass. As another guard began to lead us to the right, Vic turned his head to the left and called out a greeting.

"Hey, Ted."

About twenty feet away, in the first of several unlit steel cages the size of telephone booths, was a wiry man who looked dark, wary, and wild. My dread deepened at the flesh and blood reality of a human being who was depending on me to prevent his execution. I could barely look in his direction. We did no more than acknowledge each other with a brief, magnetic stare. I followed Vic down the opposite hallway.

I was amazed when I saw the size of the room where we were going to meet with Ted. It was not what I had envisioned at all. It looked like a grade school gymnasium/lunch room, with its high ceiling, small round tables, and short stools. Vic noticed my surprise.

"All the regular attorney interview rooms in the warden's office were booked up today," he explained. "This is the inmate visiting room, where they meet with their families on the weekend."

"All together?" I said, as I scanned the sprawling space.

"Yup. And," he added, tilting his head toward the rickety wooden toilet stalls at end of the room, "back there's where some of them have their unofficial conjugal visits."

Security arrangements apparently were a little more flexible within the prison itself than at the gates.

There was only one guard in the room, and he sat way over by the door, flipping through a magazine. To avoid being overheard, Vic and I took a seat at the back, but the long distance between us and the guard also made me feel uneasy. Ted and I were no longer strangers, but it was one thing to talk to a client on the phone and correspond by mail, and another thing entirely to be face-to-face with a brutal murderer in a cavernous hall, virtually alone. Until then I hadn't ever thought of Ted that way, as a real, actual murderer. I hadn't let myself. As my client Ted was entitled to my goodwill and respect. If I thought of Ted as a murderer my subconscious might undermine my work on his behalf—a line bent even slightly will soon be going in another direction altogether. But a little spark of realization stung me while we waited for Ted to be brought in: This man I was about to face had killed people. He was an undeniably dangerous man. And I was undeniably mortal.

Suddenly, the only door to the visitor's room burst open and Ted was led in by a guard. He was bent over, his hands were cuffed behind his back, and he was balancing a bulging file folder behind him. The stone-faced guard took the folder from Ted, inspected it, uncuffed his hands from behind and recuffed them in front. Holding his folder with his joined hands, Ted slowly unfolded his body. On the unspoken pretext of the guard's presence, none of us spoke as Ted straightened out. I didn't know where to look. I didn't want to embarrass Ted by viewing this dehumanizing spectacle, yet I didn't want to shun him either. So I looked back and forth between him and Vic. Vic's eyes were an oasis of comfort. Whenever I looked at Ted, on the other hand, he'd quickly look away. We made eye contact only at the corners of our eyes.

Ted looked smaller than I'd expected. Even after he straightened up he stayed stooped, short of his full five feet eleven inches. He was incredibly lean, taut as catgut. I could see in his face how once he had been handsome, but now he looked drawn and worn. His hair was short and coarse, a dull gray. His skin was lifeless, ashen. Ted looked like a walking cadaver—except for his eyes. Just barely blue and clear as glass, Ted's eyes looked newly born, fully alive, fully communicative. In fact, whenever I talked to him I felt like I was having two conversations at once, one with our words, and one with our eyes. It was as if Ted's eyes were peepholes someone else was peering out of. Someone deep inside, predating his horrible history and the worn-out exterior that reflected it.

Ted offered his cuffed hands to Vic and Vic shook them warmly. He gallantly did not offer them to me and I was grateful—those handcuffs spoke too loudly for me to ignore them yet. We walked silently to our table and sat down facing each other. I felt like a fake, pretending to be this man's lawyer. In his precarious position, with his life at stake, he needed someone with experience, someone who knew what lay ahead. I was working with blinders on, learning one step at a time. But I was it, and I would become competent, and for the meantime I'd have to pretend.

Ted, for his part, was trying to impress me, please me, block out for the moment what he knew I knew about him. He wanted me to see him as he liked to think of himself: sophisticated, urbane, polite, respectful. He thanked me for coming down, reiterated how grateful he was for my representation. He told me that when he was a young man he had wanted to be where I was, a successful law student, a new associate in a prestigious firm. He'd been through the first year of law school—twice. He said he was devastated to find out that the other students had something, some intellectual capacity, he did not. He found the classes completely incomprehensible, he said. "It was a great disappointment to me." He shook his head with regret.

Ted really did talk like that: "It was a great disappointment to me." So formal, so stilted, more like writing than casual speech. I always had the impression that he was consciously creating himself, his persona. His natural instincts, I think, gave him no clue how a normal person would act.

From his folder, Ted pulled out my bulky Chi Omega cert. petition. He obviously wanted to say something intelligent about it to me, but instead he stuttered and stammered and grew red with embarrassment. He had no problem, however, when he paused to condescendingly describe to Vic what was meant by the *Witherspoon* line of death qualification cases. Ted may have thought that law students had something he didn't, but that didn't stop him from thinking that he was a better lawyer than most.

But despite all the posturing and faux legal talk (from both of us), I felt very much a mere human being in the presence of another human being, who was at the same time both very dangerous and in terrible trouble. Nonetheless, we all joked about my fancy Oldsmobile.

Ted seemed mortified that I had to be aware of the very circumstances that required my representation. All his movements and conversation were designed to show me that he was not a monster, despite all documentary evidence to the contrary—which, by unspoken agreement, was never mentioned. But he knew that I knew, of course. I had just spent two months with the gruesome fifteen-thousand-page

Chi Omega trial record. It was my job to know. Besides, Ted was so acutely aware of all the publicity concerning himself that he thought every man, woman, and child in America knew. As a result, Ted's face had that perpetually-posed look of people who find themselves too often in the public eye, like politicians or famous actors.

Ted always made a point of emphasizing his family ties. On this visit he bashfully showed me Polaroid pictures routinely taken by prison guards for a fee on visiting days. There was one of Ted's wife, Carole Boone, sitting with her four-year-old daughter, Tina, at one of the same tables we were sitting at now. There was one of Tina alone, sticking her chin out and flashing a big grin in living color. There was one of Ted, with Tina riding on his shoulders.

Ted had a real soft spot for Tina, who was born after he had been on death row for almost two years. I think Tina was the key to Ted's transformation, of sorts, in prison. It wasn't that he became remorseful (he believed that he had done all he could have to lead a good life and had been victimized by his compulsion as much as anyone else had) or was born again as a Christian (although I think that, with the help of Carole, he did develop a faith—or at least an eager hope—in the abiding presence of some sort of benevolent spiritual force), but the effect of Tina in Ted's life was to give him his first glimmer of heartfelt love. Until then I think he had believed that no such emotion truly existed, that the rest of us had been faking it too. Tina's unconditional, unguarded, uncomplicated, real love for him touched him very deeply and elicited a strange new feeling that opened his mind to the possibility of the existence of love. It was then, too, I think, that he began to grieve for his own lost life.

Ted was most comfortable and relaxed when he talked about Tina; his eyes weren't as loud with subtext as they usually were. For one thing, it was a simple, lighthearted subject—it didn't tax his mind. For another, it was the one thing in his life he felt he could truly and publicly feel good about. It was a very gratifying experience for him, being a part of his own family. He was very much the *Leave It to Beaver* dad: firm, fair, and gentle. He'd describe to me stern, husbandly talks he had with Carole about child raising. They were the perfect, the pluperfect, family—except that the father lived on death row, and always had.

At this first meeting, Ted told me that Tina had traveled with Carole to the prison every week since she was born. They'd meet every Saturday in this very same room. When his execution was scheduled in February, Carole shielded Tina from the news. Nonetheless, she was deeply disturbed by the change it had created in her routine.

"When I was put on death watch in February," Ted explained, "I wasn't allowed contact visits anymore; I could only see Carole and Tina through the glass. Tina freaked out. She threw herself on the floor in a tantrum; we couldn't calm her down. We were really concerned. So, even though we weren't totally certain how things would turn out, 'cause there was always the possibility that . . ." Ted's low voice trailed off for a moment. Then he continued.

"Anyway, we decided that Carole would stop bringing her along as long as I was on death watch. Tina was really upset about that, too. She kept asking Carole, 'When's Daddy coming home?' "

Tina didn't mean when was he coming home to live with her and Carole. She'd never known that type of family life. All she wanted was for the man she knew as "Daddy" to be back in the visiting room at Florida State Prison. This was the norm within the ferociously tight-knit community of prison families to which Carole and Tina belonged in Gainesville.

When the execution was stayed in February, things, for Tina, went back to normal. Her routine, her family life, were restored.

"She's fine, now," Ted said, his otherwise immobile face shaping into a smile, "happy as ever."

Although I was spared the condescension with which he treated Vic, and despite the fact that Ted seemed to want to make a good impression on me as a worthy and cooperative client, when we finally got down to the little matter of the Lake City petition, he was unable to commit himself. I explained again the reasons I felt I had no choice but to file a cert. petition in that case in the U.S. Supreme Court. But Ted's plan all along had been to go it alone, doling out his remaining legal options carefully, only when forced to do so. It was a simplistic, unworkable plan, but he was reluctant to change course. He sighed with regret that he couldn't indulge me, averted his eyes, and said he'd let me know for sure after talking it over with Carole.

All the time we talked that day, in the mutual inspection process that was the true underlying purpose of the visit for us both, I searched for some sign that would reassure me that I would have known. All the years I'd been out in the world I'd believed I was safe when I felt safe, that my judgment and intuition protected me from harm. But I saw nothing in Ted that would have warned me. This dangerous man was not detectable by sight or sound. But not for the reasons people usually suggest. It was not because Ted exuded such charm—he was too obviously disingenuous to be truly charming. It was not because Ted was such a "diabolical genius" that he could fool you—believe me, he was not that smart. The real reason you could look Ted Bundy straight in the face—even with full knowledge of what he had done— and not see a single sign of his guilt was that he truly believed he was not guilty. There was no sense of guilt to detect. I silently gasped at my gaping vulnerability, and at the risks I had taken in my drinking days.

When Vic walked me to my car, I felt silly about having made such a big deal out of it, my luxurymobile. I could see now that, from his perspective, it was just a standard full-size car, with standard options. Vic probably drove something at least as well equipped, most lawyers probably did. For me, though, it had been a new experience.

The next day, Ted wrote me a follow-up letter in which he tempered his indecisiveness about giving me the Lake City case by including the following note of thanks:

> Polly, believe me, I don't take your help and the help of your colleagues for granted. I realize that it represents something of a personal sacrifice for you, taking time and energy away from more lucrative or entertaining pursuits. And I am aware of the special burdens and pressures that a notorious and unpopular case like mine have no doubt imposed upon you. What you are doing is exceptional and deeply appreciated by me.

I thought Ted was being melodramatic. I felt privileged to have gotten such an interesting and important case so early in my career. He concluded his letter with a wink—"I suppose you'll be buying an Oldsmobile now, one with cruise control"—and, as always, his humble, lowercase, farewell:

peace, ted.

CHAPTER 5

My April 15 eviction date was approaching fast and I'd still made no effort to find an apartment. This was highly unusual for me. In the sixteen years since I'd left home for college, I'd changed residences at least that many times. Half of my stuff had never made it out of boxes before I'd move again. I was always looking for some place that would make me feel like me. Now here I was in Washington, D.C., where real life would certainly begin, a well-credentialed lawyer well able to afford my own place. I could even hire professional movers for a change. Yet, the task of relocating myself now seemed completely beyond me. I was totally enmeshed with the Bundy case. It was a high-pitched crisis that never ended. It wasn't that I was working all the time, but that at all times I was extremely preoccupied with my awesome responsibility. My only respite came in the form of those bimonthly facials at Tatyana's Skin Care Salon. I'd spend two blissful hours in the hands of tiny, blond Tanya, a no-nonsense "medical dermatologist" from the Ukraine; and Zenaida, the beautiful Peruvian manicurist with the tall high-heels. It was during a regular Saturday session under the steam machine that I was struck by the perfect solution to my housing dilemma. I told Tanya I was moving in. I'd pay more for the full-time use of her second room than she got from renting it out sporadically to freelance masseuses. Tanya was too stunned to refuse. I thought it was a perfect arrangement, an admirably efficient use of space. Tanya would work there during the day, I'd sleep there at night, Sundays I'd have the place all to myself, and on Saturdays I'd have my facial. That may seem strange in light of my salary and position at the time—it may seem strange in any light—but to me, at the time, it seemed ideal.

The moving men were clearly intrigued. Things had not gone all that smoothly before we got to Tanya's. The movers were late and they reeked of beer at ten in the morning. They'd tried to carry whole stacks of furniture at one time and had smashed a hole in the stairwell of my old apartment (epitomizing for my roommate, no doubt, my ignominious exit). But as soon as we arrived at my new place, and they saw the name on the door and Tanya's list of services on the wall, the moving men perked right up.

"Do you do massage?"

"Is it only for women?"

"How long does it last?"

"How much does it cost?"

When I was paying them at the door, I could not bear the weight of their obvious, unsatisfied curiosity.

"Would you like to see the back room?" I asked.

"Yes!" was their enthusiastic response as they followed me down the hall. I flung open the door and shattered their fantasies. Tanya's back room more resembled a dentist's office than a bordello. There were the pristine tools of the esthestician's trade: two tilting treatment chairs, the steam machines, magnifying lights, various instruments of dermatological torture (including my personal favorite—the electrifying ultraviolet ray gun), and, on the wall, a medical illustration graphically depicting skin anatomy and disease. The movers' disappointment was palpable.

On April 13, I received an official thank you note from Ted. He dutifully acknowledged every notable occasion with a card or letter— each time I visited him at Starke or filed an extensive brief on his behalf, each time his execution was called off, and every year at Christmas. Ted's carefully constructed facade conformed rigorously to standard etiquette. In this note Ted wrote how nice it had been to meet me, how fruitful a discussion we'd had. He wrote that he still couldn't decide whether to let me file a Lake City cert. petition, though. He'd still have to consult with Carole, he wrote, because this was a "family decision," but, of course, "My wife, Carole, and I and our family are deeply appreciative of your help." Ted's surrealistic normality gave me the chills. It struck me as so phony, so cold, so obvious. Like a ten-year-old writing, "Dear Grandma, thank you very much for the nice socks." And yet I could tell it was sincere in some way. It represented Ted's best attempt to act and (I believe it was his most ardent wish) to feel like real people do. The problem was that Ted's obvious effort exposed his lack of natural human feeling and went against my image of what I was doing, whom I was protecting. I was doing this work to save a beating heart, a flesh-and-blood person with a hurting child inside. So I steadfastly projected that image onto Ted to the end—and beyond. Only a few times was my veil blown aside.

I went ahead and had Vic send up the Lake City trial record and got started on it even while Ted was still agonizing over whether or not to let me file cert. A cert. petition to the U.S. Supreme Court needed to be done and I certainly wasn't leaving any decision like that up to Ted. Not only would the Supreme Court expect to see counsel on the Lake City petition, but I had seen what Ted considered good arguments—he was not capable of making his own case.

One of the enduring Bundy myths is that Ted was "brilliant." He was not. Superficially he appeared about as intelligent as a fair-to-middling college undergraduate. And he was high-strung and driven and could sometimes produce reams of written matter when in the mood. But Ted had real deficits in judgment, awareness, and deeper thinking. He could talk and write, but he couldn't comprehend or respond. He wrote me a long letter discussing the hypnosis issue in the Lake City case, for example, accurately repeating the arguments previously made at his trial and appeal. He believed he was an expert on the legal issue of hypnosis and insisted I allow him to contribute to any legal brief on that topic. But I discovered that what he had written that first time was all he had to say. There was nothing else. He was incapable of independent thought or elaboration. If I probed his statements, he was unable to explain himself or take an idea any deeper. When I discussed different angles on the subject, he couldn't follow me. He never contributed anything of use to his case.

Ted—like almost any inmate who can write—knew how to use the right format for a filing, and he could write something that looked like an argument, but he had no judgment when it came to choosing the best argument. Again, like a precocious ten-year-old, Ted was very literal. He had language skills, but no understanding of the larger picture. Ted's deficits, though subtle and hard to pinpoint, were *real*, and they are critical to understanding who he was and what went wrong.

The next week it became imperative that work begin on the Lake City case, and even Ted reluctantly agreed. CCR called to say that the Supreme Court was going to announce its decision on the Chi Omega cert. petition on May 5. This was not public information, and CCR did not know the Court's decision, but most likely it would be thumbs-down. I was expecting that. I had hoped, however, that the Court would wait until the fall to announce a decision. As soon as the Supreme Court denied cert., their stay would automatically expire and Ted would be eligible for execution. And in the case of Ted Bundy, the governor would probably sign another death warrant as soon as possible. With a decision in Chi Omega due soon, Ted was now mildly persuaded that filing a Lake City cert. petition would help impress the Court and the governor that we were proceeding expeditiously, and maybe would forestall a Chi Omega warrant, but, he wrote, "I still have my doubts."

When we learned there would be a May 5 decision, a lot of things changed. For one, Jim Coleman had no choice but to become in-volved. A second death warrant would not be as easy to beat as the first; Ted's execution during the next few months was a real possibility. Up till now, Jim had kept me at a conspicuous arm's length. The only time I'd seen or heard from him, other than our first meeting, was when he'd grab the door frame as he flew by on his way to visit Jeff. He would stick his head in my office, say something helpful and encouraging like, "Filed that petition yet?" raise his eyebrows in mock query, and be off again. Jim had meant it when he had said, "You do it. You're Bundy's lawyer."

Part of this was due to certain assumptions about pro bono work at Wilmer. Although no one ever said it, Wilmer, Cutler & Pickering had a two-tiered pro bono policy. Big, important cases—pro bono matters with wide-ranging significance—were treated just like the pay-ing cases. They were screened for conflicts, discussed among the part-nership before they were undertaken, fully staffed with two or more partners and a half-dozen associates, and fought to the bitter end with every resource money could buy. Even though the firm received no reimbursement, these types of pro bono cases were good for public relations and allowed everyone in the firm to feel they were doing something more than just making money. During my tenure, for example, the firm took on a Tennessee textbook case, perceived by the had become difficult to find enough volunteers quickly enough. As a result, the Florida Supreme Court found itself having to issue stays of execution at the request of attorneys who had come into the case at the last minute and hadn't had any chance to prepare. Following vigorous lobbying by the Florida Supreme Court, among others, the Capital Collateral Representative was created as a state office with salaried lawyers to do the job when volunteers could not be found. They were paid by the state to litigate against the state. Public reaction to state-paid lawyers representing Ted Bundy may well have led to CCR's demise.

Whatever the reason for CCR's mysterious muteness, I got the message: I was Bundy's lawyer, for keeps.

Since Ted's mental competency was the strongest issue in the Chi Omega case, I needed expert assistance. But I was having trouble finding someone willing to conduct a mental evaluation of Ted. None of the Florida psychiatrists CCR referred me to would take the case. "No," they'd say immediately upon learning who the client was. "I won't be able to help you." With a hasty, insincere, "I wish you good luck," they were off the phone. I got the impression that they'd already made up their minds that Ted was not mentally ill; or, even if he were, was not worthy of their efforts.

I called several nationally famous psychiatrists who specialized in criminal offenders. Outside of Florida, Ted's name was a decided plus in getting people to talk to me. But as interesting, unique, and newsworthy as this case was going to be, these doctors were very firm on charging their usual rate: typically $250 an hour, including travel time to Florida. That was going to add up fast. I said I'd get back to them.

The week after the governor signed Ted's second warrant, I flew to New York to meet with Art Norman, a psychologist who had been helpful to CCR in the past, and his associate, Roy Matthews. Art and Roy were visiting New York from Florida, where they were trying to start up a forensic service especially for death penalty lawyers: Art would do the psychological evaluation, Roy would do the factual investigation. We met in the apartment of a friend of Dr. Norman. It was small and rather dark, but furnished richly with antiques and oriental rugs. In the middle of the interview Dr. Norman lay down on the floor, saying he usually napped at this time of the afternoon. It seemed strange, but I thought maybe it was some highly evolved naturalism unique to psychologists.

Jim was very reluctant to commit the firm to sizable out-of-pocket expenses such as expert fees. Whereas our own attorney time could be justified as training and public service, cash money out of the partnership shares was a different matter. It was also much more conspicuous. Jim told me to try to talk a psychiatrist into taking the case for free. In the little discussion we had on the point, he suggested that since Wilmer was donating its services, other professionals should too. Only Art Norman said he'd go ahead and interview Ted without a guarantee of payment. I asked Art and Roy to begin an investigation, and we'd discuss later whether Wilmer could pay them itself, if we couldn't get a court to pay their expenses.

The next week I flew to Florida to begin an investigation of my own. At CCR I met with Scharlette Holdman, a feisty death penalty veteran from the Volunteer Resource Center days. She had the same solicitous but condescending attitude that Mark Olive had had, giving me the impression that she tolerated private lawyers dabbling part-time in death penalty law only as necessary evils. Although freeing up resources, such lawyers (such as me) could never have the same dedication and commitment CCR lawyers gave to a case. Scharlette described all the evidence CCR routinely gathered when investigating and preparing a death penalty case: *all* medical records, *all* school records from preschool on, *all* police and prison records. I would need to contact *all* his former attorneys, interview them about their experiences with and impressions of Ted, and get copies of *all* their records. I would need to contact *all* of Ted's friends and relatives for any remembrances of him, any documents or other evidence they may have. I would have to go over Ted's life with a fine-tooth comb. Something out there could hold the key to saving his life; missing it would mean his death.

My mind was swirling with information, taking notes of what I needed to do, wondering how I could get it all done. The execution date was only a month away. It wouldn't be too difficult to gather all that information. Even thousands of dollars in postage (usually overnight, hand delivery), phone calls, and photocopying were normal expenses of litigation at Wilmer. Roy Matthews was going to dig up some of it, and Jim had authorized Roy's modest fee of thirty-five dollars an hour. We had plenty of viable legal issues—stronger than in most cases. But we would still need a psychological report. A court, partners as a present day *Stokes* trial, where the firm sided with a small school district against a mother who wanted her child excused from science class because it was based on the theory of evolution. After thousands of man-hours of preparation, the firm sent several lawyers and a whole busload of legal assistants down to the site of the ruckus. As soon as they arrived they had new phone lines installed in the little motel where they stayed in order to accommodate their computers, modems, and fax machines. The Tennessee textbook team rolled over the opposition like an armored tank. There was great celebration throughout the firm when, inevitably, they won.

The second type of pro bono case was the small, insignificant kind— like the Bundy case—handled solely by an associate as a way of getting his or her feet wet as a lawyer. Typically, these were cases of importance only to the particular clients involved, cases involving matters such as individual discrimination suits or tenants' rights. For these types of cases, no special permission was needed, just a partner willing to sign off on it and approve any minor out-of-pocket expenses. Jim Coleman had supervised more than his share of this type of pro bono case, and more than once an associate had panicked at an impending oral argument or otherwise dropped the case in his lap. He was determined it would not happen again.

With the Supreme Court's expected denial of cert., the direct appeal of the Chi Omega case would be complete. Now collateral proceedings would have to be initiated—starting again in the state trial court before winding their way to the federal district court—to raise any issues that could not have been raised before. CCR was legally bound to represent Ted at this point if no private lawyers volunteered. In theory, I could get out now if I wanted, pass the case back to CCR. In retrospect, this was nothing less than the decisive turning point of my entire life. Not that I think I had a choice in the matter—I never could have chosen to give it up. I was heavily invested spiritually as well as professionally. I'd made a moral commitment to take responsibility for Ted's plight, I knew the facts and the players better than anyone at this point, and— most important—I hadn't yet obtained that definitive satisfaction born caretakers hope to earn.

The day we learned the Supreme Court would issue its decision on May 5, Jim and Jeff appeared at my door. As usual, neither took a step inside. As usual, I stayed fastened to my desk. Over the no-man's-land between us, Jim asked me if I wanted to keep hold of Ted's case for the collateral proceedings. It didn't feel as much as though he was asking a question as throwing down a gauntlet: *Are you a corporate dilettante who would walk away from a pro bono case at the first opportunity, or a real lawyer who would tenaciously hang on to the end regardless of the consequences?* Jim and Jeff seemed to share CCR's dim view of corporate lawyers as a class.

"I can't drop him," I said. "I feel I'm Ted's lawyer now."

"It'll take up most of your time this summer," Jeff warned weakly.

If that was the worst to happen, I could handle it, I thought. One summer's work did not seem overwhelming, although I didn't have a clear idea of what Jeff meant. How were collateral proceedings any different from what I'd already been doing? I assumed they weren't, or those guys would say something. Jim and Jeff shrugged, nodded, let go of the door frame, and went back together to Jeff's office. I imagine that there they said all the things to each other that they hadn't said to me about where the case was going, what it would mean to take on collateral proceedings, how awful it would all be. Maybe they thought a full discussion would scare me off; maybe they thought they would offend me if they offered any opinions; or maybe they were just uncomfortable with me. In any case, the die was cast. I had irrevocably signed on for the duration as "Bundy's lawyer."

The first thing to do was to try preventing a second death warrant in the Chi Omega case after May 5, using a cert. petition in the Lake City case for some leverage. All the possible approaches were long shots, but I couldn't just sit there and do nothing. First, if I could let the U.S. Supreme Court know how similar the issues were in the two cases maybe the Court would hold back its decision on the Chi Omega case for possible consolidation with the Lake City case. They made a nice set—both presented issues about hypnotized witnesses, each decided differently by the Florida Supreme Court.

Second, Governor Graham, who was making a point of signing as many death warrants as possible even when inmates had not exhausted their legal options, claimed his purpose was not vengeance, but to make sure appeals proceeded expeditiously. (It also was possible his purpose was to be elected to the U.S. Senate. Execution of death row inmates is one of the few political issues for which there is no significant constituency in opposition. Not only the timing of warrants was in the hands of the governor, but the choice of who would die was also his. Among the nearly three hundred men on death row in Florida at the time, many had been eligible for execution far longer than Ted. But none would have been less controversial, more popular, or would the record. Partly it was so I wouldn't inadvertently bring nonrecord facts into my legal arguments. But it was also because I was holding myself back from learning Ted's full story. I wanted to see him as a case, as a client in need, not as a murderer or even as a real person of any kind, with a real past over which I had no control.

I sent my request to the Supreme Court to hold their Chi Omega cert. decision until they'd reviewed the so-very-similar Lake City case, which I promised to file by May 22. I thought maybe they'd be moved by the prospect that if there were an important issue in the Lake City case, it would be rendered moot by Ted's execution in the Chi Omega case. I didn't know yet that what any court looks for in a death case, first and foremost, is any way to *avoid* deciding any of it. I called Governor Graham's death penalty counsel, Art Wiedinger, and offered to agree to any litigation schedule to ensure speedy exhaustion of available remedies if the governor wouldn't sign a death warrant right away. Then I worked day and night on perfecting the Lake City cert. petition.

When the evening of Sunday, May 4, arrived, I resolutely kept the TV off and sat still in the quiet of Tatyana's Skin Care Salon, aware every minute that knives were being poked into my Ted. I was in this case to save his life and NBC was driving nails into his coffin. They were making my job even more difficult and the possibility of preventing an execution even more slim.

The next morning, Monday, May 5, 1986, at 10:00 A.M., the Supreme Court announced its cert. decisions. *Bundy* v. *State of Florida* was among the denials. I was affected more than I thought I'd be. Now it was *really* real: Ted was vulnerable to another death warrant at any time, and this one could actually go through. It was at that point that I lost my naive optimism about the case. I hadn't resolved the matter magically as I'd imagined: the justices of the Supreme Court moved and persuaded by my watertight logic and compelling writing. Now I could see Ted really might be killed no matter what I did. I couldn't guarantee it wouldn't happen. There were forces at work here beyond my control.

The realization that I might be helpless to prevent Ted's death even took the fun out of answering press calls. I wasn't amused by hearing from reporters the statements of my opponents, the governor and attorney general of Florida. I wasn't interested in discussing the possibility of another warrant and how I would respond. Reporters started looking to Jim Coleman for quotes instead. He was a litigator, he was always ready to parry and spar. But my whole self was at stake here, and I could no longer afford a sense of humor.

I tried to dismiss the effects of the miniseries and the cert. denial on the public consciousness; I tried to push it all back into a closet so it would not reverberate across the nation and into the future. As if I had the power to do that. On Monday night I kept the TV off again. But I watched the whole thing the very next day. Dara Wells, the young secretary who would eventually accompany Jim and me to Florida, had taped it in case we wanted to view it sometime. Dara was very foresightful. I could see it was silly to keep a blind eye to what the public had just seen about my client, so I had a television brought into my small office and set out chairs for the show. I planned just to scan through the tape with Jim and Jeff, laugh at its inaccuracies, and rail about the injustice of the portrayal. It didn't work out that way.

As the tape played, Jim spun in and out of my office to watch snippets of it, but I was absolutely transfixed and watched the whole thing from beginning to end. It was stunningly accurate. The movie was very careful to not portray anything that was not proven fact. I wondered if the producers had been afraid of a lawsuit after all. A lawsuit by *me*, Bundy's lawyer. That's what was so fascinating about it—it was so close to home. It was like watching a home movie, or maybe a movie I had written myself, in that it depicted scenes I had only seen before in my head gleaned from thousands of pages of dry transcripts. There on the screen were all the characters in the story I had just come to know, brought to life by actors. There was the story itself, that I'd learned piecemeal, dramatized coherently. There was Ted imitated so accurately by Mark Harmon. Harmon held his body as Ted did, rigid and stooped. He wore a constantly suspicious expression, as Ted did unless he made an effort. The difference was that Harmon couldn't hide completely that he was a fully developed person, with character and substance. It occurred to me that Ted, in contrast, seemed as empty and insubstantial as discarded packaging.

There was something else I was seeing for the first time as I watched the movie, something much more disturbing: the victims, personified. It took a little while before they got to me. I was busy analyzing the movie and marveling at seeing my own case played out on screen. At first, when Jim would pop in I would excitedly describe how some scene was portrayed, what had been included, what had been left out. Allison Zieve, the legal assistant who was rescuing me from the mounds of unread transcript, was watching it with me. She managed a faint smile when I'd turn to her with some quip, but mostly she looked as though she was seeking signs from me of how she was supposed to reconcile this story of a horrible murderer with our professionally detached and zealous representation of that same man. In my mind I tried to dismiss her apparent reaction as a nonlawyer's naïveté. Eventually, though, I fell silent too and tried not to show what I was feeling inside.

There they were: young women just living their lives, as I lived mine. There they were: for no reason other than that they were young women selected randomly for brutalization and destruction by Ted Bundy. Carole DeRonch, the one woman known to have escaped one of his abductions, was no longer a problematic witness—she was a blessed miracle. The crimes were no longer compilations of evidence to be undermined but precious lives to be mourned. As each woman was approached, I rooted for her, I willed the story to turn out differently than I knew it had. I willed her to kill Ted instead of being harmed herself. To kill him over and over, to tear him apart, to rip him to shreds. My mind shouted, *Why am I defending this merciless monster?! He doesn't deserve my help!* A wave of revulsion rose to the surface.

I pushed it back down. For better or worse, my emotions were an integral part of my work on this case. They had gotten me into it, kept me going. There was no way to separate them from my duty to provide Ted with legal representation. I was either with him or against him, I couldn't be both. I didn't dare be both. I couldn't hold such disparate impulses in my head at the same time: to save his life, to wish he'd been killed. It had been easy until now. I had felt so strongly about the case because I had felt so strongly about preventing a death, but that was when the only life there was to save was Ted's. Now I had been thrown back in time, back to when his victims' lives could have been saved, and I was rooting for that to have happened by any means possible. But I was also in the present, and in the present I did hold a life in my hand and it was Ted's. My commitment had to be pure. Otherwise, if he lost his life, how would I know I'd done all I could, that I hadn't done something unconsciously to make that happen? I may not have been the best lawyer he could have found, and I would certainly make mistakes, but I could control my thoughts and feelings and keep them pure. That much I could do for him. I had to. For me.

I was alone when the video came to the end; everyone else had left somewhere along the way. I had the television removed from my office and took the extra chairs back. I worked on paying work the rest of the day and gave the case and the tape no further thought. Even when I walked home that night in the dark, and felt a vulnerability I had never felt before, I didn't think of Ted. I felt aware, as I'd never felt before, that there really were human beings—men—out there who would attack and kill an unknown woman for no reason at all, no matter what she said or did. But I didn't think of Ted. I felt afraid for me and for all women, because of the real existence of these men. But I also felt terrified that the whole country had seen that movie and now would never let the governor get away with delaying Ted's execution no matter what I promised to do.

Ted wrote to me soon after the movie had aired, all of a sudden insisting I file a cert. petition in the Lake City case. He'd certainly changed his tune on that. He said that the movie had enraged the public more than he had ever seen before, based on the subsequent coverage and the letters he'd received. He wanted to make sure that there was some legal action going on so that the governor would be less likely to sign a warrant. It was the first time he had expressed fear to me. He truly was shook up and frightened. He, too, knew that a second warrant in the Chi Omega case wouldn't be just a warning shot, as the first had been. Second warrants had been known to be fatal.

Despite—because of—its dead-accurate movie, NBC was now my mortal enemy. It had struck my wounded bird, my ward, my charge, my Ted. All I could see was that NBC had recklessly inflamed the public without a thought that a real person, Ted, might be fatally affected. I soon got my chance for revenge, and it was satisfying.

On May 12, an NBC lawyer in Florida called, notifying me that he had filed a motion in the Tallahassee trial court to obtain the tapes of the police emergency call made from the Chi Omega sorority house on the night of the murders. NBC believed that such a tape existed in the sealed portion of the trial record. Apparently they were going to broadcast a documentary to follow up their well-received dramatization. Apparently, just as Ted Bundy sold newspapers, Ted Bundy sold TV programs. I told NBC's Florida counsel I'd oppose any attempt to unseal the records and would request a delay to give me time to respond and appear in court. He was shocked that I'd object, that I'd think I'd have some grounds upon which to object: What possible legal interest could we have in protecting a seven-year-old trial record that had resulted in conviction anyway? I didn't know what grounds, but I knew why I didn't want the tapes released. They would only provide more fuel to the fire under Ted.

I tried desperately to get in touch with Lynn Alan Thompson in Tallahassee, who had been one of Ted's public defenders at trial and was now in private practice. I wanted him to appear for us in the Tallahassee court to oppose NBC's motion. The hearing was scheduled for the next day and the judge had refused my request for a postponement. Mr. Thompson, whom I'd never contacted before, didn't return my increasingly frantic calls. That was a problem for me now, but it was even more ominous for the future. We were going to need all of Ted's former lawyers to back us up in the collateral proceedings. Was this one going to be hostile, ready to testify that Ted, while obnoxious, had been a perfectly competent defendant?

The next day the court in Tallahassee not only granted NBC's motion but, on its own initiative, crossed out NBC's description of the one tape it wanted and wrote "all video and audio recordings." It was going to be a really big show. The recordings and videos were going to be played for the public the next day and I had absolutely no idea what was in them. Things were moving too fast for me to handle this on my own. Jim Coleman stepped in and faxed an emergency appeal to the Florida Supreme Court.

The NBC lawyer was furious. This was supposed to have been a simple matter; there were no grounds to oppose it. The next morning the press gathered in the courtroom and prepared for a performance. I could imagine the resulting headlines: THE SECRET TAPES OF TED BUNDY, THE ONES HIS LAWYERS TRIED TO SUPPRESS. Just as it was about to begin, however, the Florida Supreme Court ruled in our favor, called the judge, and the show was off. CCR's paralegal arrived just in time to see the throng of disappointed reporters walking back to their cars. Ahhhhh, a little victory. I thought it was a good omen. In all likelihood, however, the Florida Supreme Court probably only wanted to prevent any judicial error or grounds of appeal that might delay the execution of Ted Bundy. Press freedom paled in comparison to such a portentous goal.

With that settled, I again turned back to the Lake City cert. petition. This fifty-page document on the single issue of hypnotizing Andy Anderson was becoming a real albatross. I had hoped to file it before the May 5 cert. decision, but hadn't made it, partly because of the NBC tapes case and partly because I was slowed by increasing anxiety now that execution was a real possibility, my first cert. petition had been unsuccessful, and Ted was back on the front pages. Finally, since the law firm was moving to fancier quarters in the fall anyway, I tacked the whole thing directly onto the wall of my office, so I could see every one of its fifty pages at the same time. This seemed to help give order to what felt like chaos.

In the midst of all this CCR called to say they were sending me the public defender's files in the Chi Omega case. When they asked whether I wanted them sent via UPS or driven up in a U-Haul truck, I thought—as I had when that first reporter had asked if I was going to have a press office—that they were kidding. Again, I was wrong. When the boxes arrived—UPS, collect—they filled a third of my office. Piled against the wall near the door, they rose all the way to the ceiling. I was completely surrounded: thirty thousand pages of transcript from Ted's two trials behind me and an entire wall of who-knows-what in front of me. Boxes and boxes, in all different shapes and sizes, of *everything* the public defender had accumulated during the eighteen-month pretrial investigation and trial of the Chi Omega case. Presumably, they were filled with pleadings, file notes, correspondence, and, worst of all, evidence. They balanced precariously atop each other, threatening at any time to topple down and spill their gruesome contents.

When they had menaced me long enough, I turned the heap of public defender files over to Allison, hoping to have them nicely inventoried and summarized for me, never having to go through them myself. But Allison wouldn't let me off that easy. Once she had arranged the files in a workroom, she insisted I come see what was there. I think she was looking for a clue, again, as to how, as part of the legal team representing this man, she was supposed to react to some of the things she was being forced to deal with other than in utter horror and revulsion. Specifically, Allison wanted me to look at the evidence. I couldn't think of any respectable reason to refuse. Some of what Allison had found was harmless enough—except that it was real. A tennis shoe in Ted's size ten, for instance, was in one box. It had been compared to the footprints that had been found leading away from the Chi Omega house and into the woods. Real, but harmless. Sort of creepy, but it also looked kind of absurd. I could handle that.

Some things were a little harder not to react to. The small, unmarked box containing plaster casts of three sets of teeth, for example, upper and lower. There was a fourth indentation in the tissue paper—one set of tooth impressions was missing. Later I found that fourth set when I dropped in on CCR and found somebody clicking them at people as if to bite them. Those were Ted's. With the discovery of the cast teeth, things were getting creepier, yet I still managed a professional assessment. One of the issues at the Chi Omega trial was whether a "forensic dentist" could testify, based on photographs alone, that the bite mark on a victim's body could have been inflicted only by the accused—and by nobody else. This was a very new and suspect concept, and Ted's public defenders had used these sets of false teeth to show that different types of teeth could leave the same mark. That was just good lawyering. Nothing wrong with that. Nothing to be upset by.

But then there were the photographs themselves, gigantic enlargements for use at trial. Close-ups of a woman's buttocks with an ordinary ruler laid across them to show scale. Dark, angry tooth marks marred the skin's surface. I tried to weave this into a lawyer's story for Allison. I started to say something like, "Look at how indistinct those marks are—they're barely visible. How could anyone claim that they could identify one man? . . ." I fell silent. It was true—the bite-mark evidence presented at trial was extremely weak. Bite marks aren't anywhere near as identifiable as fingerprints, particularly from a photograph alone. The evidence did not prove they were Ted's.

But it was hard to hold the thought that the scientific invalidity of tooth-mark identification was all the photographs stood for. I stared at the pictures, unable to avert my eyes. Blown up larger than life were the buttocks of a young woman, lifeless, exposed as she would never allow herself to be if she were alive to defend herself, a ruler lying across her as if she were merely another object. *Somebody's* tooth marks were on her. That was a fact I couldn't deny, nobody could deny. Who cared that you couldn't *prove* they were Ted's? They were *in fact* Ted's tooth marks. Ted had hurt that girl; touched and bitten and killed that girl. The same revulsion rose up in me that had surfaced with the TV dramatization. For a minute it seemed as though this woman's death and mutilation was the point, not whether the evidence was legally sound. But only for a minute. I erased that thought from my mind. I had to. I was Bundy's lawyer.

* * *

I filed the Lake City cert. petition on May 21, as I'd promised the Court and Governor Graham. So far, the governor had not signed a warrant in the Chi Omega case. So far, so good. Maybe the governor had decided to hold off, since he could see I was doing everything possible to move the legal proceedings along in both cases. It seemed only sensible. It seemed only fair.

CHAPTER 6

No such luck.

In normal appellate litigation it is the issues in the case that drive the schedule. The court can dismiss the insubstantial claims immediately, call for further briefing on the difficult legal questions, and conduct evidentiary hearings on those that require more factual development before they can be decided. The reason for the courts' careful consideration is that appellate decisions are decisions of law, not fact; they not only apply to the matter at hand but also set precedent for all future cases that raise the same legal questions. That's why it had taken the Florida Supreme Court four years to decide the Lake City case. They were not going to overturn Ted Bundy's conviction no matter what, but they clearly were disturbed by the alteration of Andy Anderson's testimony under hypnosis conducted by the police and prosecutors. They finally issued an opinion that it had been okay in his case, but that thereafter, in any *other* case, such hypnotically altered testimony was not constitutionally admissible as evidence. Not that the Constitution had changed in the meantime.

That it takes time to make appellate decisions is right and good, because each one applies to us all and becomes etched into the U.S. Constitution. The greater and greater limitations imposed in recent years by the courts and Congress on death penalty appeals, for example,

DEATH WARRANT
STATE OF FLORIDA

WHEREAS, THEODORE ROBERT BUNDY, did on the 9th day of February, 1978, murder Kimberly Diane Leach; and

WHEREAS, THEODORE ROBERT BUNDY was found guilty of murder in the first degree and was sentenced to death on the 12th day of February, 1980; and

WHEREAS, the Florida Supreme Court upheld the sentence of death imposed upon THEODORE ROBERT BUNDY on the 9th day of May, 1985, and Certiorari was denied by the United States Supreme Court on the 14th day of October, 1986; and

WHEREAS, it has been determined that Executive Clemency, as authorized by Article IV, Section 8(a), Florida Constitution, is not appropriate; and

WHEREAS, attached hereto is a copy of the record pursuant to Section 922.09, Florida Statutes;

NOW, THEREFORE, I, BOB MARTINEZ, as Governor of the State of Florida and pursuant to the authority and responsibility vested by the Constitution and Laws of Florida do hereby issue this warrant directing the Superintendent of the Florida State Prison to cause the sentence of death to be executed upon THEODORE ROBERT BUNDY on some day of the week beginning noon, Monday, the 23rd day of January, 1989 and ending noon, Monday, the day of 30th, 1989, in accord with the provisions of the laws of the State of Florida.

IN TESTIMONY WHEREOF, I have hereunto set my hand and caused the Great Seal of the State of Florida to be affixed at Tallahassee, the Capitol, this _17 72_ day of January, 1989.

GOVERNOR

ATTEST:

SECRETARY OF STATE

also automatically apply to people convicted of tax evasion, mail fraud, or reckless driving.

When U.S. Supreme Court Justice John Paul Stevens wrote, "Death is different," he meant that death penalty cases naturally deserved closer scrutiny since the consequences were so uniquely harsh and final. But the way in which "death is different" today is that death penalty cases are *expedited*—and given *less* real consideration than other types of appeals—to accommodate arbitrarily set execution dates. Once a death warrant is signed it is the execution date that drives the court schedules. Substantial issues receive real consideration only if a court is willing to stay the execution first. That's a big step and, as I found, courts are very reluctant to act like courts under these circumstances. A death penalty case under warrant is not a normal legal case; it's a hot potato.

Art Wiedinger had reason to sound a little uncomfortable, then, when he called me on May 22.

"Ms. Nelson, this is Art Wiedinger from Governor Graham's office. How are you today?"

"Fine," I said, trying to sound optimistic. "How are you?"

"Fine, thank you, ma'am." He paused. "Ah, Ms. Nelson, the governor, ah, signed a death warrant against Mr. Bundy today in the Chi Omega case." He paused again. "And, ah, the warden has scheduled the execution for July 2."

So much for litigation on the issues. We were now in a race against time. July 2, 1986, was to be an extra special execution day, a celebration of the tenth anniversary of the end of the U.S. Supreme Court's moratorium on capital punishment. The governor had taken the unprecedented step of scheduling *two* men to be executed on July 2. The other man, Gerald Stano, was being represented by a new lawyer at CCR.

I had told Jim and Jeff a few weeks back (it already seemed like a lifetime ago) that I'd stay on the case for the collateral stage. I hadn't discussed this with CCR, though. Since the warrant had been signed and the collateral stage would begin now, I wanted to talk to Mark Olive about whether he wanted the case back. After all, he was the expert. It had made sense, or at least hadn't made any difference, that the effort to get a stay from the U.S. Supreme Court in February had been handled by a Washington firm. Same for the Lake City cert.

petition. But the collateral proceedings were a different matter. Almost all the litigation would take place in Florida, and, of course, the client was there. There would be more interaction with the offices of the Florida governor and the attorney general. And collateral proceedings were much more complex than the direct appeal; involving many more pleadings and courtroom presentations. Evidence would have to be gathered and witnesses prepared. I knew this would all be very important to a death penalty litigator as impassioned as Mark. But all of a sudden he was never available when I called. This was particularly perplexing because, whatever they might think of corporate lawyers, CCR worked hard to cultivate and support its volunteers and were generally extremely responsive. It was even more surprising since a warrant had been signed. CCR would usually do anything for a man under warrant. When I'd been down there in February, the entire office had put down its other work to help me make my filing at the Florida Supreme Court. But now Mark didn't want to talk to me, and I had no idea why. I felt abandoned. What had I done wrong?

To this day I don't know why Mark Olive would not speak to me around that time, but one thing is obvious. If CCR had wanted or even been willing to take back Ted's case they would have returned my phone calls. I had already gotten the feeling that Ted was despised within CCR as much as he was by the rest of the world. CCR was in Tallahassee, for one thing, which apparently had never again felt as carefree as it had before Ted Bundy's assault on the Chi Omega sorority house had destroyed its sense of security. It also seemed that much of the staff at CCR were motivated by the belief that each particular client did not *deserve* the death penalty for one specific reason or another. Most of CCR's clients had abused or neglected childhoods; many had organic brain disorders or developmental disabilities. The staff at CCR always could find *something* that showed a particular client was not really an evil person but a victim himself in some ways. No one thought this about Ted Bundy. The apparent cold deliberateness of his crimes, his seeming mocking of justice at his trial, precluded any such sympathy. He seemed to be the boy next door who just decided one day to kidnap and kill women. Out of the blue; just for fun.

And there was also the matter of CCR's state funding. CCR was in a peculiar political position. It began as a private, nonprofit group— the Volunteer Resource Center—that found volunteer lawyers for death row inmates. As the rate of executions increased, however, it

while it is constrained to speak in legal terms, is made up of human beings. We were going to have to make our case in such a way as to raise at least a scintilla of doubt against the universal perception that Ted Bundy absolutely deserved to die. We had to develop something to at least suggest the possibility of mental mitigation. We had to provide some clue as to *why* Ted Bundy did what he did. Leaving CCR, I went up the street to the public defender's office to see Mike Minerva. Minerva was now an employee in the office he once headed—he had been voted out of office after Ted's trial. Although an especially gentle and hospitable man by nature, he greeted me with great tenuousness. He seemed shell-shocked, wary of getting involved in Ted's case again. Minerva had kept meticulous notes of his experience with Ted, but when he pulled them out and began to review them he peered over the pages and asked if I had authorization from Ted to receive this information.

I told him Ted was aware I was going to see him, I already had his other files—the ones CCR had sent up—and Ted had never raised any objection. Even though the execution date was fast approaching, my assurances were not sufficient—Minerva had been burned badly by Ted before. He did confirm for me what I already knew about the competency hearing and his staff's several attempts to re-raise the issue during trial, but he would not divulge anything else. With obvious reluctance at having to inconvenience me, he put away his file without revealing what I really needed to know: What had occurred behind the scenes? What had Ted really been doing? What had Ted really been like? I left promising to send Ted's authorization.

The next day I drove to Starke to see Ted. He signed some releases I had typed up at CCR, and we discussed my plans for fighting the death warrant. It was always important to me during my visits that I soothe the fear I imagined him to be feeling and not alarm or worry him more. Foremost, I wanted him to trust me, to know I was not judging him. Nonetheless, I had to tell him this time that I would be developing the issue of his incompetency to stand trial. And he reluctantly had to disagree.

"No one will ever believe I was incompetent—I handled myself too professionally," he said. "It will look like you have a weak case to make such a frivolous claim. Anyone who was at my trial would know I was anything but incompetent."

But I wasn't putting this to a vote; it was the only issue that was going to be of any gut-interest in this case—Ted Bundy's mental state.

Not wanting to seem ungrateful or pushy, he did not insist that I forgo the claim. But he shook his head at its uselessness and clearly was tense. That same dark color came into his face that I had seen when I first saw him in that holding cell. And then it passed. He recovered his polite and gracious client mode, expressing his great appreciation for my work, my visit, and my keeping him abreast of the case. He trusted my judgment completely, he said.

Since issues raised in collateral proceedings are necessarily those not raised or considered fully before, collateral proceedings begin again at the trial level, with the same judge who presided over the original trial. Due to the extensive pretrial publicity, Ted's 1979 trial for the Chi Omega murders had been moved from Tallahassee to Miami. Florida Circuit Court Judge Edward Cowart presided.

As luck would have it, Judge Cowart, who had gone into private practice for several years, had recently returned to the bench. I had seen pictures of him in the news clippings of the trial. He was a mammoth man, built for the flowing black robes of office, who had never failed to appreciate the Bundy case as theater. He had bantered with Ted during the trial, catered to his whims and demands, and finally allowed Ted to decimate his defense team. At every opportunity, Judge Cowart handed Ted the rope to hang himself. He even announced Ted's sentence of death in the manner of a TV Western: "You could have been a fine young man, but you took the wrong road, pardner." Ted, of course, had thought that he, too, was a character—the hero, of course—in a make-believe courtroom drama, and had responded to the judge in kind. It was not until he was sentenced to death a second time, six months later, that reality began to sink in.

On June 10 I called Judge Cowart and told him I was filing the usual *pro hac vice* and *in forma pauperis* motions as well as a motion for the payment of experts. I explained that the major issue had to do with Ted's mental state at the time of trial, especially his behind-the-scenes dealings with his lawyers, and that I needed expert testimony to investigate the case. With traditional Southern courtesy, Judge Cowart was pleased to make my acquaintance and looked forward to receiving the motions. Three days later he granted the first two and denied the last. Two out of three didn't help us at all. At least now, since the court had refused to pay, maybe Jim would be willing to commit the firm's resources for an evaluation. I had no real case without it. I invited Art Norman up to meet Jim and tell us what he'd come up with after his interviews with Ted.

Saturday, June 14, Flag Day, was also the day of the firm picnic, the only event that included everyone who worked at the firm at all levels and their families. Jim and Jeff and I met Dr. Norman in the deserted office building in a narrow, windowless conference room. I was hoping desperately that we could hire him. I did not know how else I was going to put a viable case together. Regardless of the legal issue of whether Ted had been competent to stand trial, the key would be understanding and explaining why Ted had acted the way that he had at the trial and—although it was not directly at issue at this stage— at the time of the crimes. Surprisingly, Ted Bundy had been subjected to very little psychological evaluation in the ten years since he was first incarcerated for kidnapping in Utah.

It was so still and quiet that Saturday it felt as if the conference room had been hermetically sealed. Jim, Jeff, and I were dressed in shorts for the firm picnic, and we sat back as Dr. Norman unveiled his theory, the theory I would be counting on to save Ted's life. The air-conditioning in the building was off, and we were slowly using up the available oxygen as we listened to an explanation of Ted's mental workings that was worse than my worst nightmare. Dr. Norman didn't say that Ted had brain damage, he didn't say that Ted was mentally ill, he said that Ted just had wanted to kill. For Ted, Dr. Norman said, it had been no different than a hunter shooting a deer and tying it to the hood of his car—only he'd gone after the game no one else dared to, the game that was the most highly valued: attractive young women. Ted was the "supermale," he'd gone all the way. He'd dared to break the ultimate "taboo." Dr. Norman was fascinated by what Ted had told him. He continued on in great detail about exactly how Ted himself saw his murders. The rest of us didn't speak as the room closed in. The combined horror of all that Dr. Norman was saying was too much for me. My mind stopped processing information in self-defense. When it was mercifully over, we all shook hands with Dr. Norman and parted. I had exchanged some open-eyed glances with Jim, and thought I saw the same utter dismay I felt, but he said nothing about it. I got no reaction, no feedback. What was I supposed to think about what we'd just heard? I suppose I was in the same position now that Allison had been in as she tried to put the gruesome evidence of the crimes in some professional context. And Jim was giving me no clues.

I rode to the picnic crouched in the back of Jeff's station wagon—his kids' in their car seats took up all the seating space. My mind and emotions were still numb, but my body wasn't. My stomach was turning over and I felt as if I was suffocating. The ride seemed interminable. That morning had held all sorts of horrors for me: the terrible details of the crimes, the glimpse into Ted's utter remorselessness, Dr. Norman's apparently enthusiastic embrace of Ted's self-justification. The fact was that we had less than three weeks left; no money for other experts; and no usable theory with a conclusion other than that Ted had just murdered women on purpose, to surpass men lacking the courage. To even think of the "supermale" construct: women as mere prey, the subject of pure hatred in the heart-of-hearts of all men. To think that such a theory even could be spoken by a professional man such as Dr. Norman. Did something about it ring true for him? For lots of men? I was deeply disturbed. I didn't mingle at the picnic.

On Monday we prepared to face the collateral proceedings in big-law-firm style: litigation with all the trimmings. Second-year law students were coming into the firm from their Ivy League schools for internships as summer associates, and the lucky ones were assigned to our case. Imagine them back at school in the fall, exchanging tales with their fellow students:

"How was it at your firm?" they'd ask.

"Pretty good," their classmate would answer. "First I did secondary-source research on nonpreferred-stockholder liability for negligent omissions of material-but-insignificant facts, and then, because I'd done so well, they let me go with them to the printers one night, where we proofread a draft prospectus until dawn. What did you do?"

"I helped save Bundy from the chair." It had a nice ring to it. And besides, our issues were genuinely interesting.

With Judge Cowart we would raise only those issues that could not have been raised before. If we didn't get a stay there, we'd appeal to the Florida Supreme Court. When, inevitably, that failed, we'd file a habeas corpus petition in the Federal District Court for the Southern District of Florida. There we could present for the first time in federal court all the claims that had been made in Ted's original Florida appeal, along with those we'd just raised in collateral proceedings. If we failed in the U.S. District Court we could appeal to the Eleventh Circuit Court of Appeals in Atlanta, and, finally, if worse came to worse, to the U.S. Supreme Court. I didn't expect to have to go anywhere near that far, though. We had good issues. The only way a court could refuse to grant us a stay of execution would be to dismiss every one of our claims on the spot. Our issues were too strong and numerous for that. I was utterly certain that once we got to the first federal court—where the judges are appointed for life and not elected for terms like Florida state judges—we would get our stay of execution.

We still had the hypnosis, grand jury, and death-qualification issues I'd included in my first cert. petition, and the free choice of counsel and ineffective assistance of counsel issues I'd left out. We also had prejudicial pretrial publicity, scientifically unreliable bite-mark evidence, Judge Cowart's improper ruling that Ted could represent himself when it became clear he could not cooperate with his public defenders, and even a sleeping juror. We also had a couple of boilerplate death penalty issues—constitutional claims common to capital cases that were included in every appropriate case so as to percolate through the system toward the U.S. Supreme Court. In all, we had seventeen broad categories of claims. But the strongest claim by far was incompetency.

Mike Minerva had first formally raised the issue of Ted's competency on June 1, 1979, with a motion suggesting that Ted was incapable of assisting his lawyers in his own defense, and was uncomprehending of the strength of the evidence against him in the Chi Omega case. Minerva had observed Ted's irrational behavior over the entire sixteen-month period since his arrest. When first arrested Ted had asked his lawyers for a court order preventing law enforcement personnel from interviewing him outside the lawyers' presence. Then, at night, he'd invite those same police officers into his cell for long, rambling talks. As the investigation progressed, he had been unable to decide whether to accept the public defender's services or to represent himself. In the meantime, he announced to the court that he was ready to proceed to trial but believing the state had no evidence against him, he had done nothing to prepare. When the trial was postponed, he had switched gears and flown into a frenzy, taking ninety depositions of potential witnesses in the fall of 1978. None of them served any useful purpose, other than, perhaps, helping to solidify witnesses' identification of him—a decided plus for the prosecution.

Always referring to himself in the third person, Ted would ask questions such as "Are you familiar with Ted Bundy?" "Do you see him in the room with you today?"

By the spring of 1979 Ted finally had accepted the representation of Mike Minerva and his staff and had agreed to allow them to pursue a plea bargain to encompass both the Chi Omega and Lake City cases. But even though Minerva told him this would mean they would not be prepared to go to trial, that the plea negotiations would damage his case at any subsequent trial, Ted simultaneously had continued to suggest to the assistant public defenders ways they could prepare for trial. In May Minerva had asked the advice of Dr. Emanuel Tanay, a Detroit psychiatrist and prominent expert on violent offenders, who had suggested that although Ted seemed to have a tenuous grasp on reality, he might be competent to enter a plea bargain. His agreement to enter a plea would show he understood the weight of the evidence and the gravity of the charges. A rejection of it, however, would indicate that Ted was controlled by his delusions and impulses and incompetent to assist in his defense.

The carefully negotiated plea was lost on May 31, when Ted was to have affirmed it in court. Instead he had made a ranting motion to fire Mike Minerva, who had moved immediately for a judicial determination of Ted's competence to stand trial. Ted had objected to the hearing and had filed a motion for special counsel "to protect him"—again referring to himself in the third person—"from an attempt by his public defender to find him incompetent."

Judge Cowart had gladly granted Ted's motion, given him special counsel for the competency hearing, and excluded his public defenders—who had all the evidence and had requested the hearing in the first place—from the proceeding. The special counsel, Brian Hayes, at Ted's request, had argued that he was competent. The state had argued the same thing. Dr. Tanay was put on the stand, but only to discredit his report. Judge Cowart had noted the uniqueness of the situation as the proceeding reached its inevitable conclusion: "Gentlemen, it is very seldom, at least in this court's career, that we have an opportunity to rule consistent with what both lawyers argued. I don't think I've ever been able to do that." Since no evidence had been solicited to the contrary, Judge Cowart found Ted competent to stand trial, fully able to assist and cooperate with his lawyers—who'd been left out in the hall without a say in the matter. Trial was set to commence in less than two weeks, and Ted's public defenders would be starting virtually from scratch.

At the trial, Ted had conducted himself exactly as Dr. Tanay had predicted he would: He had sabotaged the entire defense effort out of spite, distrust, and grandiose delusion. Ted had disrupted the proceedings, bantered with the press, and obstructed his lawyers. When his lawyers had attempted again to raise the issue of Ted's competency, the court had decided to resolve the arguments between them by first making Ted co-counsel of his defense team, then finally chief counsel, relegating the assistant public defenders to "stand-by counsel." During the penalty phase, Ted had barred his lawyers from introducing any evidence (such as Dr. Tanay's report) of any mental disturbance. The jury never learned his mental competence had ever been at issue. Ted was convicted and sentenced to death. Brian Hayes, who spoke with him immediately afterward, had found him to be "blasé about the conviction" and unconcerned that he had just been sentenced to death.

Thanks to Ted and Judge Cowart's bizarre collusion in making sure no one argued or testified against Ted's competency at the supposed competency hearing that issue had not been tried before. We were certain to win the right to have an evidentiary hearing on it. Judge Cowart's kangaroo competency hearing, and Ted's demonstrated incompetence to assist his lawyers at the trial that followed, were great substantive issues as well. Not only were they on a solid legal foundation, but the facts made intuitive sense. The real Ted Bundy, who had seemed such an enigma at trial, began to come into focus. There was something driving Ted's self-defeating behavior, something other than "diabolical genius," something beyond his control. I doled out our seventeen issues to the Bundy team's legion of summer associates for research and development. Jim planned our litigation strategy as the execution date drew near. We did a little bit of preliminary legal sparring while we were still in Washington. In one such action, Judge Cowart actually granted our request, despite opposition from the state, to hold the state court proceeding in Miami (where the trial had been held), rather than in Tallahassee (where it had originated). We were glad for that. In addition to being the scene of the crime, the Tallahassee trial court's recent actions in the NBC tapes case had not been encouraging.

On Sunday, June 22, I headed down to Florida for the duration of the death warrant, stopping first in Starke to see Ted, and, for the first time, his wife, Carole. I needed Ted to sign the pleadings, verifying that the facts were true to the best of his knowledge. I was apprehensive about how he'd take my very prominent claim that he had been mentally incompetent at the time of the trial. If he refused to sign, with the execution scheduled for only a week away, we'd have to consider whether he was *presently* competent to proceed.

CHAPTER 7

I dropped off a copy of our pleadings at the prison and drove back into Starke. I wanted to give Ted time to read our claims before signing them—and to have time to do it in private. I cringed at his reading the competency claim, given that he still liked to think of himself as co-counsel on the case. But Mike Minerva's fastidious private notes—which he had forwarded to me promptly upon receiving Ted's signed release—had told a different story.

While Ted read, I went back to Starke's fast-food strip to meet Carole Boone. This was a woman who had come to the aid of an accused murderer she'd known only casually several years before, when they'd worked in the same office. She had married him after he'd been sentenced to death and convicted of murder a *second* time. Her life apparently revolved around his needs; she moved from Seattle to be close by and visit as often as the prison allowed. I had a picture in my mind of what such a woman would be like. I imagined her as young, flighty, mindless, dependent, totally vulnerable to manipulation. I pictured her all dolled up for a prison visit. But that's not what Carole Boone was like.

At the McDonald's where Carole had suggested we meet, a woman approached me with a child and a young man in tow. She was tall and big boned, with long auburn hair hanging straight and unattended to.

She wore eyeglasses. The child hopping up and down beside Carole was a girl about four years old, her own brown hair hanging in her eyes. The young man was about nineteen, with thick black hair and a strong, compact build. Carole was very businesslike. After a firm handshake she identified the child as her daughter, Tina, the young man as her son, Jamey. The warmth and strong bond among the three was apparent. They were obviously a very close family. Jamey was silent but extremely vigilant. His protective stance was heightened by his imposing bodybuilder's physique.

We had lunch inside and tried to make small talk. Carole asked politely about my trip and thanked me for all my efforts, telling me how pleased Ted was with my work. She asked how we expected the case to go for Ted over the next few days. She reminded me to keep in close contact with Ted; Ted was entitled to that. She asked for nothing for herself. I was impressed with how caring and confident a mother she was. She treated both her children with great respect and handled Tina's growing impatience with ease. Nonetheless, it was difficult to continue talking in code words to avoid tipping off Tina that Ted was in trouble, although she seemed to sense the tension enough to want to stay close to her mother. Carole and I tried to talk more frankly in the play yard, while Jamey entertained his sister, but Tina would not leave Carole alone. Finally, Carole reluctantly agreed to take a walk with me, away from her brood.

At the edge of the highway, on a little piece of dirt under a scrawny tree, I explained the competency claim to Carole. I told her why it was such a strong issue, how well it was supported by the facts. It was the best issue we had for stopping this execution and, maybe eventually, to removing his death sentences altogether. After a while I noticed that Carole was not responding. She stood stiffly, staring grimly ahead. I asked her if I could count on her support. Carole did not turn to face me as she spoke.

"Ted was not incompetent. I was there at the trial; he was anything but incompetent. There is nothing mentally wrong with him."

I switched tactics, telling her I could understand if she didn't agree with the facts of the claim, but wouldn't she at least help impress Ted with how necessary it was to save his life? Through her clenched jaw, I got my answer:

"Ted will never go for it. He'll never let you claim he was incompetent."

Our conversation was over. This issue was obviously not negotiable;

it was extremely important to her, maybe because Ted had been so vehement about it at the trial, or maybe for some reason of her own. In any case, it surprised me. I had thought a woman who had dedicated her life to a man on death row would support *anything* to save his life. Apparently not. It seemed as though there was something more complex at stake here for Carole than I'd imagined, perhaps some image of Ted even more important to keep alive than Ted himself.

I drove back to the prison dreading the confrontation ahead. Did Ted feel the same way as Carole did? The two of them were so closely in sync, and Ted has stressed before that all crucial decisions were "family decisions." I thought over the factual validity of the competency issue to reassure myself that it was an honest claim. Ted had had good, dedicated lawyers at his trial and *they* had believed he was incompetent. Kindly and scrupulous Mike Minerva would not have raised it otherwise, particularly in the face of the obvious disbelief of both Ted and the court. Ted himself, in what appeared to have been a state of extreme confusion and excitement, had destroyed his only clear chance to avoid the death penalty. The plea bargain had been a done deal when he went nuts in court, fired Mike Minerva and accused him of sabotage, and then calmly asked him to proceed with the plea hearing. Dr. Tanay had said that Ted had a mental illness that prevented him from acting in his own best interest, that he would even aid the prosecution if he could. The competency hearing had been a clear sham, the trial a disaster. Ted had been facing murder charges, with a possible death sentence, and all that had mattered to him apparently was that he be in charge.

Not only was the competency claim very strong on its own, I told myself, it was also the window we needed on what really had been going on underneath Ted's otherwise inexplicable behavior at the trial. Such as his obnoxious posturing for the press, his disrespectful and destructive bantering with Judge Cowart, his utter lack of concern for what the jury saw or heard. This public behavior seemed to have contributed to the public's heated insistence on execution. He appeared to have murdered those women with deliberate stealth and then mocked justice to its face besides. But if, instead, Ted's self-destructive behavior at the trial was a manifestation of a mental illness over which he had no control, a responsible, humane, and honest judge would not be able to ignore the implication that Ted had been mentally unable to assist in his own defense. We could not go to court without the competency issue. Not with the stakes as they were. Ted had to sign. I had to convince him right now, or we couldn't carry out our plan to save him.

When I got to the prison, I learned to my dismay that, for the first time, because it was so close to the scheduled execution date, I was not to be allowed in the same room with Ted. I would have to speak with him through a glass barrier. Ted was now on "phase II" of death watch. It was not a good situation for discussing something so sensitive with Ted. When I was led in I found him sitting glumly at one of the stalls; the other fifteen or so were empty. Two guards were sitting directly behind him. It wasn't possible to whisper, it was difficult enough to communicate in a regular voice through the little speaker in the window. Ted was bent over his copy of my brief. I expected the worst. To my surprise, though, it was the interview conditions that had Ted the most upset, not our brief. His rights were being violated by the prison, he whispered angrily, and he would not stand for that. He said that the prison was wrong, he was entitled to contact visits with his attorney even while on death watch. He was being singled out for extra restrictions again. Ted was in a bad mood. It was left to me to begin discussing the claims in the petition.

I spoke rapidly to keep from hearing an objection. I emphasized his pet issue, hypnosis. I told him the hypnosis issue looked good, I was very optimistic that we'd get a stay. It had been a good sign that we had won our motion to have the case heard in Miami rather than in Tallahassee. Then I talked of his family, another favorite topic. I had had a good meeting with Carole, I told him. She sent her love; Tina was adorable; Jamey seemed very nice. Finally, my babble segued into the competency claim, how it was primarily the procedural deficiencies in the competency hearing we were emphasizing, not Ted's behavior. We'd had to put a little of that in, but he already knew all the facts that had prompted Minerva to ask for that hearing in the first place. It was a form of insanity on my part that I thought I could put a spin on my 125-page brief when he'd just spent three hours reading it. Ted already knew the full extent of what I'd written, describing incidents where he had thought he was being brilliant when he was acting stupidly, out of irrational motivation. I guess I wanted to overwhelm him with words so he wouldn't tell me what he thought about it, and so I wouldn't have to deal with his refusal to allow the claim. Carole knew him better than I did—and she was certain Ted would choose death over disgrace.

Finally I stopped talking. Like Carole, Ted hadn't said anything while I talked on. He looked tense and wound up, dark again. We both looked at the petition in front of him. Without a word, Ted dropped his shoulders with a sigh, signaled the officers behind him for a pen, and slowly signed the verification with his usual belabored scrawl: "Theodore Robert Bundy."

Mission accomplished, I flew to Miami, rented a car, and met Dara to set up shop. Dara, the secretary who had volunteered to go to Florida with us, had arrived earlier in the day. She was twenty-one years old and had never left home before, much less flown on a plane. But she'd never mentioned that. She had made the reservations for all of us, taken an advance from the law firm, arranged for her replacement, learned how to operate the telecommunications system, and then her whole extended family had seen her off at the airport. Dara was on her own for the first time. We checked into the Hotel St. Michel in Coral Gables, across the street from Zuckerman, Spaeder & Evans, the law firm that had agreed to act as local counsel and to provide office space. (Under Florida court rules, we were required to designate local counsel to receive notices and to be available to advise us on local practice.) The St. Michel was really more of a *pensione* than a hotel. It had a few small rooms furnished in antiques, a large dining room that catered to the local crowd as well, and an ice cream parlor. Soon we would be on the news constantly—we would *be* the news in Florida—and the staff of the St. Michel would smile with pride as we passed through the tiny lobby. We may have been representing Florida's public enemy number one, but we were celebrities nonetheless. Today, however, we were just welcome customers renting four rooms for the week—Dara's, mine, Jim's, and one for Bill Davis, the summer associate along for the ride. He'd have tales to tell back at law school.

When the Bundy team walked down the street we looked like the Mod Squad—earnest young bespectacled Bill; tall, cool Jim; and me, the blonde. We were easy to spot once you'd seen us on TV—and people did spot us. Dara, on the other hand, was never seen with us in public, because if she wasn't needed at the office she snuck some sleep or disappeared with the rented car. When it was time to return to Washington, Dara's room bore the incriminating evidence: every inch of space was covered with unsteady piles of new clothes from The Gap. Homesick, Dara had sought haven in a familiar environment.

Dara and I spent the first two days of our stay in Miami rather leisurely. We'd spend about nine hours at work editing the motions we were going to file in state court, drafting the inevitable appeals we had to anticipate might follow, working on the word-processing system that was supposed to allow us to have the documents researched and drafted in Washington and transmitted electronically to us. Then we'd go out to eat on the firm. Dara was impressed. This was The Life.

On Wednesday, June 25, with seven days to go before the execution date, we had our first court hearing in the case, our first outing in public, and our first experience with the cameras. We arrived at the courthouse at 9:00 A.M. and were surprised when the bailiff said that the judge wanted to see Jim and me in chambers. Must be something important. The enormous Judge Cowart greeted us warmly and offered us coffee; he asked generally about our plans. We chatted noncommittally and wondered why we were there; we hadn't thought to ask who the man at the other end of the room was (we'd assumed he was a court employee) but we were introduced on the way out: he was a Miami *Herald* reporter. Judge Cowart apparently had engineered the meeting to provide him with a scoop. That was typical of the judge's approach to this case. After pronouncing Ted's death sentence, for example, Judge Cowart had invited the entire press corps into his chamber for interviews and had had his wife serve cake. Now he had a second chance to step into the limelight.

The actual hearing was brief. Jim made the oral argument. A lawyer for the state responded. Judge Cowart ruled against us. There was no need for an expert to examine Ted Bundy, he said. He himself had seen Ted in action and if there had been any evidence of mental illness he would have seen it. He also didn't see as how we needed any more time to investigate and prepare claims. Motion for stay DENIED. No real surprises but maddening all the same. I needed that expert assistance.

There were cameras in the courtroom that day, and when we left we were pursued by a pack of photographers and reporters shouting questions. When we kept on walking, one reporter told us we had to at least stop to allow photographs or risk the photographers in front of us tumbling backward over some balcony. It sounded like blackmail. By what right could they tell us what to do? This was not a show and we were not performers.

We spent the entire night drafting an appeal to the Florida Supreme Court and flew to Tallahassee the next day, Thursday, for the appeal hearing. Ever expectantly leaning in the direction in which he wanted to go, Jim declared we would win in Tallahassee and go straight home to Washington from there. It was wishful thinking at best, delusion at worst, but Jim maintained absolute confidence of success every step of the way. It's what kept him going, I guess. And his confidence kept me going. And mine kept Ted from freaking out. I hoped his trust was not misplaced.

So Jim, Bill Davis, and I checked out of the St. Michel and took our clothes with us to Tallahassee. A bewildered Dara rode with us to the airport and looked terrified as suddenly she was put in charge of the rental car and of clearing out the office now that we were on our way to Tallahassee to win our appeal and get a stay of execution. When we boarded the plane, a roar of enthusiasm arose from the rear: We were seated smack dab in the middle of the reporters and photographers flying up to cover our Florida Supreme Court appeal. They had us now.

Once in Tallahassee we dropped off our lengthy appeal papers and stopped by CCR to make phone calls. Within the hour the court was ready for argument. If it were any other type of case we would not have moved to the argument stage for months, with a decision months or even years later. But death is different. The court welcomed Jim back—he had represented Stephen Booker before them—and ruled against us immediately. When we inevitably flew right back down to Miami the very same day, the St. Michel was overjoyed. The manager was so chagrined that the maid had thrown out the shampoo I had inadvertently left behind that he offered to fire her. I said that that wasn't necessary.

The next day we worked around the clock to prepare the final motion for Judge Cowart, asking for relief on the merits of our claims, rather than just assistance and time. The newspapers were making the most of this horse race between Ted Bundy and the state of Florida. Even though the reporters, who were well informed, knew that we were probably going to succeed in getting a stay in federal court, their articles played the story as if Ted was certain to die. Interestingly enough, a couple of years later, during our doomed fight against Ted's fourth warrant, the press fanned the flames by suggesting that we had a good chance of succeeding. Ted Bundy's execution was entertainment, not news, and the proper mix of thrills and suspense had to be maintained.

So in false anticipation of Ted's imminent demise, the newspapers came out with extensive retrospectives of his history. Topping every one would be high school graduation pictures of six or eight of the young women he had murdered. Allegedly, I'd think to myself. I couldn't look at them. They couldn't be real. Each time, I ignored that spread of pictures as if it didn't exist. Then the text. The text would appear to describe the killings in Utah and Colorado in detail, including a map with the locations of the crimes, emphasizing their reality. I ignored all that, too. Basically, even though my very own case was in the headlines of every Florida paper, radiating from every newsrack, I never read past the first three paragraphs. The rest, Ted's past, threatened me.

Another measure of how seriously the press played this second death warrant was the sudden barrage of urgent messages from writers and reporters asking for a "final interview" with Ted Bundy before his execution. They'd "uh-huh" politely when I told them he was *not* going to be executed, so there was no need for a final interview, then they'd go on to repeat their request for one, "just in case." I said "no" to them all.

But none of this was helping my state of mind. I was getting more and more anxious, particularly now that we were going through a court or two every day. Then, on Friday, I got a little break. Jim Coleman, the last computer illiterate lawyer in Washington, had made plans for us to use Zuckerman, Spaeder's phones to connect us to our Washington office via modem. He had assumed this was possible with utter reliance on his baseless belief that computers were perfect, simple, and instantly responsive (at the same time reserving the right to say "I've always known those things were no damn good" when something went wrong). Naturally, then, while I had spent most of June writing briefs and, along with Jeff, supervising the summer associates and law clerks, Jim had been ordering the computer team into action. They were supposed to devise a system so that we could easily continue to receive supporting memoranda, drafts, and research from the team in Washington. Dara and I had spent nearly all of Thursday—a whole precious day during the final week of the death warrant—trying to realize this vision, but discovered we could not, due to some idiosyncrasy in Zuckerman, Spader's phone system. I jumped at the offer of the managing partner, John Evans, to work out of his home, where our modems presumably would work. On Friday, we moved to the cool den of his house, where there was a swimming pool just outside the sliding glass door, a wide-screen TV, a kitchenette well stocked with treats— consulting hopelessly with the computer team back in Washington.

Dara was in a panic, mindful that receiving the documents was truly a matter of life and death and, worse, her responsibility. I was blissfully enjoying this respite away from the real crisis, as we careened toward the execution date less than four days away. Life felt so different, so private, so *pleasant*, out there by the pool.

Telecommunications-wise, however, this attempt yielded only limited success—we got the documents, but they were garbled because the files were too big. When we gave up and went back to the office, Dara and I worked on piercing together the document ourselves on the computer. Bill Davis was, as usual, in the firm's tiny library, trying to find case support for some new argument that Jim had just invented but just *knew* there had to be precedent for. Jim was drafting motions and pacing around the office, maintaining a wide berth around the word-processing vortex, like a cartoon father helplessly awaiting the birth of his child. I, as usual, took over, inventing amateurish procedures for splitting this stupid document and officiously demonstrating them to Dara, naming the files Polly.1, Polly.2, etc.; not trusting to hand the problem over, not really wanting to face the larger, real task As if I could delay the execution date by burying myself in word-processing matters. Finally I took a walk in the dark and deserted halls of the office building around 3:00 A.M. Making good use of my absence, Dara expertly split the files we'd already received into usable segments and began printing them. I saw that they were named Dara.1, Dara.2, Dara.3. We were able to file the full brief the next morning, a Saturday. Judge Cowart set a hearing for Monday at 9:00 A.M.

The headlines continued: FOUR DAYS UNTIL BUNDY'S EXECUTION; BUNDY'S LAWYERS START TO RUN OUT OF TIME IN FIGHT TO BEAT OL' SPARKY. The press spoke with one voice—Bundy was going to die. Every day we received a hundred calls. The small law office had seen nothing like it before, and the receptionist was shocked that we weren't returning urgent phone calls from the likes of Connie Chung or *People* magazine. My ad hoc policy was to answer questions when a reporter happened to reach me, but not to return phone calls. The few interviews I gave in this haphazard manner served the same redemptive purpose that they had during the first death warrant back in February. It felt good to talk to people whose primary purpose was to draw me out, to keep me talking for more quotable quotes, and who cared only about the broadest parameters of the case—never coming near the real legal hurdles that were scaring me into an emotional coma. Only occasionally did someone dare ask the question I still didn't have an answer for, the question that would guarantee that the interview was over: "What about the victims?"

We actually got a full night's sleep on Saturday and, on Sunday morning, the Florida Bundy team met downstairs at the hotel for brunch. It was really mid morning already, the sun was streaming in from the windows, and the banquet tables were piled high with food, including tantalizing tropical fruits and sumptuous platters of breads and pastries. Calm and attractive locals in Sunday clothes milled about. There was a pot of coffee on our table and real half-and-half. Jim had bought a couple of Sunday papers and was reading the sports section. The troublesome front pages and editorials screaming "Death to Bundy" were strewn on the floor, upside down. Bill Davis was contributing to morale by joking around, teasing Jim to elicit good-natured growls. Dara was quiet and suppressing her smiles, trying her best to pretend there was nothing unusual for her about having a fancy brunch in a hotel in Miami. And I felt very cheery. Another break in the drama.

But then Jim and I got to talking. Jeff Robinson was supposed to be preparing the federal habeas corpus petition back in Washington that weekend. But we knew he also was working on another project that weekend—for a paying client and a demanding partner—and it would be hard for him to get away to work on our case. He had been assuring us that he'd have no problem putting the petition together and sending it down with a law clerk on Monday. The execution was set for Tuesday. We were certain to lose our stay motion before Judge Cowart Monday morning, and then the Florida Supreme Court appeal that afternoon. We wanted to have something sitting in federal court by the end of the day Monday. At the same moment, without a word between us, Jim and I stared at each other and both realized *it was not going to happen*.

With a full plate in front of me at the first relaxed meal we'd had since Jim had arrived in Florida, intended to be only the first of many other helpings from the buffet table, I leapt up and told a disbelieving Dara that she was driving me to the airport immediately. I was flying to Washington.

I felt high on the plane, giddy with the fast pace of events, glad to be leaving Miami, happy to have the kind of task ahead I was best at:

overnight production of a brief on the merits, the facts about Ted's trial I knew so well. I enjoyed writing the story. As fate would have it I was bumped up to first class because the flight was overbooked. So was the guy next to me. As he knocked down the free drinks, I reinvented myself for the ride. I told him that I was a free spirit, that the purpose of my life was to enjoy myself and then move on. For three hours the struggle back in Florida, murder, execution, seemed but a distant memory. This guy, it turned out, lived on an island in the Caribbean and made his living by providing support services to marijuana magnates. He sailed their boats to Miami or wherever, any safe harbor, helping them to avoid tax assessors and police. He was on his way to his mother's funeral. When he was soaked so thoroughly in alcohol he would have ignited in the presence of flame, this modern-day pirate gave me his phone number and made me promise to visit him on his island. Such a free, unencumbered spirit as I was hard to find, he said. I felt a flash of imaginary freedom from the formidable complexities in which I had mired myself.

I arrived in Washington late Sunday afternoon and burst in on Jeff. Just as Jim and I had suspected, he was trapped in an endless meeting with another partner and his client. My unexpected arrival from Florida gave Jeff an excuse to ditch them to work with me to complete the habeas petition. All 210 pages of it. We cut and pasted, drafted and edited, and stood behind the operators in the word-processing center, urging them on like galley slaves.

I kept thinking of my home in the beauty parlor, only a few blocks away. My bed, my fresh clothes, my bountiful selection of beauty supplies. But I never had even ten minutes to spare. I left for Florida at 7:00 A.M. with a briefcase full of copies of the petition that was supposed to save Ted's life. One of the clients of my environmental law partner told me later that he had been on that same flight, but he found me fast asleep when he came back to say hello. I guess I must have dozed off.

That morning, Jim and Bill Davis went to court for the second hearing before Judge Cowart. The ruling was as expected: Judge Cowart decided that he had indeed conducted an adequate competency hearing, and that none of our other claims had any merit warranting even a day's consideration. Stay DENIED. We appealed to the Florida Supreme Court and received its decision the same day. AFFIRMED.

When we filed the habeas corpus petition with the federal district court we were told that the hearing would be held the next morning before Judge William J. Zloch in Ft. Lauderdale. That first hearing before Judge Zloch would shatter forever my ingenuous confidence in the federal judicial system. It was Tuesday, less than twenty-four hours before the time the execution was to take place. Ted had been moved onto phase III of death watch, where he had been measured for a casket and asked for his final requests and how he wanted his property disposed of after his death. They hadn't yet shaved his head. For the first time, Ted's voice sounded shaky on the phone. But he remained steadfast.

"If you're confident, Polly, I'm confident."

After Judge Zloch's hearing, though, I wasn't so sure we could count on anything. He was a very gentlemanly young judge, new to the bench, a Reagan appointee. He had been a divorce lawyer in private practice. He had warmed and humanized his courtroom bench with a shaded desk lamp and an old-fashioned caned chair—it even may have been a rocker. He was not at all stern or unapproachable. He was tall, blond, handsome, and friendly, a former football player at Notre Dame. He had no clue as to how to handle a death case. But he knew that he was not going to be the judge that caused Ted Bundy's execution to be stayed. I had expected that from the state courts, but not from the federal judges. I had assumed they'd apply the law impartially.

When the hearing began, Judge Zloch told us that he had read our entire 210-page petition the evening before and had thoroughly researched the legal issues. He was denying all seventeen claims on their merits—without a hearing. The prosecutors, surprised at the breadth and swiftness of the decision, asked if the judge would like to see the record, because it was still locked in their car. Judge Zloch said that wouldn't be necessary, he could tell by the petition that the acts claimed to be the result of ineffective assistance of counsel, for example, could have had reasonable explanations. From the petition alone he could tell, as a matter of fact, that there were no signs in the record that Ted Bundy might have been incompetent.

Judge Zloch's mistake was that he bypassed the purpose of a habeas corpus petition, which is simply to state issues that can be proven with the record. It is not supposed to contain all the evidence for the claims. In effect, Judge Zloch was saying that real issues *had* been raised but he could decide them without any evidence. This was a big mistake.

Jim kept sparring politely, always on his toes, asking Judge Zloch questions about his ruling. Of course a judge is not required to answer questions from counsel, but Judge Zloch was too courteous to refuse. When Jim asked him something, Judge Zloch would gaze at the ceiling for the longest time, then, sometimes, recess so he could look it up. He seemed to have no idea of his essential error: He should not have been talking about the facts at all. If we had made a viable claim we were entitled to present facts on that claim, and we were entitled to a stay of execution to allow time for that to take place.

Then Judge Zloch voluntarily made things worse for himself. It suddenly occurred to him that the Florida Supreme Court had ruled on our appeal the day before. He criticized us (gently) for making him waste his entire evening the night before reading our lengthy petition. Obviously, if the state courts had fully heard and decided these same claims, they could not also be brought into federal court. This was his *really* big mistake. Under the "doctrine of exhaustion," as a federal courtesy to the states, claims brought against state judgments *must* first be decided by the state courts. The petitioner must have exhausted his state remedies before coming into federal court. Otherwise, of course, we would never have bothered with Judge Cowart at all.

To top it all off, even though he denied our stay, Judge Zloch did in fact become the judge directly responsible for Ted Bundy receiving a stay of execution. At the end of the hearing, Jim asked him if he'd grant us a certificate of probable cause to appeal to the Eleventh Circuit Court of Appeals. That is, would he certify to the Eleventh Circuit that we had arguable grounds to appeal? We waited in silence for the answer as the judge searched the ceiling. Finally, gallantly, he said yes. With that "yes" the Eleventh Circuit's stay was guaranteed. The Eleventh Circuit then had *no choice* but to accept the case for appeal, and thus no choice but to issue a stay of execution in order to hear the appeal. And, within hours, that's what happened.

We were back at Zuckerman, Spaeder when the news came. Though no friends of Ted Bundy's, the staff at the firm were happy for our personal victory—and for the privilege of being the first to know. Particularly when the handsome local news anchor came to interview Jim, and a helicopter hovered overhead to transmit it live on television. Jim didn't share my superstition about press interviews.

Ted was glad to get the stay, of course, but a bit miffed that the other inmate, Gerald Stano, had gotten his days before. "And he didn't even have any issues!" said Ted, indignantly. Ted's keen sense of justice.

There are benefits to having your work covered daily in the press.

Beyond the far, far horizon,
Where we cannot see . . . .
Lies the glory of eternal tomorrow,
How beautiful heaven must be!

For here have we no continuing city, but we seek
one to come.   Hebrews 13:14

Thank-you card from Ted

Your family knows your whereabouts. My cousin Bruce and his family, following the case on their sailboat's radio and hearing of the stay, knew just when to sail into Nantucket to pick me up for a visit. I flew to meet them on July 5, my thirty-fourth birthday, and spent a week giving manicures to my young cousins and enjoying the tranquil muteness imposed by the noisy sea.

PART III

CHAPTER 8

"Ted Bundy" is to serial killers as "Kleenex" is to disposable handkerchiefs: The brand name that stands for all others. I learned this was true even among death penalty defense lawyers at their annual conference at a retreat center in rural Virginia that August. Jim had received an invitation to this exclusive gathering because of his work on the Booker case, but sent me in his place as a way of further indoctrinating me into the cult of death penalty law—or maybe it was just supposed to be a nice vacation. The conference was held when the U.S. Supreme Court justices are on vacation and states observe a voluntary cease-fire in scheduling executions.

So there they were, 150 or so murderers' lawyers, all together in an isolated conference center out in the country, all talking about their clients, their clients' crimes, their clients' death sentences. They were *real* death penalty lawyers, not corporate dilettantes. Unlike me, the others didn't have only one case to work on nearly full-time, with the seemingly-endless rich resources of a large private law firm at their disposal. Most were paid by the government and had to squeeze every dime. Unlike mine, their cases were not front-page news in *USA Today*, did not attract any special attention, did not elicit any special acknowledgment. Their clients had not become celebrities, they were just people, mostly young, mostly male, mostly brutally victimized themselves, who had killed someone, usually horribly. And these were mostly trial, not appellate, lawyers, which meant the death sentence hadn't been imposed yet and they had the responsibility of preventing it. As an appellate lawyer I would have the luxury of trying to build my case by blaming the trial lawyers for their shortcomings—if I could. And it also meant that if they did a very good job and the planets were in a particular alignment, their client would not only avoid the death penalty, he would go free. They had to be ready to embrace as success that possible result of their efforts. That was not something I had to be prepared for in Ted's case. My goal was to overturn the conviction, win a new trial and hope that the state of Florida would offer another plea bargain to avoid going through it all again. My ultimate goal was a life sentence. There was no realistic possibility that Ted would go free—and that was fine with me. I don't think Ted himself even had hopes his conviction would be overturned; he was just looking for time, just hoping for delays.

So again I felt uncomfortably "pretty," a dandified corporate lawyer toying with one high-profile postconviction death penalty case. At the first evening's reception the other participants shared the stuff of the work they had in common, the stuff they could share only with colleagues. Without fear of judgment they recounted their clients' tortured childhoods as well as their murderous adolescences. They described outrageous summary trials and the efforts they'd made to hold back death's gaping jaw. I had nothing to say. I felt so small, so useless, so different from the others. I was, in fact, a death penalty lawyer. I did, in fact, have a story to tell. But I felt a fraud nonetheless and kept silent.

It was about eleven that night when I slipped out of the reception to ride back to my dormitory, about a half mile away, on one of the conference center's balloon-tire bicycles. I had ridden this route once before, in the daytime, and it had seemed simple enough: down a winding path through a small woods, up the highway a little way, a short turn to the right. The dorm was a relatively big building, covered in white plaster, like a small, unadorned motel. I thought nothing about setting out in the dark, though I did feel pretty goofy bouncing up and down on the springy seat of a bicycle with only one gear. I'd been doing a lot of riding lately on my hard-saddle ten-speed back in Washington, fast-pedaling to blasting rock music on earphones until as Judge Sharp was losing his patience, Kennedy wandered in and I was able to question my first witness in open court. (Lynn Thompson later pouted, "I thought *I* was going to be your first!") But Kennedy didn't seem to be picking up my hints as to the subject matter of his testimony. And during my examination of Lynn, the judge took a dislike to me and impatiently ruled that all of Ted's conduct before the Lake City trial itself was irrelevant. I could toss out my notes after that. Finally, Mark Menser, the state's attorney, smelling blood and a chance for revenge, started objecting to everything I said, and the judge kept automatically ruling in his favor. It was not my shining hour.

Now, the state is at a distinct disadvantage in any claim based on the defendant's mental state. Nearly all the facts of the claim are solely within the knowledge of the defendant, the defendant's lawyers and doctors, and the defendant's family and friends. So, if it appears as if I am giving the witnesses for the state short shrift as I recount the testimony presented at the competency hearing in December 1987, I am. They had nothing useful to contribute—our real opponents throughout this case were the courts, not the prosecutor. But, in order to be fair, I'll sum up the testimony elicited by the state at this hearing: State's witness, on direct exam—Bundy was a genius. Our witness, on cross-exam—yes, I admit that if that one example you mention of Ted's strange behavior were taken completely out of context, it would not be impossible to concoct some imaginable rational explanation for it.

In fact, the resolution of a question of mental competency, such as this, especially the defendant's ability to assist his attorneys rationally in his own defense, turns on the credibility of the testimony of the defense lawyers and other persons who knew him best. Thus, it is their testimony I emphasize.

Our first witness was Bruce Lubek, by then an Assistant U.S. Attorney in Utah, who had represented Ted as a private attorney from 1975 through 1976 for the aggravated kidnapping of Carole DeRonch in Salt Lake City. His testimony showed how consistent Ted's pattern had been over time: his lack of comprehension about the weight of the evidence against him; his inability to conform to legal advice; his self-defeating concern for appearance over substance.

BRUCE LUBEK: In the early stages he seemed to me to be a fairly typical law student, one who found himself in an unusual predicament, and I felt his behavior was pretty standard for such a situation, if there was such a thing as standard behavior for a law student charged with a serious crime.

JIM COLEMAN: Did there come a time when his behavior changed?

B.L.: Well, it was particularly during the trial and shortly before. I would describe it as very concerned about how he appeared as opposed to as much concern about the actual case itself.

J.C.: And did this change in concern manifest itself in his behavior during the trial?

B.L.: I felt it did. At the trial I felt he appeared as not a humble law student who was in trouble but rather as a combatant with the prosecutor.

J.C.: Did Mr. Bundy testify at the trial?

B.L.: He did.

J.C.: And what was your assessment of his testimony, his behavior during this testimony?

B.L.: It was that he was attempting to match wits with the prosecutor, that he was playing a game with the prosecutor.

J.C.: And do you have an opinion about whether that behavior affected the decision in the case?

B.L.: I do.

J.C.: What is your opinion?

B.L.: It affected it greatly. Negatively for Mr. Bundy.

Bruce Lubek testified that, even in his trial in Utah, Ted did not understand the strength of the evidence against him. In that case, Ted was accused of attempting to force nineteen-year-old Carole DeRonch into his car. He was arrested a few days later after being stopped by the police for erratic driving. Lubek noted that Ted "was arrested in a residential neighborhood in the early morning hours parked in front of a home; a search of the vehicle revealed a pair of handcuffs, an ice pick, some lengths of rope, and a plastic garbage bag." Ted's view, however, which he noted in a letter to Lubek's co-counsel, was that using the facts of that arrest, a "completely immaterial event," to support his subsequent kidnapping case "was just a ploy advanced by a desperate prosecution." His attorney, Lubek, in contrast, thought the arrest and the contents of his vehicle would be *very* relevant in his kidnapping trial. Ted wrote letters to the judge behind his lawyers' backs. After his conviction for aggravated kidnapping, Ted was served in Lubek's presence with an arrest warrant for a homicide in Colorado:

my senses were exhausted. Then I could relax. But now, with my dormitory less than a mile away, this jalopy was adequate to the task.

When I started out I was still in city-darkness, the lights from the conference center still with me as I entered the woods. I could still see perfectly well. But after a short while, without my noticing it, the light faded. I had forgotten how dark night really is. Out in the country, into the woods, night is completely dark. I could barely see the road beneath me, much less the road up ahead or the bushes to the side. I hadn't thought to bring along a flashlight. I thought of turning back and asking for a ride, but I was far enough along to think that I could make it the rest of the way in the dark. I slowed down, riding cautiously so as not to miss the curves and fall off the road. I grew wary. Anything could happen in the dark, in the woods. Anyone could be there.

When I reached the highway I thought I'd made it. A faint moon in the overcast sky allowed me to follow the white line on the edge of the road. I'd be home soon. I started looking for the side road that led to the dorm, the one on the right, soon after the woods. I kept riding, finding nothing that looked right. Finally, I knew for certain I'd gone too far and turned around to retrace the route. A car passed, full speed ahead, briefly providing then snatching back the bright illumination of its headlights. I was growing hungry for light. I rode back to where the woods met the highway and started up the right side again. Still nothing. When I'd again gone what I knew was too far, I took the only side road I found. As I rode down it, I kept straining to see an outline of a man-made structure, the dorm building, sometimes getting off the bicycle and walking beside it because actually feeling the surface was the only way I could find the road. It was so dark. It was then I realized that there are no guarantees. That I would find the dorm. That I wouldn't be some other angry man's victim. It occurred to me that I was completely vulnerable.

I couldn't rationalize away the vulnerability, as I had in the past. When as a student I'd worked in an isolated carrel in forsaken stacks of the library; when as a social worker I'd entered the homes of violent child-abusers and out-of-control schizophrenics; when as a drunk I'd depended on the kindness of strangers; when as a lawyer I had walked home gaily on an unpeopled side street on a dark February night, exultant about the "little pro bono case" I'd just accepted—I'd believed I was invulnerable. I was not the victim "type," and serial rapists and killers had been largely invented by newspapers. That's what I'd always believed.

But now I knew one. I personally knew a flesh-and-blood human being who looked just like everybody else and had killed women at random. Women like me, women not even as helpless as I was now. Lost in the dark on a wrong road in a strange place.

Riding, sometimes walking, down the asphalt road, I no longer trusted my memory that the dorm building was right off the highway. Maybe it was just a little further ahead. Nothing. Nothing but an occasional patch of tall bushes. I rode past them quickly. I heard the stirring of small animals and the crack of tree branches. The clouds shifted away from the moon. I could see houses. There were houses by the side of the road. I wasn't alone. My brief relief vanished when I saw that they were still under construction, empty, like ghost houses. Now it really hit me. I was defending one. One of the men I couldn't admit even existed. And I had just come from a room where people were sharing stories about the hundreds of killers they had defended. Sympathetic stories. We'd laughed about them.

Now I knew I'd gone too far. Without stepping down, I turned the bicycle around and headed back the way I'd come. At first the dim moonlight allowed me to ride faster, because I could see the road— although a fat-tire one-speed will go only so fast, particularly under a rider who has grown weak in the knees. Suddenly, just as I came up to a patch of tall bushes a large form burst out. I couldn't see it in the darkness, but I could hear its weight when it hit the pavement. It was heavy. My heart contracted with a jolt. This was it, perfect justice. Bundy's lawyer becomes another's victim. The form passed, probably a deer. A little way ahead I saw a yard light and rode toward it seeking help. When I got there I saw it was the dorm itself. I was safe. I'd been spared.

At the general sessions of the death penalty conference, my client's name came up often. Not his case, of course, not the fact that he had been scheduled to be executed twice that year already. No, even these ardent death penalty opponents appeared willing to let Ted Bundy be executed—he gave capital defendants a bad name. His name stood for the unmitigated evildoer that their own clients certainly were not.

"Unlike Ted Bundy," someone would start out, "most criminal defendants present sympathetic circumstances that would mitigate against imposition of the death penalty in the mind of the jurors."

"We've got to get the word out," another would say, "that Ted Bundy is not typical of death row inmates."

Unable to stand it any longer, I rose to object and was promptly in participating in a scheme to subvert Florida's "Son of Sam" law? The room was infused with a great stillness as I awaited his advice. "In my day," he began, "we did not try our cases in the press. But," he continued, "things seem to have changed." In other words, he would not give me his opinion either.

So, unarmed with any guidance and with great reluctance, I met Linda Gomez for lunch. She had arranged for us to meet at the fanciest hotel in Washington—the Willard. As soon as I entered the still, cool lobby I knew this was wrong. We were seated in a discreet enclave in the dining room—the entire dining room was divided into discreet enclaves. It was made for clandestine meetings. Ms. Gomez urged me to order something expensive. Wrong. She showed me samples of other articles she'd written; she assured me her article would be sympathetic to Ted. Wrong, wrong. When the check finally came she grabbed it, insisted on paying. I put my money on the table and dashed out, unable to take another moment. I could hear her chasing after me with the money I'd thrown down: "Don't be silly, let me pay!" Wrong, wrong, wrong. I guess I had my answer on what to do—my body had told me. That was the last time I gave any consideration to a request for an interview with Ted, although they never stopped coming.

Under Florida law a condemned prisoner has a right to apply for clemency and to a lawyer to represent him in any clemency proceedings. The only hope of preventing a warrant in the Lake City case if (when) the Supreme Court denied cert. in October would be to have other legal proceedings in the case pending at the time. Even if the governor signed a warrant anyway, the court conducting those proceedings would be hard-pressed to not grant a stay of execution to allow them to be completed. So in August I applied to the trial court in Lake City to be appointed Ted's clemency counsel. Ted was not happy with this approach. He still believed the best way to handle his case was to wait for a death warrant, and only then file any claims we had. But beginning clemency proceedings had a chance of *preventing* a warrant in the case, at least for a few months, and courts are much more likely to take a real look at the issues in a case that does not have an execution date set. Even if we got a warrant in October, the fact that I had been expeditiously seeking the next logical level of relief—executive clemency—might prompt a higher court to grant a stay to allow me to see that through. Theoretically.

I went ahead in August and wrote all the motions necessary to be appointed Ted's clemency counsel in the Lake City case. (Ted had had the chance to apply for clemency in the Chi Omega case but, typically, had fired his counsel and blown his opportunity to present any reason he should not be executed in that case.) I filed these with Judge Wallace Jopling, the trial judge in the Lake City case, and he promptly ruled that my motions were premature because the case was currently before the U.S. Supreme Court, and that if they ultimately overturned the conviction any application for clemency would be moot. What a kind fib. That was the best ruling I could have gotten, though. I didn't have to do anything before the Supreme Court acted and, when they did deny cert., I could start clemency proceedings in the Lake City case—and maybe avoid or oppose a warrant—without being accused of "last-minute delay tactics"; my motions and Jopling's decision would show I had tried to move the case along.

Ted's cozy and stabilizing family life, his routine of Saturday visits with Carole and Tina, ended abruptly in August of 1986. Carole's mother was badly injured in a car accident in Seattle and Carole, Tina, and Jamey rushed to her side. Furthermore, they were going to have to stay there for a while—Carole's mother was going to need months of rehabilitation. But Ted seemed to know the move would end up being permanent—and it was. After the fright of two death warrants, Carole needed to put some distance between them, if not for herself, certainly for Tina. "Not being able to see them anymore will be more difficult than I can say," he wrote, maintaining a stiff upper lip, "but that's the way it has to be." He seemed more anxious than ever for me to try to get a phone call through to him—not to abandon him as well.

> I hope that representing me hasn't been too demanding or unpleasant. I realize that a lot of work is involved. I know, too, that I am an intensely unpopular figure. There was much hostility directed at my attorneys following the stay. Did it bother you? If this case is causing you problems, let's talk about it. Please don't keep it from me.

As always, he signed off with "peace, ted" and added an imploring P.S.: "And call . . . please."

CCR persuaded Dr. Lewis to include Ted in her neuropsychology tests at FSP—without using the results in her study. I wrote Ted asking him to cooperate and to send a release to Dr. Lewis. Ted complied but clearly still thought any claim based on some alleged mental defect was as false as it was useless. True, at this point we didn't have much to go on. Art Norman was continuing to see Ted in the hope we would be able to formally hire him, but I'd heard nothing from him since June. We had Dr. Tanay's evaluation from the time of the competency hearing, but his diagnosis, while highly predictive of Ted's behavior, was not very specific as to its cause. One thing about Ted's case was that we were never going to get the benefit of any doubt; we had to nail down his specific psychiatric problem before we got to a hearing. We had to have expert testimony. The courts had refused to pay for an expert, CCR had not responded to my letter asking for investigative services, and Jim still was not willing to spend the firm's money. But then Dr. Lewis called, and things started to fall into place.

"*Did you know that your client is bipolar?!*" Dr. Lewis is not one to mince words. Even though this was the first time we'd spoken, she bypassed the small talk and blurted out her diagnosis as if to say, *Are you incompetent?! How could you have missed this?!* Dr. Lewis had worked on several criminal cases and seemed to approach lawyers assuming they were not interested in saving their clients and purpose-fully avoided potentially useful evidence of mental illness. It would be a while before she trusted me.

"Uh, no . . ." I said, struck as if by lightning with the first ray of hope in the case. A real mental illness? Ted had a real, definable, recognized mental illness? Dr. Lewis's unbounded self-assurance and certainty about her diagnosis, which meant that Ted was manic-depressive and went through uncontrollable mood changes that might have impaired his judgment at the trial, was like a hand to a woman on a leaky raft. The more we compared notes—her test and interview results with my history of the case—the more the entire story fell into place.

That was why Ted had invited the police into his cell in the middle of the night, and rambled on and on about the compulsions of the "Other Ted," while pleading with his lawyers during the day to stop the uncounseled interrogations! *That* was why he had asked for and signed a carefully negotiated plea agreement in which he admitted his guilt, but then stayed up all night typing a fifteen-page, single-spaced motion to have his lawyers replaced because they thought he was guilty! *That* was why he pranced around the courtroom like a dandy in his bow tie, playing to the press, destructive of his lawyers' strategies and oblivious to the horrified reaction of the jurors! He had an abnormal brain chemistry, he had been responding to impulses beyond his rational control. Best of all, it could be documented for years before the trial or even the crimes.

The case was shaping up. We had a real handle now, the kind that a court could hang on to. Not just for a stay of execution, either, but for a real reversal of the conviction and maybe another chance at a plea bargain for life in prison.

Between July and October 1986, Ted was protected against a warrant in either case. The Chi Omega case was on appeal in the Eleventh Circuit; the Lake City case was awaiting a Supreme Court decision on cert. I was able to turn my full attention to work for other partners and paying clients, and even take a significant role in a large insurance defense case: a fully funded, fully staffed, bread-and-butter legal matter helping a big insurance company avoid paying on a big claim by the government for hugely expensive environmental damages caused by the insured's toxic-waste dumping. In another of the firm's cases, one of my best friends was working diligently to keep a drug company's insurance company from having to pay damages for the injuries suffered by a child inoculated with its drug. One thing I learned from my corporate law experience was that insurance companies would rather use your premiums to pay their lawyers to defend themselves against you than to pay your claim. It's a question of avoiding bad precedent.

I still was fishing around for a role to slip into, a way of being a lawyer that felt competent, comfortable, and real. I wasn't looking to reject any possibility out of hand, even corporate law, with its professionally blind eye to questions of morality. The lawyers at Wilmer were uniformly brilliant and skillful, at the top of their profession. Each one had had their pick of jobs out of law school. Any of us could have chosen to work for the government, for legal services, in small law offices. We could have been prosecutors or criminal defense attorneys anywhere in the United States, we could have worked for the rights and advancement of the abused and disadvantaged, we could have helped to guide public policy. We believed in all those things. Instead we had gone to the highest bidder, the law firm with the most prestige and the highest starting salaries. Like me, when they first arrived at the firm many of these lawyers would say they were there just to receive the training and experience a big firm could provide and then go do what they really wanted to do, in a better position to be effective. But, in fact, very few left the firm voluntarily. There were several reasons for this. There were the "golden handcuffs" of salaries that rose eight thousand dollars a year without a struggle. There was the same competitiveness and urge for approval from superiors that had made us successful students in the first place. There was the brass ring of partnership dangling at the end of seven years as an associate. There was the "Swedish hostage syndrome" of coming to identify with the goals of your captors, the result of working long hours days, nights, and weekends. Another thing I've learned, not just at the firm but in going to law school without intending to practice law: Be careful the company you keep. I was more permeable than I liked to think.

In law school you learn to set aside your own principles and prejudices in order to see clearly the structure of the law. In theory, the purpose is that you will thereby be in a better position to use the law in the service of your personal vision. But though law school accomplishes the destruction of assumptions and biases very well, it pays only lip service to the moral application of the law, the reconstruction of individual principles. In this nonjudgmental frame of mind you are perfectly suited to the work of a large law firm, where you might get any kind of case, for any kind of client. To be fair, one reason I chose Wilmer was that it had expressed more of a social commitment than most. In the past it had taken stands against serving antisocial interests. They would not represent the tobacco industry, for example. They had a substantial and enthusiastic commitment to pro bono work. But the time I was at Wilmer was a critical period for the practice of law. The partners' corporate clients were making more money than ever, their friends had fantastic salaries as investment bankers, partners in New York law firms were making a half million dollars a year, and public service was not in vogue. Lost was the idea of being an officer of the court, an intermediary between the desires of the client and public policy as expressed in the law. Instead, the goal was to get whatever the client wanted—exemption from environmental laws, protection against liability for damage caused by their products, whatever—in any way that minimally met the standards of professional responsibility.

So there I was, straining my brain to misinterpret insurance agreements convincingly so that the insurers would not have to pay. That's what I was paid so well to do—turn black to white. I was trying hard to participate in litigation as practiced by the best of the best. I was open-minded to the possibility that a moral balance could be struck somehow. No one else seemed uncomfortable. The few times the issue came up—from some cheeky summer associate or brand-new lawyer—some partners would say that, for them, it seemed better to have a good guy than a bad guy on the wrong side. They believed that they helped to modify the client's demands for complete exemption from legal or regulatory authority. Others contributed generously to liberal causes, believing they were a conduit through which the ill-gotten gains of their clients flowed to their victims. I really tried to believe it myself. More than anything else, I needed to fit in here. This had to be real life. I had no alternate plan.

CHAPTER 9

One way in which Ted was not typical of the men on Florida's death
row was that he had been free most of his life. It showed in his two
escape attempts soon after arriving at Florida State Prison, one of which
had exposed him to the other. The first he had initiated on his own
and had worked at nightly, filing away at his cell bars and pasting them
back together with dirt-dyed toothpaste. When his work was discovered
by a guard during a routine tapping of the cell bars, he was transferred
to the disciplinary cell block. There, to his surprise and delight, he
found himself in the middle of another plot in progress. His first night
in solitary, Ted told me with some relish, he had heard scurrying
outside his cell. He couldn't see what was going on because the cell
had double doors, with the outside door having just enough room to
shove meal trays through. The noise had sounded like rats, but the
shadows cast had looked much larger.

On the second night Ted had sent out a coded message on a bar of
soap attached to a string: "I know there's something going on, let me
in." No answer. The next night Ted had sent his message out again,
this time including a threat to squeal. By return soap bar he learned
they had fashioned keys with their toothbrushes and were able to let
themselves out at night to roam the hallway and smoke marijuana they
bought from the guards. Ted wanted a key, so, as often as he could,

he would send his toothbrush out into the hallway attached to his line, and another inmate would retrieve it with another string with a hook attached. The unofficial locksmith would make some tentative cuts and send it back down the line. Ted would test it in his door and return it. He had been in love with the project.

Finally, the night came when he stepped out into the hallway. There were the other inmates, mingling, lounging, getting high.

Ted had said, "Let's go. It's just a matter of time before this operation is blown. We've got to go now."

"We can't go," the others had protested. "The razor wire would tear us to shreds."

Ted's reaction was, "So what? It's better than sitting here waiting to die. At least we'd have a chance to be free!" Then their real reason for staying behind came out.

"But where would we go once we got out?"

Ted was dumbfounded.

"Where *wouldn't* you go?"

In late September 1986 I received a call from a woman who identified herself as Diana Weiner, a Florida attorney. She said that she had been hired by Art Norman to assist him in his psychological evaluation of Ted for us, to explain to him the legal context of the evaluation. I had no idea Dr. Norman had been confused about what we wanted. After all this time. He seemed to promise even less hope of a solution than I'd thought, but, still, he was willing to work on spec. Dr. Lewis was very anxious to follow up on her preliminary evaluation of Ted's mental condition, but Jim still would not commit the funds. I told Ms. Weiner I'd add her to the list of Ted's authorized legal visitors.

Jim's reluctance to authorize payment for experts in this case was not only a matter of firm politics—although that entered into it. Throughout this case there was an ethical dilemma we could never (particularly since the client was Ted Bundy, for whom there was extraordinary pressure to execute) allow to come to the surface. But it was always there in the back of Jim's mind: The *system* had to work. The *system* had to provide the experts necessary for indigent defendants— particularly indigent capital defendants—regardless of whether they had lucked out and were represented by a big law firm that presumably could absorb those costs. The *system* had to set reasonable filing dead- lines in death cases—as they did in most other cases—that could be met by normal lawyers under normal circumstances, not just by lawyers in big law firms who could round up six associates, three paralegals, and two secretaries to prepare an appeal brief overnight—or even in a matter of hours—if they had to. Jim was not as naïve as I had been in expecting the judicial system to work, but he felt a strong obligation to *make* it work. Wilmer, Cutler & Pickering was a private business volunteering its professional services to aid the courts in carrying out their legal responsibility to uphold the law. The law provided for this. The law provided for court appointed experts when necessary for an indigent to prove a legitimate claim. Ted Bundy was indigent, the law firm was already providing tens of thousands of dollars in free legal services, as well as support services. We had made a well-based legal claim that Ted was mentally incompetent to assist his lawyers at the time of his trial and this claim could not be proved without the assistance of expert testimony. There was no reason the law firm should have to pick up the tab.

I began to brace for the return of the Bundy blitz in the fall. The U.S. Supreme Court would reconvene on the first Monday in October, October 6, and the Lake City case would probably be on its list of cert. decisions. And that decision would probably be: DENIED. Ted then would be vulnerable for the first time to a warrant in the Lake City case. At the same time, the Chi Omega case was under consideration by the Eleventh Circuit Court of Appeals in Atlanta. I had filed the appeal brief (on an expedited schedule, of course) in August, and soon the Eleventh Circuit would schedule oral arguments. And I was still, of course, sorting insurance documents.

Jeff Robinson left Wilmer to become counsel to the Senate Judiciary Committee—a plum. The summer associates had all gone back to school. I circulated a memo to all the lawyers and, after describing the two cases, pleaded for assistance:

> The virtual unanimity of public opinion—even among those who claim to be opposed to the death penalty—is that our client should be put to death by the State of Florida regardless of whether he received a fair trial or was even given the opportunity to challenge the fairness of his trial. As lawyers, we beg to differ. In our experience, however, the Governor of Florida and the state and federal district courts have acted in accord with the public view and will not take notice of the constitutional issues at stake here unless absolutely forced to do so.
>
> With the recent departure of our brother-in-arms Jeff Robinson, the

number of associates on the Bundy team has now dwindled by half. We need help. In the political climate now prevailing in Florida, this case requires more than even the rigorous representation usually necessary in capital cases. Specifically, we need another lawyer to assume responsibility for the Lake City case as soon as possible—today would be nice. We also need lawyers to research and develop discrete issues over the next few months.

Although the odds are great, the task is in no way grim. Consider the company. Besides, the two Bundy cases raise substantial issues of constitutional law in a rich factual environment—we are not grasping at straws. The absence of any post-conviction evidentiary hearing thus far means an opportunity to create our record on a virtually clean slate. The intense press attention lends undeniable excitement to the case, as well as another factor to contend with. As Jim Coleman so frequently reminds me, as far as a learning experience, "You couldn't *buy* this case!"

Polly Nelson
x6111

No one responded.

October 6 came and went without a U.S. Supreme Court decision on the Lake City cert. petition. Now this was a result I didn't expect, and I read it as a favorable sign. Perhaps there was a struggle among the justices over granting cert. in the case; after all, the admission of Andy Anderson's hypnotically altered testimony had created a very dangerous precedent, particularly since a majority of the Florida Supreme Court had found that the only alleged eyewitness testimony in the case *had indeed been rendered unreliable by the hypnosis* yet still upheld the conviction. Perhaps the U.S. Supreme Court actually was going to *grant* cert. My hopes rose a little. This might not be a bad autumn after all. The Lake City stay order might stay in effect. We might get to brief and argue our case in the U.S. Supreme Court. We might even win.

Not likely. The next week, on Tuesday, October 14 (Monday was Columbus Day), the Lake City case appeared on the U.S. Supreme Court's weekly list of cert. denials. Its absence the week before apparently had not meant anything at all. Then the clerk of the Eleventh Circuit Court of Appeals called to say oral argument would be held in the Chi Omega case the next week, on October 23. In the meantime I had to try to prevent a death warrant in the Lake City case, now that the Supreme Court stay had been lifted. I renewed my motions with Judge Jopling to be appointed Ted's clemency counsel in that case, and on October 20 he granted them. Governor Graham did not care.

On the twenty-first the governor signed a warrant ordering the execution of Ted's death sentence, noting, "It has been determined that Executive Clemency . . . is not appropriate." I applied to Judge Jopling for a stay of execution based on a prisoner's right to clemency proceedings. Judge Jopling set his hearing for November 7. So now I had two hearings scheduled in two different cases within three weeks of the Supreme Court announcement—and an execution scheduled ten days later. How quickly things change.

Jim and I flew to Atlanta for oral argument on the twenty-third. The Eleventh Circuit was where our hopes for relief from Ted's Chi Omega death sentence ultimately lay. The appellate judges were better versed in the law than Judge Zloch and presumably suffered less local pressure to ensure Ted Bundy was executed. And, unlike the Supreme Court, the Eleventh Circuit *had* to accept our case for appeal because Judge Zloch had so kindly certified that there was probable cause to appeal.

We had the best three-judge panel we could have hoped for in the Eleventh Circuit. The chief judge of the Circuit had chosen Frank M. Johnson, Jr., who was among the most liberal on the court and who was still revered as a civil rights hero for his steadfast integration stands as a trial judge in the 1960s; John C. Godbold, former chief judge of the circuit, whose integrity and honesty about the requirements of the law were impeccable; and Robert S. Vance, who was conservative on law and order but a Democratic appointment with a good civil rights record (for which he was assassinated by mail bomb two years later). It wasn't the most liberal panel we could have had, or the most skeptical about the death penalty, but that was good. We needed a panel that would be respected by the nineteen other appellate judges on the Eleventh Circuit, as well as the U.S. Supreme Court. If we convinced this panel that the law required Ted Bundy's conviction to be overturned, their decision would stand. We needed a smart panel, an honest panel, a panel strong enough to uphold the law.

It was clear at the oral argument that the panel understood how egregiously Judge Zloch had erred. Jim made our argument virtually without interruption, whereas the assistant state attorney was immediately pelted with questions and statements of amazement that the state had allowed this to happen. In fact, the assistant state attorney had tried to a hint to Judge Zloch that he needed the record if he was going to rule on the merits but he had declined to receive it. Nonetheless, the state's attorney was an easier target for the panel than the judge, and he got it full force. Judge Vance asked Jim whether we had an expert who would be able to testify that our client had a mental illness. Now that Dr. Lewis had discovered Ted's bipolar mood disorder, he could honestly say we did. After the hearing concluded, we commiserated with the shaken state's attorney and left the courtroom elated. It looked certain that the Chi Omega case would be sent back down.

Jim went back to Washington and I flew down to Jacksonville. Since Ted was now under warrant for the Lake City case, I needed to review Vic Africano's files from representing him at trial. I also needed to interview Vic about his encounters with Ted and Ted's conduct at the trial, for evidence of incompetency. Vic's office in Live Oak was just one town over from Lake City, Kimberly Leach's hometown. According to Vic, representing Ted Bundy had been pretty much of a wash in terms of his career in Live Oak. It had provided steady income for a while, but he'd had to give up most of the rest of his practice for the duration of the trial. The extensive publicity about the case had certainly given him name recognition greater than any other lawyer in the region, but that had not always turned out to be a plus, given his client's crime. After the trial was over, Vic had first thought he'd expand his practice, take on an associate; but despite the publicity, legal work in those parts still came in handshake by handshake, and Vic had found he couldn't delegate that part.

I found his office off a dusty road on the outskirts of town. It was in a small, one-story professional building with a large parking lot surrounded by trees. The friendly receptionist greeted me with evident surprise at an unfamiliar face, and called down the hall to let Vic know he had a visitor. Vic was always Vic, always a joy to see. With a warm, well-intended, "Hey, Sweetie!" he escorted me into his office. "Come in, have a seat. Can I get you an iced tea?" Always so solicitous. I think he thought this was no case for a woman to be involved with. Too harsh, too ugly. His office was dominated by a thick burlwood coffee table and large pictures of his wife and children in country-western wear. I myself wasn't much good at small talk, so I came right to the point: "Vic, we need to prove Ted was incompetent during the Lake City trial. It's our only real hope. How did he seem to you? Can you remember anything that happened that might be helpful?" Vic's kindness and hospitality did not extend to saying anything he didn't believe. "Nope. He was no trouble to me at all," he said. "He was perfectly competent in every way. More than competent, even."

This was not good. If called to the stand in an evidentiary hearing, Vic would not corroborate our competency claim. We would have to prove our case—that Ted had been incompetent to assist Vic in his defense—without the concurrence of Vic himself. Vic was rock solid in his opinion that Ted had been competent; he had no doubts. He obviously was sorry to give me bad news, and that he could not be more helpful to my case, but that was the bottom line.

Well, I could still draw my own conclusions from Vic's files, so I looked forward to seeing them next. The public defenders' files in the Chi Omega case had filled an entire wall in my office. Vic presumably had had as much, but by this time they had been scattered to various locations; preserving them intact had not been a priority for this solo practitioner's budget. But I needed to track down at least some of them. The trial transcript Vic had sent me in the spring was missing some of its volumes, and I wanted to see at least some of the investigation files to get a feeling for what was going on outside of the courtroom. And, with great reluctance, Vic entrusted me with his most prized memento of the case: a gigantic album of news clippings. They would be a great source of press observations of Ted's behavior. Reporters had been so scrupulous during the trials to note *everything* Ted did, or said, or wore, or looked like, especially, of course, anything weird. That would be very helpful to me now.

As I sat in Vic's conference room reviewing the files he had close at hand, one investigation memo caught my eye. And my desperate imagination. There was a folder on alleged sightings of Kimberly Leach after she was supposed to have disappeared, raising the possibility that she had run away from school that day and possibly been killed by someone else later. Though these leads had apparently gone nowhere, since Vic had not emphasized them in his defense case, I eagerly grasped this straw of hope that Ted was not guilty of this one at all.

It had seemed a possibility before. The evidence in the Lake City case, other than Andy Anderson's dubious testimony, was the expert testimony identifying some of the fibers found in the van Ted allegedly used to abduct Kimberly Leach as the same type as in their clothing from that day. Without Anderson's testimony and Ted's prior conviction in the highly publicized Chi Omega trial, the jury might have had trouble finding Ted's guilt proven beyond a reasonable doubt. That was why the hypnotic manipulation of Anderson's testimony could not have been "harmless error." But now, armed with Vic's unused file on other sightings, I indulged in the thought that I had a case of actual innocence. After all, following the Chi Omega trial, *everyone* in Florida had known who Ted Bundy was and what he'd done, and they'd seen on TV what he'd acted like at trial. As one juror in the Lake City case had answered when asked if he'd heard of the defendant: "You'd have to be in Siberia not to have heard of Ted Bundy." It was not hard to imagine that Ted could have been convicted of *anything* after he was convicted in the Chi Omega case. Maybe this one had been a mistake. Then it wouldn't matter at all that Vic thought Ted had been competent. I could base my appeal on innocence.

That night I stayed at a motel outside of Lake City that was on the way to the prison, where I was going to see Ted the next day. All sorts of thoughts came to mind as I drove into that parking lot. What if someone recognized my name on the register, for one thing. What if they knew Bundy's lawyer was staying there? I felt that eerie feeling of vulnerability again. The vans and pickup campers in the lot reminded me of Ted's modus operandi: snatch and drive. I felt again that acute awareness of the reality of random murder, something that usually seemed completely outside the realm of possibility. I was not comfortable as it was, then, as I tried to settle down in my room. And then I turned on the TV, and, on every channel, I heard "Ted Bundy," "Ted Bundy," "Ted Bundy." It was not my imagination. It was election time in Florida and every candidate was running against Ted Bundy. According to news accounts, Ted Bundy's name was mentioned in the campaign commericals more often than the candidates'. There was a candidates' debate that night, and the very first issue mentioned by every single one of them was how much faster he would kill Ted Bundy than his opponents would. I spent the evening in nightmarish silence: unable to watch TV, too spooked to go out.

I had a lot on my mind the next morning as I drove to see Ted. I had a lot to prepare for in the next three weeks: my first solo court appearance and oral argument on Ted's right to apply for executive clemency; the execution scheduled for two weeks later. A stay of that execution would not be simple to obtain, even though it was the first warrant in the Lake City case. Unlike the first Chi Omega warrant, this time the U.S. Supreme Court had already denied cert. in the case; the direct appeal was over; and the only way to apply for a stay would be in collateral proceedings. It would involve all the same levels of courts and variety of pleadings as we'd gone through in June and July on the Chi Omega case—when we'd had a much bigger Bundy team, more time to prepare, a well-documented competency claim, only one active case, and my naive optimism. We had none of that now. No wonder I found myself focusing on the minuscule possibility that Ted had been convicted falsely in this instance. That would be a whole other ball game. It certainly would have given me energy.

Ted and I hadn't talked about the crimes up to this point. He had seemed so worried that I was or would be so revolted by what he had done that I would stop representing him. And I hadn't really had a need to know, since our cases had concerned the trials, not the crimes. But I had had those moments of overwhelming revulsion that Ted feared. I had tamped them down and kept them from my conscious-ness, for fear they'd interfere with my work. If there were any chance Ted had not in fact killed Kimberly Leach, I *really* needed to know. I'd be free, on this one. Free of shadowy feelings of betraying the victim. Free to feel completely right. Free to feel the power of my client's cause without conflict. A bad man, yes; even a murderer, yes; but guilty of this one—NO! That was my brief fantasy.

Ted and I sat together in one of the three glass-enclosed attorney interview rooms within the superintendent's offices. Ted was glad with the room we'd gotten because one of the others had an open air duct, and he was afraid of being overheard. He sat with his handcuffed hands on the table between us. He always made a point of not leaning in too closely so as not to offend or frighten me. After some pleasant talk about what Tina was doing in Seattle and how well Carole's mother's recovery was going, I finally brought up the question:

"Ted, when I was at Vic's yesterday, I saw a file of statements from people who claimed to have seen Kimberly Leach some time after she'd disappeared from school."

Ted said nothing, but grew still. He could see where this was headed.

"One was from a man who reported seeing her at a truck stop outside of town a week after the disappearance," I continued. Ted kept staring at me with an unchanging expression. "Another was someone who said he'd seen her on the street with another girl two days after."

Ted volunteered nothing. This was the first time I was talking to him as the perpetrator of the crimes, not just as a trial participant, but I still didn't dare be direct.

"Ted," I finally asked, after thinking of exactly how to word this, "is there any possibility these reports could have been true?"

Continuing to stare at me, Ted waited another moment more, then shook his head. That was his first direct admission of guilt.

My heart sank with disappointment. It had been a long shot. Vic would have used it if there'd been any chance it was true. Ted never would have put up with being convicted of a murder he hadn't done— it would have deeply offended his fine-tuned sense of justice. My fantasy evaporated.

I turned to the main purpose for my visit—to explore any possible grounds for clemency, to pursue if Judge Jopling granted a stay for that purpose. Ted only cared to talk about how the governor had violated his rights by not allowing him to apply before signing a warrant. He continued to believe that there was no point in trying to raise the question of his mental state, even as grounds for clemency, because his mind was perfectly sound and always had been. He shook his head regretfully though, as if he wished he could oblige me.

I was fine until I left the prison and started back down the road to Starke. Then I was overcome with weakness. Ted was not innocent of killing Kimberly Leach. In fact, he had now told me he had done it. He'd never told me that before. I'd never really had to tie his corporeal body, the Ted I knew, to the act of murder. Added to that, we had no case. Vic did not think Ted had been incompetent to stand trial and I had no other documented proof. I needed help. I needed the psychological report, even though I still did not have permission to pay for one.

I pulled over and called Art Norman from a pay phone. "Please, Art," I said. "Please see him. I need something I can use to stop this execution." Art said he would try. I headed back to Washington to prepare for all that lay ahead in the next three weeks.

The partners chose this time to complain that I was spending too much time on the Bundy case. The insurance partner was angry that I was not as available as I had been the month before. An impending execution date seemed a flimsy excuse to him. Three partners swooped into my office soon after I got back from Starke to ask why I was not doing "the work of the firm." Their presence filled the room. I couldn't believe that the situation was not obvious. A man's life was in imminent jeopardy and I was in charge of representing him. A few associates were helping me with research on specific issues, but I had full responsibility for the case, and those other associates dropped *my* case when a partner wanted their time on another matter. They were protecting their careers at the firm. I still had hopes myself of fitting in. But I couldn't get around the fact that while other associates were available to do "the work of the firm," there was no one to take responsibility for the Bundy case but me.

The partners knew this, and I explained it again, but it seemed to make no impression. It was if we were speaking different languages. What did they expect me to do? Do less to try to stop the execution? "Balance" my responsibility to prevent my client from being killed in three weeks with my responsibility to categorize insurance documents? The confrontation ended with utter frustration on both sides. I was shaken deeply. How could my view of my commitment to this case be so different from what the partners apparently thought was appropriate? And why did they approach me directly? What was the point of this personal intimidation? Why not go to my supervisor, Jim? Or, if they had talked to him already, why hadn't he warned me?

Ironically, on the other side I had CCR, who obviously believed I was not committed *enough* to saving Ted. Mike Mello had been aghast when he saw my appellate brief in the Chi Omega case. I had been so certain of Judge Zloch's procedural errors—and wanted to communicate that certainty to the Eleventh Circuit—that I'd addressed only that issue in the appeal brief. When CCR received a copy, Mike called me in a dread-filled tone of voice. He couldn't believe I had not included our claims on the merits, such as competency and hypnosis, on which the court had ruled without reviewing the evidence. My tactic was always to file briefs that were as clean and confident as Wilmer's on corporate matters. Pleas for compassion not only would be useless in Ted's case, they'd be counterproductive—it would look like we had no real legal issues. I had wanted the judges on the appeals court to forget about Ted and to think about the law. But Mike clearly thought I was placing legal niceties above saving a man's life.

There was no follow-up to my visit from the partners—when I told Jim about it he looked angry, but said nothing—and I proceeded as I felt I had to. The next event would be my hearing before Judge Jopling on Ted's right to make a case for executive clemency. I wanted my first oral argument in court to be perfect, of course. It was a discrete issue: whether the governor had a right under Florida law and practice to deny a particular inmate an opportunity even to apply for clemency. The argument would be straightforward. The state would argue that the U.S. Constitution does not grant inmates the right to be considered for clemency. That was true. I would argue that Florida law and the governor's rules and standard practices had created a statutory right to clemency proceedings, and that Ted had been singled out for exclusion, in violation of his U.S. constitutional right to equal protection under the law. That, I think, was also true. I knew it would be covered by the press, and I wanted to do and look my best. But fate would have it otherwise.

I was preparing, at the same time, for the collateral proceedings that would commence immediately if I lost in Judge Jopling's court. Although many of the claims were similar to those in the Chi Omega case, the evidence would be completely different. For example, there was extensive prejudicial pretrial publicity in both cases. But different jurors were involved, different press reports. Most significantly, when the Lake City trial was held, there had been all of the additional publicity about the recent Chi Omega case, conviction, and death sentence.

Several associates had volunteered to help with the various briefs, mostly at Jim's chiding, so I was able to farm out some of the substantive claims. But given the pace of events, the brief was not ready the day before my hearing in Lake City. Instead, my secretary, Pat Bennett, and I worked through the night. Pat became more and more concerned with how I was going to get some sleep before my court appearance— Pat worried about my personal health and circumstances for me. (Whenever I was fighting an active warrant, my mother would quit asking for me when she called. It was too scary. Instead, she'd just ask Pat how I was doing and Pat would reassure her.)

Near morning I knew sleep was not a possibility, but I never guessed I wouldn't even have the half hour to spare to run home and change clothes. But that's what happened. Right before my flight I dumped the collateral pleading on Jim's chair, picked up my clemency materials, and took a cab to the airport. I was met in Jacksonville by Margaret Vandiver, a volunteer legal assistant who had worked with CCR. When I told her I needed to buy clothes before we drove halfway across northern Florida to the one o'clock hearing in Lake City, Margaret's face registered her alarm. We dashed to a department store, where I bought the first dark dress that fit, a slip, stockings, and a pair of shoes. We went back to Margaret's so I could shower and change, and then we drove out to Lake City in time for the hearing. This was not how I had pictured the day of my first solo court appearance.

*   *   *

In Lake City we were met by Diane, another volunteer. These two women were my entourage. They were in my corner, encouraging me, offering to run errands, getting coffee. I was buoyed by their gentle support, given so freely. With the television cameras beside my table, and reporters ready with questions, Margaret and Diane stood nearby protectively. The hearing proceeded uneventfully. I was so nervous I shook as I spoke in court for the first time blandly rectifying a dry and technical argument on statutorily created clemency rights—no doubt deadly boring for the television audience tuned in to hear Bundy's lawyer plead for a stay of execution. Judge Jopling graciously refrained from interrupting me. The state's attorney presented his rebuttal. The judge asked a few polite questions and then promptly ruled against me: The governor could properly deny only Ted Bundy the opportunity even to apply for clemency and, thus, a stay of execution was not warranted. When the hearing concluded the press converged and I was questioned about what I was going to do next. Apparently it was broadcast nationwide, because my cousin in Montana later told me she'd been excited to see me on TV, but why was I wearing such a dopey dress?

Press attention is as brief as it is intense. For five minutes a dozen people were pointing microphones at me, reporters with notepads competed to get their questions in. Then it was over. My handlers, Margaret and Diane, praised my awkward efforts and escorted me out of the courthouse. I called Jim with the results from a phone by the side of the state highway and drove on to Starke to see Ted again briefly before I flew home. It was November 13, and he was scheduled to be executed in five days.

I arrived in Jim's office at about eleven that night. I threw myself onto the couch with exhilarated exhaustion and exclaimed, "Today I am a lawyer!" My exaltation at completing my first courtroom appearance was short-lived. Jim handed me the collateral brief that he had finalized in my absence and already sent down to be hand delivered to Judge Jopling and the prosecutors in Florida that same day. This was Friday and the execution was scheduled for Tuesday. At midnight, still draped over the couch in Jim's office like a melted chocolate bar, I casually started reading the brief and noticed that most of the changes Pat and I had made the night before were now missing. It was not like Jim to reject my edits, so I started to protest, then noticed that the last few lines of every page were missing, too. Major word-processing snafu.

I sprang off the couch, Jim ran down the hall to grab a secretary, and we spent the rest of the night cleaning up the mess and figuring out how to get the new copies to all the people we had served so that we could have our hearing first thing on Monday. Another couple of hundred dollars in overnight delivery expenses—and another lost night's sleep. There was one savings, though. Judge Jopling and the state's attorney were attending the Lake City High School football game together on Saturday night, so they could receive their copies at the same time. How convenient.

Sunday was November 16, two days before the scheduled execution. Jim and I and our ad hoc team of associates and legal assistants finalized all the papers we would need—if we were denied relief—all the way up to the Supreme Court. We would have to file a motion to reopen the case with Judge Jopling, primarily on the claim that he should have held a hearing at the time of the Lake City trial on Ted's mental competence. We'd have to be ready to file an appeal in the Florida Supreme Court if (when) Judge Jopling ruled against us. If (when) we lost our appeal there, we'd have to file a habeas corpus petition in the federal district court. If (not likely, I thought) we failed to get a stay in federal district court, we'd instantly be forced to file an appeal in the Eleventh Circuit. Finally, if all else failed, we would file a motion for a stay in the U.S. Supreme Court to allow time to file a cert. petition challenging the Eleventh Circuit's refusal to accept our appeal. And we had to be ready to do it all in the course of one day, Monday, if we had to.

On Sunday I "lodged" our motion in the Supreme Court, not filing it officially but allowing the court to be prepared when the time came. Then I set out for Starke. As he had in June for the Chi Omega case, Ted would have to verify the facts of our claims. When I changed planes in Atlanta I was met by a volunteer from the Southern Poverty Law Center, who took the required ten copies of our Eleventh Circuit appeal brief to be lodged there as well. When I saw Ted he was tense but optimistic. We believed we would be successful in getting a stay of execution because this was the first death warrant in the Lake City case. We didn't have great support for the competency claim in that case, but the hypnosis of Andy Anderson had been hard for even the Florida Supreme Court to accept in the appeal that followed his trial. But we were very, very close to the deadline, and anything could happen.

I spent Sunday night in Jacksonville and asked Margaret Vandiver to assist us the next day. Jim arrived late that night. The next morning, as we prepared to leave for the 9:00 A.M. hearing in Lake City, he declared we would leave our things there, not check out of the hotel in the morning because we were sure to win and return to Jacksonville that evening. Jim's boundless optimism.

Monday morning Jim, Margaret, and I drove to Lake City. Mere minutes after we filed the two-hundred-plus-page motion with the clerk, Judge Jopling announced he was ready to hear the case. Jim presented our case, one of the half dozen state attorneys at the prosecutor's table argued "delay tactics," and Jopling promptly ruled against us, recalling that "Ted Bundy was one of the most competent lawyers I ever had in my courtroom." I could only imagine the reaction of the state attorneys, lawyers who often appeared there in Judge Jopling's courtroom.

Upon learning that Jopling had concluded his hearing before noon, the Florida Supreme Court had moved up their hearing on our expected appeal that afternoon to 1:00 P.M. Margaret rented a car and drove to Orlando to lodge the federal habeas corpus claim in district court, and Jim and I raced on to Tallahassee. Lake City was in the middle of northern Florida, the federal district court in Orlando was on the shore to the southeast, and the Florida Supreme Court was in the northwestern panhandle. If Ted Bundy's lawyers couldn't be in two or three places at once, well, they'd just have to go ahead and execute him then. We went directly to CCR to update our appeal papers with Judge Jopling's decision. At one o'clock Jim left to argue our appeal in the Florida Supreme Court and I stayed behind to work on updating the appeal papers to the Eleventh Circuit and keep contact with Margaret in Orlando. Our case had been assigned to District Court Judge Kendall Sharp.

Jim wasn't gone long, and the Florida Supreme Court's decision came in right behind him: APPEAL DENIED. In other words, the court had ruled that we hadn't raised even one arguable issue worthy of even one more day's consideration. Yeah, right. I told Margaret to file the habeas petition with Judge Sharp officially and to find out when our hearing would be. Judge Sharp's clerk called back to say a hearing "would not be necessary." We waited helplessly in Tallahassee for the decision. Margaret reported later that a law clerk would run out of Judge Sharp's chambers from time to time, saying, "Only ten more

left," then "Five," then "One more to go!" Judge Sharp was ruling
on—and denying—every claim individually without even providing
us an opportunity to stand before him. It was 5:00 P.M. when Margaret
called with Judge Sharp's decision: STAY DENIED. He had written
a twenty-page opinion in support of his judgment. This judge had
learned from Judge Zloch's mistakes. He had had the state deliver the
entire fifteen-thousand-page trial transcript before the case was even in
his jurisdiction, and in his written opinion he claimed he had read the
entire thing. He was trying to make his decision appeal-proof so that
Ted's execution could go through. He even refused to certify the case
for appeal. I called the Eleventh Circuit's death clerk (each court had
a clerk designated for capital cases under warrants, which required
around-the-clock availability) to formally file the appeal I'd dropped
off in Atlanta on the way down to the court the day before.

Dark fell as we sat in CCR's cluttered offices waiting for an answer
from the Eleventh Circuit. In the Chi Omega case we'd had a stay by
four in the afternoon. This time, at eight the court's death clerk admitted they were having a problem getting the papers to the three judges
on our panel, the same panel as in the Chi Omega case. They were
all in their hometowns, scattered among the five states covered by the
Eleventh Circuit. She asked me to read her the list of claims covered
by the appeal. After all that writing, my emergency handoff of appeal
papers Sunday in the Atlanta airport, keeping the court informed every
step of the way, it had come down to reading a bare list of claims over
the phone the night before the execution. I became very discouraged.
At 11:00 P.M. there was still no word.

I couldn't stand to spend another minute in CCR's office. I felt
confined, suffocated; I wanted to run away, or scream. I left to stand
out in the street, to get out of that pressure cooker, but Scharlette
Holdman sent Mike Mello to bring me back because the streets were
not safe. CCR was smack in the middle of the Florida State University
campus where, before Ted Bundy, people hadn't even locked their
doors at night.

I was talking to Ted every two hours. The prison had started serious
preparations for the execution. Ted remained steadfast, refusing to
make his last requests. They measured him for his coffin. By midnight
we still hadn't heard, although we continued to believe we would get
a stay.

"Polly, I'm confident if you're confident," Ted said again, "but if it
ever looks like it's going the other way, *promise* me you'll let me know

right away. Promise me you won't hide it from me. It's important. If it's going the other way, there are some things I need to do."

I had no idea what those "things" were, but it sounded ominous. Ted and I had never talked about the possibility of a real execution. And I wasn't at all prepared myself. We'd fully expected a stay this time. We hadn't gotten a decision in the Chi Omega case yet, but we'd certainly had the strong impression at the oral argument that the panel was going to send the case back for further proceedings, and Judge Vance had asked specifically if we had an expert to back up our incompetency claim. Why were they hesitating so long this time?

It was nearly 1:00 A.M. when the Eleventh Circuit issued a stay of execution, not recognizing any of our issues or the inappropriateness of Judge Sharp's refusal to see us or his preprepared opinion, but saying only that there was insufficient time for them to review the case before the execution. I called the prison and, thinking that I had reached the warden, told the person who answered the phone that Bundy had received a stay. There was a long pause on the other end of the line; the surprised prison guard's disappointment was palpable. There would be no execution that morning. After all that preparation.

When I told Ted, he let go a deep sigh. "Oh, Polly," he whispered. I felt a rare moment of honest emotional expression from Ted.

Jim and I checked into a hotel in Tallahassee at two o'clock in the morning, our clothes and toiletries all the way across the state in Jacksonville, spending the night in a different hotel, on the firm.

CHAPTER 10

While we were fighting Ted's third death warrant in November 1986, Dr. Lewis was finishing up her study of juveniles on death row at FSP. She'd informed me she would be at the prison in November, and Jim had said we'd pay her hourly fee for the interview, but not her other expenses. The next thing I know, Jim gets a call from the Legal Defense Fund in New York, asking what kind of case we were running, why was such an inexperienced person as me being allowed to handle it, and *why was I letting Dr. Norman bring a scantily clad young woman in to see Ted?* Dorothy Lewis, he said, was extremely alarmed. Not knowing what he was talking about, I called Dr. Lewis. It turned out that when she went to see Ted he was just finishing an interview with Dr. Norman and that with Dr. Norman was an attractive young woman. A CCR legal assistant who had observed this encounter later called especially to tell me what the mystery woman was wearing: "Not much, and nothing under it." Dr. Lewis said Dr. Norman told her he'd brought the woman in to "soften Ted up."

I realized that this must be Diana Weiner. Dr. Norman had assured me her visits were necessary to "help explain to me the legal context of my examination." He was essentially volunteering his work at this point, and I was still hoping he'd come up with some useful insight.

I had assumed that after the stay Dr. Norman would quit visiting, since that was the purpose for which I'd asked him to see Ted again—and we had never found a way to pay him. Dr. Lewis was very relieved to know that what she had seen was not what I'd intended by my authorization.

What I did not realize after the stay was that Diana Weiner continued to see Ted on her own—alone—and still on the basis of my original authorization. By the time I knew this for certain, it was too late.

Three death warrants were enough for me. I was glad to get the stays, but they were granted only to allow further proceedings, more appeal briefs, another oral argument. I didn't see any way out of this quagmire as long as I stayed at the firm. I would always be the one ultimately responsible for getting the work done. I tried to start easing out of the case, to pass it on to someone else. But there were no takers. In retrospect, I can see that what I really wanted was some real help and support. I felt as if I were drowning

When the Eleventh Circuit finally had granted its stay at 1:00 A.M. on November 18, it had ordered an expedited appeal schedule; our briefs were due December 1—two weeks to prepare documents that in normal litigation took months. Even in the Chi Omega case we'd been allowed a month to complete the appeal brief. Although my plan for farming out the issues in this appeal had seemed to be working, on the date the brief was due some associates hadn't completed their sections; they had been called away on other work, "the work of the firm." So I found myself once again standing behind Pat at the word processor after hours on the first, dictating changes and drafting the auxiliary documents up until just minutes before midnight, when the waiting messenger from the airline delivery service verified the time and marked them RECEIVED. Jim had come by around ten and then had fled when the printers broke down. "Like sausage," he said, "law is something you shouldn't see being made."

Each of these last-minute sprints to the deadline was like another death warrant to me. While deadlines are important in all legal cases, they generally can be extended for necessity or technical problems. But I never dared test this with Ted Bundy's case. A missed deadline would be all the excuse a court would need to avoid having to deal with our appeal, allow the execution to take place, and be done with it. Forever. I knew for a fact that the governor faced each court deadline with pen poised over a fresh death warrant, hoping for a slipup. By me.

I was saved each time, as the minutes ticked toward midnight and the other lawyers scattered, by Pat (who, I suspected, could care less if Ted's life were lost, but who knew *my* life was at stake in those moments) and Chuck Halcombe, services' night supervisor, who would call the delivery service with the promise that the documents really were ready to be picked up, and then cajole the antsy messenger into waiting just a minute longer, then another minute, until one minute before midnight, one minute before the deadline. It seemed that the briefs were never done sooner than that. One minute *after* midnight and they could have been deemed late by the court—and the case lost. And I had no reason to think a court wouldn't be that harsh when it came to the case of Ted Bundy.

After filing the appeal brief in the Lake City case, I applied for teaching positions at several law schools. Jim finally took seriously my threats to quit when he received a call asking for a recommendation. He came flying up to my office, a shocked look on his face. He had told the caller, "She can't leave, and if she does, she's taking Bundy with her." That was not likely to enhance my standing as a candidate, but at least it was the acknowledgment I was hungry to hear.

Part of me knew I needed to get rid of this case, but the other part knew I could never drop it. A man's life was at stake, and I had taken responsibility for it. So, part of me went on the job interview circuit, and the other part held me back. It was a disaster. The interview would go well at first, I'd feel a rush of optimism at the possibility of new work, a new environment. Inevitably, though, we'd come to the question of what kind of work I'd been doing at the law firm. And then the question, What would happen to the Bundy case, how could I leave it? That would always stump me. A tremendous smothering weight would descend on me and few coherent words would come out.

On December 12, 1986, Ted urgently wrote that he was being disciplined—refused outside exercise privileges for thirty days—as the result of receiving the stay in November. "This has gone too far, Polly," he wrote. "I am tired of being singled out for abuse."

I made some halfhearted attempts to intervene, calling Assistant Superintendent O'Neill and writing Ted for more information about the DR (disciplinary report). But in fact I was in no mood to help. After all the work I had done to save his life in November, I was frankly not interested in exerting myself to protect his exercise rights. I wanted my own life back. I wanted Ted to take care of himself for a while. But that wasn't his style.

On January 14 I received a call from John Tanner, a Florida attorney who visited Ted as part of his lay Christian ministry. He told me Ted was frustrated that I was not keeping in closer touch, and that I was not sufficiently following up on details Ted thought were important in the case. I wrote Ted a crisp, schoolmarmish letter reminding him that he had not answered my last letter himself, and that although I was working on getting the state attorney files—including those he had expressed concern about—"focusing on the deficiency of the State's evidence did not prove to be a successful strategy for your trial, and will not be any more likely to bring you post-conviction relief."

Later, when I began to track Ted's behavior based on Dr. Lewis's diagnosis of manic-depression, these periods of tension between Ted and me, and especially his lack of letter writing, stood out as depressed periods. He responded to my letter on January 20, 1987, also enclosing a belated Christmas card:

Dear Polly, Christmas, New Years and the 12 days of Christmas have come and gone. I felt reclusive during the holidays and couldn't bring myself to send season's greetings to anyone. So it goes. But I got over it. So please accept my heartfelt thanks for all you have done and my wishes that the coming year will give you much Peace and Joy. Ted.

In his letter, Ted was contrite. I always felt I abused my power when I reprimanded him. I held the ultimate weapon—I could quit at any time. Or at least Ted thought I could. He wrote, "You're right. The ball is in my court. I do owe you a letter as well as many thank you's to you, Jim, and associates for the splendid work you did on the Lake City case brief recently filed with the 11th Circuit. So thank you. The brief is superb." Ted noted that FSP had rescinded the DR with a memo affirming that it had been a misunderstanding, but he offered me no thanks for that. It would be a while before I realized Ted was now relying on Diana Weiner to handle personal matters for him.

Next to come would be the Eleventh Circuit oral argument in the Lake City case, and I was beginning to prepare for that when Jim came by to say he and Mike Mello had talked about it and decided Jim should do the argument, not me. He said they were afraid the court

January 20, 1987

Dear Polly,

Christmas, New Years and the 12 days of Christmas have come and gone. I felt reclusive during the holidays and couldn't bring myself to send season's greetings to anyone. So it goes. But I got over it.

So please accept my heartfelt thanks for all you have done and for my wishes that the coming year will give you much Peace and Joy

ted

A Christmas card from Ted, 1986

would think we weren't taking the case very seriously if I, a lowly associate, did it. So much for "You do it, you're Bundy's lawyer." I was relieved, because I didn't really feel up to it, but I felt crushed that Jim—and now he was relying on Mike Mello's opinion, too—didn't think I was either.

I had began to feel as if I were walking around with a wet blanket around my shoulders. And the change was beginning to show. My father noticed it first: the flatness in my voice, my lack of interest in carrying on a conversation. That was not like me. "What's happened to you?" he said. "You used to be the life of the party. Everyone would look forward to when Polly would come around. What's wrong?" I'd reply that his calling and bugging me was what was wrong. But Tanya noticed it too. Sometimes when I came home to the beauty parlor, Tanya would still be there, finishing up a facial. As her last client lay in the back room under an herbal mask, Tanya would take my face in her hands, expertly reading signs of stress. "This Ted Bundy case is not good for you," she'd say. "That case is all right for a man, but it is not a case for a woman to handle." She apparently shared Vic Africano's feelings on that. "You should take a drink," she'd say. "I don't drink," I'd answer. "You need to take a drink now and then," she said. "This is too much strain on you."

Well, I wasn't about to do that. I was a teeth-gritting nondrinker and I wasn't going to let anything set me back. I had been surprised at how easy it had been to quit. I'd been consuming the equivalent of two bottles of wine at home every night for almost two years when I did, following several years of bar drinking. Although it had given me some sense of fitting in—and certainly relieved me of my overdeveloped sense of responsibility—public drinking had become too dangerous. And drinking alone at home had been too dismal. When I quit cold turkey in February 1986 I had thought for sure I'd have some physical reaction and, when I did, I'd call Alcoholics Anonymous. But it didn't happen, so I didn't call. Instead, I laid on the couch licking frozen fruit bars for those same evening hours I had been drinking.

Through the spring of my new sobriety I'd still had in mind that I'd start again, with a clean body. Get my tolerance down, be satisfied with one or two drinks. But when we went to Miami in June to fight Ted's second warrant, I knew I could never drink again. The stress and fear were killing me, my ignorance of the collateral appeal process had made the experience one of hurtling forward toward a black abyss. The thought of drinking had come to mind, though, and to my surprise I had found that I was very grateful I was not drinking, I thought how lucky it was my six months were not up yet. For one thing, timing was everything. We were going through two or three courts a day. I had to be available, I had to keep up with it, I needed to be sober. But, more importantly, if I had had a drink I would have been unable to stand the unbreachable distance Jim always maintained between us. I would have had to breach it. Even under those combat conditions, when we were totally dependent on each other, where it was us against the world—quite literally—Jim never said anything to me that couldn't be printed in the newspaper. No expression of personal emotion over the court losses—just occasional professional outrage at systemic injustice—as the execution hour neared. No shared confidences, no personal interaction. As I had thought about what would happen if I took a drink, I knew that I would drink until I was drunk. I would drink to an alcoholic epiphany and then force Jim to deal with me—personally. I knew then I would never "dry out" and become a normal drinker. I knew then I could never drink again.

On January 15, 1987, the Eleventh Circuit Court of Appeals issued its decision in the Chi Omega case:

> The judgment of the district court must be reversed and the case remanded for orderly, careful, and deliberate consideration of the constitutional issues that are involved.

Writing for the three-judge panel, former chief judge John Godbold echoed the court's mood at the oral argument in November in a terse and quietly seething opinion. While painstakingly detailing, minute-by-minute, Judge Zloch's fundamental procedural errors in refusing to grant a stay of execution and dismissing the case on its merits, Judge Godbold socked it to the state's attorney again:

> We cannot identify with certainty the district court's rationale for dismissing the petition. The confusion at the oral argument on the motion to stay was substantially contributed to by the state. In the district court and before this court on appeal the state's less-than-candid and misleading presentations are deeply disturbing. Litigants, the judicial system, and society at large are entitled to have habeas corpus cases, and especially death penalty cases, proceed promptly, effectively, and fairly. Counsel for Florida and for other states in this circuit now work cooperatively and with high professional standards toward this end. But somehow this case went astray.

Judge Godbold noted that far from being insufficient, our petition had been "overextensive," including arguments and facts that did not need to be put forth until a hearing was granted. At the end of his opinion,

Judge Godbold, while noting that he was not prejudging the outcome of the case, described our two main claims in ways that made it clear the panel understood them well:

> [W]ithout analyzing all of his numerous claims, the petition demonstrates a likelihood of success in at least some respects sufficient to justify a stay. These include permitting the testimony of the only eyewitness after she had been hypnotized. The Florida Supreme Court held this testimony was admissible. Eight months later in Bundy's separate appeal arising out of the Lake City murder, the same court held that hypnotically refreshed testimony was per se inadmissible in Florida but that its decision was to be prospective only. It may be that these two cases can be distinguished. But the interplay between them, and the constitutional implications of the two cases, raise serious questions that can be neither ignored nor brushed aside.
>
> Another serious question is raised by the state court determination of Bundy's competency to stand trial. . . . No one participating in the hearing adequately developed in an adversary manner the issue of whether Bundy was competent, which was what the hearing was all about. Obviously, it is not an answer to questions raised concerning the constitutional adequacy of the hearing that Bundy did not wish to be found incompetent—if in fact he was incompetent, he was not competent to make such a decision.

I felt heard. The Chi Omega case was going back to Judge Zloch on an opinion that specifically noted the apparent merits of the two major claims it shared with the Lake City case, which was still pending with the panel. Things were looking good. For the case.

Word came to me that the firm was unhappy with my attempts to recruit more lawyers for the Bundy team. As if it were a cult, something other than a real case. A new rule was silently instituted at Wilmer: No pro bono work in the first six months at the firm, and then not without official approval.

I also heard that the women partners were questioning their partnership shares going to represent a man who had specifically targeted women, for murder. Wasn't this like Jews contributing to the representation of Adolf Hitler, they wondered? But no one discussed it with me.

On February 5, 1987, Ted had his first panic attack. Although he'd maintained an unperturbed exterior, always in control, always cool and superrational, inside, he apparently was destabilizing after the events of the past year. Until his first death warrant his life at Florida State Prison had been relatively peaceful, especially after he and Carole and Tina had settled into their weekly routine. The disruption caused by the first warrant was only the first tremor of the crumbling of that existence. The TV movie had brought more public attention, hatred, and unavoidable reminders of the crimes he had put out of his mind for six years. The second warrant had made the possibility of execution real to him—and to Carole. Then Carole had left for Seattle, and Ted's six-year pattern of Saturday visits with his attentive "family" were over. Bad memories were being dredged up from the past as Dr. Norman visited sporadically, spending several hours each time probing Ted's recollections, his dark side. He was spending time alone with Diana Weiner. He'd always expected to be permitted time to apply for clemency in the Lake City case after cert. was denied. Instead, he had found himself on death watch again, receiving a stay only six hours before his execution was to take place. Then, to top it off, he'd been wrongly placed in disciplinary status upon receiving the stay and deprived of outdoor exercise—his most treasured privilege. The pressure was mounting, his peaceful existence was slowly unraveling. Even the Eleventh Circuit ruling in our favor and remanding the Chi Omega case for further consideration was not necessarily a great comfort to Ted. For him, the mere resolution of a court case—whether in his favor or not—meant that he was that much closer to running out of legal ammunition.

Ted later told me he thought he was going to die that morning of February 5. He said he had been feeling fine since his release from the DR, exercising as usual, doing yoga, avoiding coffee and chemicals. Ted valued self-discipline. The panic attack hit at six in the morning, without warning. He said he lost his short-term memory; lost all perspective; he felt "waves of adrenaline, terror and panic"; he was trembling and his hands were shaking; he felt "numbness, pinpricks on top of my brain"; he was dizzy, heard echoes, and had ringing in his ears. He writhed on the floor of his cell for half a day before it passed. Subsequent attacks would last longer.

"May your daughters all befall the same fate as Bundy's victims, and may you remain without vindication for their deaths, and rot in hell."

On the day the Eleventh Circuit heard oral argument in the Lake

City case, March 5, 1987, the St. Petersburg *Times* noted that the court had received more angry phone calls and hate mail than ever before as the result of granting stays of execution to Ted Bundy. One letter began: "The criminal justice system in America has a festering, pus-dripping sore called the U.S. 11th Circuit Court of Appeals." Another contained death threats deemed serious enough to be turned over to the FBI. The clerk of court described it as an "I know where you live, and there's a contract out on you, and they're going to find your bodies floating in the river" letter. Some, including one addressed to the "Three Blind Judges," merely charged our panel with gross ineptitude. Still others used stronger language: "Judges like you cast shame on the entire justice system. In a civilized society, I don't think you have any excuse for being."

On April 2, 1987, the Eleventh Circuit issued its decision in the Lake City case. This time, rather than identifying a single author, it was a per curiam opinion of the entire panel. Per curiam opinions are used in especially controversial cases or in cases in which the panel wants to emphasize that the decision is without dissent, since the correct resolution of the case is self-evident. In this case, I suspected it was used to prevent any one judge from shouldering the blame. Certainly the Lake City case had been a little trickier for the panel than the Chi Omega case had been. For one thing, Vic had never raised the issue of Ted's competency at trial. For another, Judge Sharp had covered his procedural bases. As a result, the panel felt compelled to accept at face value Judge Sharp's implausible assertion that before he ever heard from us, he'd read the entire record, considered all the possible claims and all answers to rebuttals that could be made on the basis of the fifteen-thousand-page record, and been ready to rule on the merits of every claim within hours of filing, without even allowing us to appear before him to argue our case. Given that assumption, Judge Sharp's factual findings carried a presumption of correctness on appeal, and could be overturned only if we had shown that they were "clearly erroneous," a very high standard to meet. But the panel ruled that we had.

[A] defendant is mentally incompetent to stand trial if he lacks a "sufficient present ability to consult with his lawyer with a reasonable degree of rational understanding" and if he lacks "a rational as well as factual understanding of the proceedings against him." A defendant is not entitled to an evidentiary hearing on his claim of incompetency unless he "presents clear and convincing evidence to create a 'real, substantial and legitimate doubt as to [his] mental capacity . . . to meaningfully participate and cooperate with counsel.' " The standard of proof is high. The facts must " 'positively, unequivocally and clearly generate' the legitimate doubt."

The district court dismissed this claim, finding that Bundy was not entitled to an evidentiary hearing because he had failed to present sufficient evidence raising a legitimate doubt as to his competence to stand trial. In making that finding, the district court first noted that a trial court in Leon County [the Chi Omega case] had found Bundy competent to stand trial. The district court then stated that Bundy's failure to raise this claim at trial in this case was "highly significant" and that "[i]t would be a 'perversion of the judicial process' to allow petitioner to waive any challenge to his competence at trial and then permit a new trial on the grounds that he was not granted a hearing on his competence."

Admittedly, we must accept the district court's finding that Bundy failed to produce sufficient evidence generating a legitimate doubt as to his competence to stand trial unless that finding is clearly erroneous. However, our review of the record convinces us that the district court erred in concluding that Bundy was not entitled to an evidentiary hearing on this claim.

[T]he district court improperly weighed the evidence in the record. Although defense counsel's failure to question at trial his client's competency can be highly persuasive evidence that the petitioner's competence to stand trial was not in doubt, the district court unduly emphasized defense counsel's [Vic Africano's] failure to do so here. As indicated, the trial court in the Leon County case determined that Bundy was competent to stand trial. Because this case and the Leon County prosecution were contemporaneous and because a competency claim in this case would have rested on much of the same evidence that the Leon County court apparently rejected, defense counsel may have concluded that the trial court here also would have denied any relief on a competency claim. He could have reached that conclusion even though he seriously doubted Bundy's competency to stand trial. Therefore, because trial counsel's failure to raise this claim gives rise to conflicting inferences, the district court attached too much weight to the failure to raise this claim at trial.

Whether the defendant believed he was competent to stand trial is irrelevant for, if a defendant is incompetent to stand trial, his belief that he is able to do so is without import. We note that any instruction from Bundy to his trial counsel not to challenge his competency does not foreclose our inquiry. If defense counsel suspects that the defendant is unable to consult with him "with a reasonable degree of rational understanding," he cannot blindly accept his client's demand that his competency not be challenged.

· · ·

In contrast, the district court seemingly ignored strong indicia of Bundy's incompetence to stand trial. After the sentencing jury recommended the death sentence, defense counsel offered to the court the report of Dr. Tanay. The trial court in the Leon County case appointed Dr. Tanay, a clinical psychiatrist, to examine Bundy. Dr. Tanay interviewed Bundy and defense counsel in the Leon County case and examined Bundy's behavior during police interrogations and in the courtroom. As a result, Dr. Tanay concluded that Bundy "lacks a rational understanding of what is facing him" and that he probably lacks "sufficient present ability to consult with his lawyers with a reasonable degree of rational understanding," and recommended that the court conduct an inquiry into Bundy's competence to stand trial. Such evidence—the uncontradicted opinion of a qualified psychiatrist directed expressly towards the relevant legal standard—is far more significant than defense counsel's failure to raise this claim at trial. The district court, however, failed even to mention Dr. Tanay's report.

In addition, the record contains several instances in which Bundy apparently ignored the advice of his counsel such as when he gave statements to the police and when he reneged on the plea agreement. Furthermore, despite his counsel's urging to the contrary, Bundy refused to offer any mitigating evidence to the sentencing jury. Instead, Bundy insisted on performing a mock wedding ceremony with his fiancee before them. Such conduct standing alone may not constitute a "history of pronounced irrational behavior" warranting a competency hearing. However, a court must consider the aggregate effect of the indicia of a defendant's incompetence. Bundy's behavior throughout this prosecution reinforces Dr. Tanay's conclusion that Bundy lacked a rational understanding of the case against him and that Bundy could not rationally consult with counsel. We believe that the district court gave too little weight to that fact.

Furthermore, it is highly significant that both defense counsel and the state moved for a competency hearing in the Leon County case after Bundy refused to accept a joint plea offer. Bundy's behavior in rejecting the plea offer was central to the state's decision to request a competency hearing in the Leon County case. Because the joint plea agreement covered both this case and the Leon County case, the trial judge in this case attended the hearing where Bundy theatrically rejected the plea offer. Bundy's behavior at that hearing, atop his already suspect behavior, sufficed to question seriously his competency to stand trial in the Leon County case. It has the same effect here.

Finally, the district court erred in denying a hearing on the ground that, because Bundy did not raise this claim at trial, granting him a hearing now would be a "perversion of justice." A defendant cannot waive his right not to stand trial if he is incompetent. Thus, a defendant can challenge his competency to stand trial for the first time in his initial habeas petition and, if he presents facts raising a legitimate doubt as to his competency to stand trial, he is entitled to an evidentiary hearing in the district court. [Citations omitted.]

Our case in a nutshell. The Eleventh Circuit remanded the Lake City case back to Judge Sharp so a "full and fair determination of Bundy's competence at the time of his trial" could be conducted. It also ordered the proceeding to be consolidated with the competency hearing to be held in the Chi Omega case, both to be considered by Judge Sharp—not Judge Zloch. For a few days after receiving this opinion, Jim and I were elated. Both cases were under control, both were remanded, they were now one case for the competency hearing. We could quit fighting warrants and procedural battles, do our investigation, prepare our case, and put on our evidence. Instead of juggling two live hand grenades, I'd have one normal, consolidated litigation case. I thought. Judge Sharp brought me up short by immediately setting the date for the competency hearing—it was to take place in only two weeks.

Suddenly it was now "drop everything" time again on the Bundy case. Sometimes it seemed as if executing Ted Bundy was right up there with ridding the world of communism in terms of national priorities. Why couldn't we have time to prepare a real case? We'd been prevented from doing this for over a year through no fault of our own, forced by death warrants into wasteful stay litigation and unwarranted rejections by courts anxious to toss away the hot potato. Why the rush to have a hearing? If an inmate has, say, only a life sentence, his habeas petition will languish for years waiting for a hearing, along with all the other civil litigants whose cases are backed up in district court. But Judge Sharp pushed all other cases, all the other litigants, off his calendar to make room for the Bundy case so he could deny it again and be done with it.

Asked by a television reporter if he thought a hearing on Bundy's competency would be a waste of time, Judge Sharp replied, "Absolutely."

PART IV

CHAPTER 11

Considering that I was born to represent Ted Bundy, I was always surprised that I wasn't enjoying myself more. It was a privilege to be in charge of such an important case at the very beginning of my legal career. The stakes couldn't have been more meaningful to me—a man's life. I set my own schedule, determined the work flow. I traveled to Florida on the firm at my own discretion. Most of the legal issues involved compelling questions of constitutional criminal law. Certainly other associates thought I had it made—one example was the associate who announced at a meeting that he didn't feel free to do pro bono work because I was doing more than I was entitled to. I didn't have a nasty partner hovering over me; I wasn't researching bits of dry, technical, legal esoterica; and I certainly wasn't drafting footnotes to suggested comments on proposed regulations. Far from it. *Everything* I wrote made it into the final product, one of my seemingly biweekly court filings. And my very name appeared in newspapers.

But that first year on the case, when I was trying to get my footing, was an unending series of crises. And by the end of that first year, when I finally felt as if I knew what I was doing and should have been able to hit my stride, it was too late. I was shell-shocked, constantly braced for the next emergency, the next disaster, unable to let my guard down. But there was one bright spot. The concentrated factual investigation for Judge Sharp's sudden competency hearing proved to be a virtual oasis of pleasurable activity. People told their stories and, for the most part, all I had to do was listen.

First came Dr. Lewis, miraculously already in Washington for a professional conference the weekend after Judge Sharp scheduled the competency hearing. Dr. Lewis had interviewed Ted twice by then, in September and November 1986. We'd never met in person before, although we'd had many phone conversations. The first was when she'd demanded to know if I knew my client was bipolar, and if not, was I blind? Another, of course, was when she set off the death penalty community alarm that I was mishandling the case after she got a look at Diana Weiner. Most of our other conversations had concerned her travel arrangements to and from FSP. Other than calling me in Washington, D.C., Dr. Lewis apparently had no means of getting a taxicab to her home in New Haven, Connecticut, for a ride to the airport. After all, she was doing us a big, big favor by tacking Ted onto her study and, by the way, how was she supposed to get from the airport in Florida to the prison? Was I going to send a car to pick her up? How would she know where to go? I had handled her requests as best I could, and was careful to refer to her as "Doctor," rather than by her first name. I didn't want to presume. Clearly Dr. Lewis had had very bad experiences with lawyers. On that Saturday, April 4, 1987, I knew it was her the instant she arrived, tumbling out of the taxicab with handfuls of bags and briefcases, looking as young and lively as the Vassar girl she had been thirty years before—and as eccentric as Mary Poppins.

Dr. Lewis mesmerized us all—me, Jim, and two other associates working part-time on the case, John Sandage and Andy Munro. There was no doubt in Dr. Lewis's mind that Ted was suffering from manic depression, which had contributed both to his crimes and to his self-destructive behavior during his Chi Omega trial. The crimes, she said, most likely were committed during depressive phases, which he had attempted to end through the stimulus of stalking and capturing his victim. Much of his trial behavior illustrated his manic phase: talking to the Pensacola police all night; writing his long tirade against Mike Minerva the night before the plea bargain hearing; and acting as though he were invincible. That much, as far as Dr. Lewis was concerned, was settled. What most intrigued her was the possibility that Ted also suffered from multiple personalities.

It was a chilly, drizzly day in Washington. My brother Ivar had come to visit me from Minneapolis on a plane ticket I'd given him for

Christmas, but he ended up exploring Washington on his own that overcast day. Every few hours he'd call from a phone booth to see if I was free yet. But that afternoon, as we sat in a conference room of the firm's brand-new office building, Dr. Lewis charged the room with energy, as if she were a walking, talking nuclear generator. She was so intense, so fascinating, so fascinated by the puzzles posed by the human mind. After we'd discussed Ted's case, and even though we all had other things to do, we could not let her go. She didn't waste words, Dr. Lewis; she didn't waste thoughts. Her power of concentration sparked and illuminated our minds and imaginations for six hours. It was one of those rare moments when you become aware of the real human potential of time, of mere hours.

During the course of the afternoon, Dr. Lewis described her first face-to-face experience with a bona fide multiple personality, a condemned murderer in North Carolina. Dr. Lewis had met with Thelma Barfield, a demure middle-aged woman, while her attorneys were attempting to save her from being executed. She was certain Barfield had been sexually abused as a child, but was unable to get her to admit to it. She'd also been told Barfield had multiple personalities, but she hadn't seen any sign of this. As Dr. Lewis was giving up, however, and turning her back to leave the room, she heard a rough, growling voice rise up behind her. Barfield's other personality, "Billy," had emerged spontaneously. Dr. Lewis became a true believer in multiples. "Billy" told her of the sexual abuse Barfield had endured, but said he had told Thelma he would kill her if she told anyone. In the end, in the typically Alice-in-Wonderland way in which the courts deal with the mentally ill, "Billy's" subsequent appearance at trial only confirmed for the judge that Barfield should be executed. "One of them did it," the judge declared. "I don't care which one." Thelma Barfield was the first woman to be executed after the Supreme Court's moratorium was lifted. Ever the curious scientist, Dr. Lewis seemed to stand in equal awestruck wonder both at "Billy's" cruel victimization of Thelma and the judge's spectacular ignorance in refusing to find her insane.

The next week I was raring to go. Dr. Lewis had suggested all sorts of materials that would be helpful for her evaluation of Ted: the depositions he had taken on his own; transcripts of him at hearings; videotapes of the trials, if they still existed; school records—the works. I had a clear context for the investigation now. I was going to document Ted's pattern of manic-depressive behavior; possibly find periods of amnesia or other signs of multiple personality disorder; and otherwise to show Ted incapable of assisting his lawyers during his trials. I also wanted to find anything in Ted's early childhood that might point to the origins of his mental disturbance, and thereby reinforce the truth of its existence. This competency hearing would be our only chance to present the case. All the evidence would have to be dug up now or lost forever. There was so much to do.

The first series of interviews took place over the phone, in my office. If we hadn't been under such a tight deadline, with the evidentiary hearing coming up like a train at full speed in less than two weeks, I probably would have felt shy about calling up as many of Ted's relatives as I could find, without warning, without a previous introduction, to ask them to tell me everything they remembered about him and his family. If I'd had more time, I probably would have spent it compiling a list of addresses and phone numbers, writing lawyerly letters to each of them, assuring them that I was indeed representing Ted, and that the investigation, as painful as it might be, was necessary to save his life, et cetera, et cetera.

Instead, I was on the phone each night, so I'd catch people at home. I started making guesses as to the whereabouts of certain relatives, calling directory assistance, and reaching them unaware. The results were enlightening and gratifying. Once they got over the shock of the unexpected call, and had also overcome the apparent family rule against talking about Ted, his aunts and uncles and cousins, cognizant of the very real possibility of his execution, almost involuntarily began to open up and reminisce. I was moved by how they entrusted me with their stories. Sometimes Jim would sit in my office for a while listening on an extension, but he'd never speak. The facts were my territory.

I learned that, contrary to Ted's description of an idyllic family background, his grandfather had been a violent and bizarre man who beat his wife and talked aloud to unseen presences. Ted's grandmother had been hospitalized for depression several times and treated with electroshock therapy. I learned that Ted had had episodes where he would seem to turn into another, unrecognizable, person. A great-aunt who had witnessed one such episode suddenly, inexplicably, found herself afraid of her favorite nephew as they waited together at a dusk-darkened train station. He'd turned into a stranger. The same aunt, by then over eighty years old, also volunteered that she had known for sure that something was wrong when, some time later, he changed "from a nice, sweet, normal boy to a Nixon Republican." Ted's cousin talked about the time they lived together, how Ted could charm any woman in the bar, how he could be the life of the party. Aunt Audie, Ted's mother's sister in Philadelphia, was the most helpful. Ted was three months old by the time his mother retrieved him from the foundling home where she'd placed him for adoption after his birth. They then lived with her parents and two sisters until Ted was five years old. He had come back to stay with Aunt Audie twice as a young man. She recalled that, at the age of three, Ted was discovered slipping knives into the bed of his sleeping teenage aunt, her other sister, and how he had just stood there in a daze as she awoke in amazement. The family had conspired to get Ted and his mother out of her father's house—and out to Seattle to start a new life.

Ted's mother denied there had been any problems.

With time ticking away till the scheduled hearing, I headed south for interviews with Ted and his former lawyers.

But first, of course, in this case where surprises were hardly a surprise, another diversion. Changing planes in Atlanta on my way down to see Ted, I was assaulted from the newsstands with brand new information about my client. I couldn't believe my eyes. Sometimes representing Ted was like living a strange dream. There was my client's name splashed boldly across the headlines. For something I knew nothing about; something tying him to another one of the more famous criminals of our time:

JOHN HINCKLEY CORRESPONDS WITH SERIAL MURDERER TED BUNDY
SECRET SERVICE TO INVESTIGATE HINCKLEY-BUNDY CONNECTION

Great. We finally get the case turned around, won the opportunity to prove a claim that might result in his convictions being overturned, and Ted acts up and makes the headlines. I felt betrayed. What was all our careful positioning for, if Ted could act so recklessly?

By the time I got to the prison, the Secret Service had already come and gone, meeting with Ted to inquire about his relationship with John Hinckley and asking to see the letters Hinckley had sent him, while at the same time the prison officials ransacked his cell, looking for those letters themselves. Ted was outraged at this invasion of privacy, and by the time I got there had already drafted a long letter to the judge who had denied Hinckley's furlough pass because of his letters to Ted. He remained in a tizzy my entire visit and we were unable to get any work done on Sharp's upcoming hearing—it was all I could do to get Ted to agree not to take any steps on his own to respond to this. As the result of this revelation, Ted was charged with a disciplinary infraction for "corresponding with another inmate

without authorization." He eventually beat that one, arguing successfully that John Hinckley was technically not an inmate in a prison,
but a patient in a hospital (albeit for the criminally insane).

I went on to Tallahassee, after seeing Ted, checked into a hotel,
and phoned more of Ted's family and old acquaintances. Again, my
calls came to them right out of the blue. Bluntly, I'd say something
like "Hello. I am Polly Nelson and I represent Ted Bundy. We have
one shot at preventing his execution, an evidentiary hearing next week.
Tell me everything you know." As before, I was touched by how
generously people opened up and told me what they could remember.
His only brother, Richard, remembered Ted taking him to a basketball
game when he was a young child, and how flattered he had been that
his older brother would bother to do that for him. Richard told me he
thought Ted had been framed; he was certain Ted was innocent. But
then, why did he seem so accepting of Ted's fate?

That afternoon I paid a visit to Dr. Peter Macaluso, who had been
the jail's physician-on-call at the time Ted was being held for trial. He
now practiced as an "addictionologist" in Tallahassee. Roy Matthews
had discovered jail records showing that Dr. Macaluso had been prescribing tranquilizers and other psychotropic medication for Ted at
the very time he was being evaluated for his mental competency.
Apparently, no one else had known this—not Mike Minerva, who was
finding Ted inexplicably erratic and impossible to deal with; not Dr.
Tanay, who was examining him. Dr. Macaluso told me he had absolutely no recall of this period and had nothing to say. He told me he
could remember absolutely nothing outside of his scant notes in the
jail's medical records. He seemed afraid.

I picked Jim up at the Tallahassee airport that night, and in the
morning we had breakfast with Margaret Good, another of Ted's lawyers at the Chi Omega trial. Ted had seen her around the public
defenders office and—even though she was strictly an appellate lawyer—had insisted that she be added to the defense team when Minerva
had stepped aside after the plea fiasco. Ms. Good had only good things
to say about Ted. He was smart, she said, completely rational. He did
not cause any problems that she, at least, could not handle. She did,
though, describe the time Ted jumped up from the counsel table to
question the crime scene technician, walking him through every detail
of what he'd seen, where the blood was, what the bodies looked like,
etc. Ms. Good told us the jurors had watched in open-eyed amazement, looking back and forth between Ted and Captain Poitinger like

spectators at a tennis match. They knew at that moment they were watching the killer relive his crimes.

A few miles outside of town, the humidity that blankets Tallahassee gives way to the breeze of the Gulf that is its source. Jim and I rode out later that morning to see Ted's other trial lawyers in the Chi Omega case, Lynn Thompson and Ed Harvey. The sun was bright and the sky was clear and it felt good to be driving into the country, 'gator country. We interviewed the two men in Ed Harvey's office, a trailer behind a county courthouse, on the one street in the small town where he now practiced. I could smell the bay miles away; and in hearing their stories I could feel the heartbeat of the real people who had lived with this case at its most crucial and confounding stage—the doomed plea negotiations and the Chi Omega trial. These lawyers, like Mike Minerva, were reluctant to talk. For one thing, they apparently despised Ted; he had been nothing but trouble as a client. They told us how Ted had decimated their plans, how his actions had made no sense, how Judge Cowart would not listen to what the problems were, how it had seemed as if Ted were working for the other side. They were relatively new lawyers at that time, and both men said that now they would have handled it differently, would have been more firm about Ted taking his place as the defendant in the case, not as the lawyer. On the way back, Jim decided I had a crush on Lynn Thompson, and referred to him thereafter as the "Robert Redford of the South." No comment.

We interviewed Joe Aloi in Tallahassee. Compact, dark-haired, and hard talking, Joe was now a bail bondsman in a prefabricated office near the jail on the outskirts of town. His paneled office was dark; the shades were drawn. He told us about the days when he was an investigator for the public defender, the days that he spent in the cell with Ted Bundy, at Minerva's request, to allow Ted to get things off his chest so that he would stop inviting the police into his cell to talk to him. Joe and Ted would each lie in a bunk, and Ted would talk about sex. Joe said that when he went home afterwards he'd feel dirty and find it difficult to face his wife. Jim asked him if he thought Ted was insane; his answer both reinforced and undermined our case. "Oh, yeah," Joe said, "he was as insane as they come." That was the helpful part. "But he could control it," he continued, dashing our thoughts of calling him as a witness. "He had a bunch of boxes in his head, see, and he could open one when he wanted to, he could open an insane one when he wanted to. He had all these boxes, see." While Joe believed that Ted could exercise some control over his changes, twice he had seen Ted turn into another person right in front of him. Joe said the transformation was so complete that Ted would change color and emit some strange odor; and he would become incoherent.

The room seemed to darken as Joe spoke, even though the sun was beating on the closed blinds. The three of us seemed to recess into the shadows. While all of Ted's former lawyers other than Margaret Good had conveyed a strong sense of personal foreboding, Joe expressed it outright. "Bundy's got a power, a special kind of power. He'll ruin your lives. I've seen it happen before. You'll see," he said, turning to Jim, "he'll make you impotent." "And you," he said to me, with a bit more gallantry, "he'll make your husband leave you, if you have a husband." Joe shook his head gravely as he leaned back in his big leather chair. "Yeah, he'll ruin both your lives."

At the end of the day Jim and I tracked down the videotapes of the trial, which had been recorded daily by Florida State University and broadcast nightly on television. Jim laid out a large chunk of the firm's cash for a copy of them, in the hope that they captured Ted's behavior and could be used to bolster Dr. Lewis's evaluation. He was crushed when we played them back at the hotel and they turned out to be only brief excerpts. The next morning we learned Judge Sharp was canceling the hearing because the state had appealed the Eleventh Circuit's decision to the U.S. Supreme Court. But not before Ted's mother, Louise, thinking that it was really her final chance to say something that would save Ted, called me at the hotel to admit that her father had been violent and probably had beat her mother. It was clearly a very, very difficult thing for her to say.

So the hearing was off for now, which was good, since we could use a lot more time to digest and follow up on all the new information and materials we had. But it was sort of a letdown after that terrific buildup. And we were let down further when, soon afterward, the Eleventh Circuit unconsolidated the two cases, agreeing with the state that the Chi Omega case was not far enough along to have a competency hearing—it had been sent back to Judge Zloch to start from *scratch*. The court noted, however, that they would consider reconsolidating the cases if Judge Zloch brought his up to speed before Judge Sharp held his hearing. Until then, I was back to two hand grenades—but at least they both had pins in them for the time being.

Ted had been anxious to meet Jim—he had only seen him on television before, standing on the steps of one courthouse or another,

LINKAGE INTERVIEW FORM

1. Need to *expand* section J. Crime scene with
more input from offender. (See also p 29 question 45)
and page 68 Past Offense Behavior).　§ 46

　　The question of whether or not an
offender returns to the place where body is left
is touched on in passing, is not fully explored
and is essentially overlooked.

　　If it can be determined if, where and under
what conditions certain offenders return to a scene it
could be of enormous benefit to those offices
investigating such crimes.

　　Additional questions on p. 47.

1=yes, 2=no, 9=no recall, no data

manipulative, conning				47-49/
threatening; intimidating; gives orders				50-52/
abusive/degrading/insulting				53-55/
inquisitive; asks victim about self; about sex				56-58/
polite, friendly talk; apologizes to victim				59-61/
personal				62-64/
threatens victim's family/children				65-67/
complementary				68-70/
silent; no conversation				71-73/
other_____				74-76/
describe E7				79-80/

ID ☐☐☐☐   1-4/

45. Did subject engage in any of the following behaviors after the event?

1=yes, 2=no, 9=no recall, no data

followed the case in the newspapers or other media				5-7/
kept souvenirs of victim:_____				8-10/
describe				
communicated with police/news media				11-13/
communicated with victim or victim's family				14-16/
interjected himself somehow into the investigation				17-19/
confided in someone/hints about his crime				20-22/
increased drug/alcohol use				23-25/
changed his residence				26-28/
religiousity increased				29-31/
changed his job				32-34/
experienced physical deterioration				35-37/
left town				38-40/
overall behavior changed				41-43/
revisited scene of crime _see question 46_				44-46/
visited residence or workplace of victim				47-49/
reassaults victim				50-52/
felt remorse/sad/guilty				53-55/
Other:_____				56-58/

E8   79-80/

	ID				1-4/
		A	B	C	

46. If the offender revisited the scene of the assault, what was his purpose in doing so?

    1=re-live the offense or engage in further fantasy
       about the crime
    2=to determine progress of police investigation
    3=to engage in further sex acts
    4=to mutilate body
    5=to recommit acts with other victims at same location
    6=other:_____

    _____
                    describe
    8=didn't re-visit scene, does not apply
    9=no recall, no data

    5-7/

47. What actions did subject take to preclude identification/evidence retrieval?

    1=blindfold victim
    2=disguise
    3=wear gloves/type:_____
    4=force victim to bathe/douche
    5=take evidentiary items
    6=other:_____
                    describe
    8=none
    9=no recall, no data

    8-10/

48. Was anything else taken from the the assault scene by subject?
    1=valuables
    2=personal items
    3=other:_____
                    describe
    8=nothing taken
    9=no recall, no data

    11-13/

49. Driving habits of subject:

    1=drives when necessary
    2=does not drive
    3=compulsive driver/cruises a lot
    4=night driving preferred
    5=aggressive driver
    6=other:_____
                    describe
    9=no recall, no data

    14-16/

50. Accessories on car: (1=yes, 2=no, 9=no recall, no data)

    CB   17-19/
    police scanner   20-22/
    siren   23-25/
    red lights   26-28/
    spot light   29-31/
    antenna placement/police   32-34/
    equipped for offense   35-37/
    modification for entrapment   38-40/
    other:_____   41-43/
                    describe

SECTION J   CRIME SCENE SEXUAL HOMICIDE ONLY

DIRECTIONS: COMPLETE ONLY IF REPORTING ON SEXUAL HOMICIDES. OTHERWISE,
             LEAVE BLANK.

DATA ARE DRAWN FROM PRE-SENTENCE RECORDS ONLY

This section should be expanded to include data from offender about place where body was found. Among areas to be explored include:

1. Reason for selecting site where body disposed
   a. to conceal crime (check all which apply)
   b. to facilitate post mortem activities w/ body (i.e. sexual molestation)
   c. to display victim's body
   d. to facilitate discovery of body
   d. impulse
   e. convenience
   g. no reason
   h. other (impulse)

2. Picked site prior to / time made contact w/ victim
   □ yes   □ no

3. Return to site after body placed there
   □ yes   □ no

4. Number of times
   □ 1   □ 2   □ 3   □ 4   □ 5   □ 6   □ more than six _____

5. Time lapse between visits to site (days)
   Between disposition of body and first visit _____
   first to second visit _____
   second to third _____
   etc

6.

(15) 6. Time of day ~~returned~~ travelling ~~from~~ to site

    ☐ early morning   ☐ midnight - 4:00
    ☒ midday   ☐ 4:00 - 8:00
    ☒ evening (after dark)   ☐ 8:00 - 4:00
    ☒ late night   ☐ 4:00 - 12:00
    ☒ variable   ☐ time varied

(17) 7. ~~How~~ Manner in which offender returned to site

    ☐ Drove by site only without stopping
    ☐ approach site on foot but kept distance from body
    ☐   and came right up to body

18

(19)(18) 8. Reason(s) for returning to site (check all that apply)

    ☐ ~~check felt~~ Check for and retrieve evidence
    ☐ retrieve personal belongings of victim
    ☐ ~~observe~~ To observe body
    ☐ to mutilate body
    ☐ to further conceal (bury, decapitate, etc) body
    ☐ to engage in sexual activity with body
    ☐ no reason
    ☐ other (photograph, general curiosity, etc) _____

19. when you were ~~returning~~ ~~to~~ site, did ~~you ever think that~~ the police _____

    An questionnaire based on these eight questions should be prepared and administered to the 36 subjects in the FBI's sexual homicide study.

20 Did you ~~feel that~~ concern stop you ☐yes ☐no
(see #4 **)

    There needs to be additional discussion about how to use data obtained from the questions above in maintaining surveillance at a site where a body has been discovered.

(right margin, vertical:) might be watching the site ☐yes ☐no

Also need question on characteristics of body recovery site (see VI-CAP form questions 101 to 105. Interpret in connection with data from section I, 8-14.)

⑥ 9. How far (miles) was site from place where victim contacted / abducted _____ (miles

④ 10. How far was site from offender's residence _____ (miles)

① 11. ⎫
② 12. ⎬ Question 101-104 from VI-CAP form
③ 13. ⎭
⑤ 14. → Did offender transport victim from point contact to
14a. site where body
⑧ 15. How far was victim's body taken from roadway offender used to transport victim / discovered

☐ not applicable. Did not transport   ☐ yes ☐ no
☐ along roadside   if no go to
☐ 10 ft - 50   quest 13
☐ 50 - 100
☐ 100 - 300
☐ 300 or more
☐ don't know

(8) 16 what attempt made to conceal victim body
    ☐ yes ☑ no

(9) 17 what was done (check all which apply)
    ☐ transported to remote area
    ☐ carried off roadway
    ☐ buried
    ☐ covered with debris (brush, trash)
    ☐ left in thickly wooded area   body of water
    ☐ other (i.e. placed in dumpster, dumped in roads,
        cremated, dismembered, etc)

20. What precautions would you take when
returning to site (check all that apply)
☐ would drive by area first
☐ would park car at distance from
   site and carefully approach on foot
☐ would approach under cover of darkness
☐ would look for out-of-place vehicle in area
☐ would look for fresh footprints near body
☐ would look to see if body had been
   moved or disturbed.
☐ other ——————
☐ took no unusual precautions

December 22, 1987

Dear Polly,

Have you recovered from the
stresses of Orlando? All of you
worked so hard on that hearing.
I am grateful. You did superb.

I hope you had a wonderful
Christmas.

peace
ted

SEASON'S GREETINGS

defending Ted's right to a hearing on his collateral claims before being put to death. Now that we were in Florida together, and Judge Sharp had canceled his hearing, Jim and I took the opportunity to visit Ted and get him to start talking about his past.

At the beginning of the visit, Ted sheepishly slid a thick sheaf of paper toward me and warned, "You're not going to like this." He was right about that. While Jim began the interview, my attention was fixed on the document in my hands. It was a questionnaire used by the FBI to interview serial killers for research purposes. Ted had been seeing an FBI officer, Bill Haigmeier, behind my back. On top of the Hinckley correspondence, this was another blow to my dearly held belief that I held control over this case. What had he told the FBI? What would the FBI say about his competency if the state called them to testify? Keeping Ted out of the public eye and away from anyone who might report on his demeanor was important to our strategy of positioning Bundy as the mentally ill person he was, as opposed to the clever master planner he was usually portrayed as.

> 1. Need to expand section J. Crime scene with more input from offender. (See also p. 29 question 45, 46 and page 68 Past Offense Behavior).

Worse, though, was what Ted Bundy, serial killer expert, had done with the questionnaire—without any apparent understanding of what it said about Ted Bundy, defendant—or about Ted Bundy, the man. He apparently had been especially fascinated by one area he thought the questionnaire authors had not emphasized enough: "The question of whether or not an offender returns to the place where body left is touched on in passing, is not fully examined and is essentially over-looked. If it can be determined if, when and under what conditions certain offenders return to a scene it could be of enormous benefit to agencies investigating such crimes." Assistant Professor Bundy had written in a complete set of questions, complete with little hand-drawn checkboxes. I read them in horror:

> This section should be expanded to include data from offender about place where body was found. Among areas to be explored include:
> 1. Reason for selecting site where body disposed (check all which apply)
>   a. to conceal crime

   b. to facilitate post mortem activities with body (i.e. sexual molestation)

   c. to display victim's body

   d. to facilitate discovery of body

   e. impulse

   f. convenience

   g. no reason

   h. other _____

2. Picked site prior to time made contact with victim
   □ yes   □ no

3. Return to site after body placed there
   □ yes   □ no

4. Number of times
   □ 1   □ 2   □ 3   □ 4   □ 5   □ 6
   □ more than six _____ (no.)

5. Time lapse between visits to site (days)
   Between original disposal of body and
       first visit   _____
       first and second visit   _____
       second and third   _____

6 Time of day usually returned to site
   □ early morning   □ midnight to 4:00
   □ midday   □ 4:00–8:00
   □ evening (after dark)   □ 8:00–4:00
   □ late night   □ 4:00–12:00
   □ variable   □ time varied

7. Manner in which offender returned to site
   □ drove by site only without stopping
   □ approach site on foot but kept distance from body
   □ approach site on foot and came right up to body

8. Reason(s) for returning to site (check all that apply)
   □ To check for and retrieve evidence
   □ to retrieve personal belongings of victim
   □ to observe body
   □ to mutilate body
   □ to further conceal (bury, decapitate, etc.) body
   □ to engage in sexual activity with body
   □ other (photograph, general curiosity, etc.) _____

9. When you were returning to site, did you ever think that the police might be watching the site?
   □ yes   □ no

A questionnaire based on these eight questions should be prepared and administered to the 36 subjects on the FBI's sexual homicide study.

> 10. Did you let that concern stop you?
>   ☐ yes   ☐ no

There needs to be additional discussion about how to use data from the questions above in maintaining surveillance of a site where a body has been discovered.

For the next section, Ted edited the FBI's own questions, noting "Also need questions on characteristics of body recovery site. (See VI-CAP form questions 101 to 105. Interpret in connection with data from Section I, 8-14.)"

> 9. How far (miles) was site from place where victim contacted/
>   abducted? _____*(miles
> 10. How far was site from offender's residence?
>   _____ (miles)
> 11.) ⎫
> 12.) ⎬ question 101-104 from VI-CAP form
> 13.) ⎪
> 14.) ⎭
> 14a. Did offender transport victim from point contact [sic] to site
>   where body discovered
>   ☐ yes   ☐ no   if no go to question 13
> 15. How far was victim's body taken from roadway offender used to
>   transport victim
>   ☐ not applicable. Did not transport
>   ☐ along roadside
>   ☐ 10 ft–50
>   ☐ 50–100
>   ☐ 100–300
>   ☐ 300 or more
>   ☐ don't know
> 16. What attempt made to conceal victim body
>   ☐ yes   ☐ no
> 17. What was done (check all which apply)
>   ☐ transported to remote area
>   ☐ carried off roadway
>   ☐ buried
>   ☐ covered with debris (brush, trash)
>   ☐ left in thickly wooded area

□ other (i.e. placed in dumpster, dumped in body of water, cremated, dismembered, etc.)

20. What precautions would you take when returning to site (check all that apply)
   □ took no unusual precautions
   □ would drive by area first
   □ would park car at distance from site and carefully approach on foot
   □ would approach under cover of darkness
   □ would look for out-of-place vehicles near body
   □ would look for fresh footprints near body
   □ would look to see if body had been moved or disturbed
   □ other _____

I was speechless. I was stunned. I tucked the documents into my brief case. I was firm.

"I'm taking this, Ted."

He started to protest. He had *promised* it to the FBI agent. He had to be true to his word.

"Forget it, Ted," I said, staring down his piercing eyes.

Never was I so curt with him. Never had I felt so betrayed on so many levels. That he should communicate with law enforcement behind my back. That he should incriminate himself so thoroughly, so carelessly, as if he were untouchable. That he should have such total disregard for the horror of his crimes. That he, instead, should have such evident pride. Why couldn't he at least *pretend* he was sorry?

I said nothing more about the questionnaire and let Jim handle the rest of the interview. I didn't really feel like talking to Ted right then. Jim asked him to recount his childhood. Ted was extremely uncomfortable at first, always qualifying or recanting any statement that he felt reflected poorly on any member of his family. It wasn't until our time was almost up that Ted stopped censoring himself and his story began to flow. But it was too late. The superintendent refused to give us more time and we all parted frustrated that we couldn't continue.

I wrote to Ted as soon as we got back to Washington, saying I felt we'd had a productive interview with him and were anxious to come back down to finish what we'd begun as soon as possible. But Ted was not happy to have let himself go at the end of the interview, and he wrote back that we needn't hurry down. Nonetheless, Jim and I went back and, this time our goal was to get him to describe a murder in the first person, not pretending to be talking theoretically or hypothetically.

Ted began with a string of disclaimers: "This is very difficult for me, I have a lot of resistance to bringing this into the open—it's a part of me that needed silence to survive," and "I'll use the term 'I' because I know it was me, in the conventional sense, but you have to understand that it was not the same person who is talking to you now." Then he described the steps leading up to one of his first murders, a blonde in the vestibule of her apartment building. He stopped after recounting his still clear vision of her unconscious body laid out on the floor, after he had hit her with a club, her long hair spread out like a fan above her head. He could not go further, he could not describe what happened next, he choked, he heaved with sighs.

"I can't. It won't let me."

After a moment, he skipped ahead and talked about pulling the woman's body into the weeds at the back of the building, his searing remorse and horror, his mantra of assurance to himself that it would never happen again, the beast had been satisfied, the Good Ted would take back his life. He still could not admit to the murder itself, the actual moment of killing, or maybe there was a reason he couldn't remember. Maybe he was a multiple personality and had amnesia from the point the "Bad Ted" took over.

Two weeks later we had a rare status conference on the Chi Omega case before Judge Zloch in Ft. Lauderdale. With the state's cert. petition challenging the remand order in the Lake City case pending in the U.S. Supreme Court, this was our opportunity to play catch-up with Chi Omega and try to get the cases reconsolidated. We raised several motions at this hearing to move the case forward, including a motion, again, for the appointment of experts so that we could pay for Dr. Lewis's psychiatric evaluation. The hearing lasted all day, with lengthy pauses from the bench, but nothing was accomplished. We had lunch with the state's attorney for the case, Greg Costas, with whom it looked like we were going to have a very long association.

I had not spoken to Dr. Norman since Ted's last stay of execution six months earlier. But one day I was informed that Dr. Norman was out in Tacoma and had burst in on Ted's mother, implying that I had authorized him to see her. Apparently he had attempted to interview her, but ended up browbeating her, telling her she must have been a bad mother not to have seen the signs in Ted as he was growing up. Suddenly, Diana Weiner's continuing visits to Ted—which Ted had been trying to conceal from me—did not seem so innocuous. What were she and Dr. Norman up to? What news would I wake up to hear tomorrow? I wrote to the prison and told them that Ms. Weiner was no longer authorized to see Ted on our behalf.

Thus began the low point in my relationship with Ted—the angry period. Ted was furious when he learned I had caused the prison to cancel Diana's visits. I was tired of bearing all the responsibility for the case and annoyed that Ted didn't share my view that his legal case was the only thing that mattered.

June of 1987 was a bad month for both of us. Ted suffered a whole series of painful and frightening panic attacks that landed him in the prison infirmary. Their intensity scared him nearly to death. He wrote me with detailed descriptions of his symptoms—it seemed to be his way of trying to maintain control. Over the course of his life, Ted had learned to dread being out of control. During one of these episodes I was able to get Ted on the phone and hook him up with Dr. Lewis. It calmed him to be able to discuss his experience with her. Immediately after the panic attacks, however, Ted suddenly became a very active letter writer, ending up in trouble with prison authorities again. One letter he wrote to Dr. Lewis showed his state of mind: in contrast to his usual serious and etiquette-bound writing style, instead of "Dear Dr. Lewis" it began "Hi, Dorothy!" He picked up a new DR, for another letter, and this time it stuck. Even though he had just squeaked by on the last one, Ted walked right back into trouble by trying to smuggle a letter out to John Hinckley's *parents*. Ted wanted to assure them that John was a nice boy and that it meant nothing that he was writing to an admittedly famous serial killer such as himself. Ted had tucked it in a package of materials he mailed to John Tanner that he marked CONFIDENTIAL—LEGAL MAIL, which meant it shouldn't be opened by the prison censors. Unfortunately for Ted, however, the prison knew that John Tanner, though a lawyer, was not Ted's lawyer. Ted was enraged at being charged with a DR for abusing the legal mail privilege and forced to spend sixty days without outdoor exercise. He wrote angry letters to me, demanding that I assist him. I was not sympathetic. How could he have been so reckless, how could he risk the confidentiality of our correspondence by abusing the legal mail privilege? The answer was probably that it was because of who he was, because of the same drives, delusions of grandeur, and lack of impulse control that got him to death row, that made him my client in the first place. But it was annoying all the same.

The upshot was that Ted moved closer to Diana, who had regained

CHAPTER 12

To my surprise, Ted didn't want to attend the evidentiary hearing in Orlando any more than I wanted to have him there. He had not been outside the Florida State Prison since the end of the Lake City trial in February 1980. He liked his routine, he felt comfortable in the prison, and he had no idea what it would be like to be in public again.

I didn't want him there for other reasons. First of all, his presence was unnecessary. We were not going to call him as a witness, and the issue was his competency at the time of his trials, not at the present time. Second, I was worried about security—his and ours—because this would be his first public appearance in over seven years. Third, we were not sure whether, when it came down to it, if actually, directly, asked by the judge about it, Ted would indeed cooperate with our attempt to establish his incompetency. He did not find that claim any more believable—or flattering—than he ever had.

I of course asked Judge Sharp to reconsider his arbitrary time limits on the evidentiary hearing and he of course declined. I filed an appeal in the Eleventh Circuit, and though the court denied the appeal, somehow word got to Judge Sharp that he had better allow us to put on *all* our evidence, not just two hours' worth, if he wanted his decision to stick this time. At the last minute before the hearing, Judge Sharp added four more days in December for the hearing to continue.

Ted was in a lather on October 22 when John Sandage and I went down to meet him in the holding cell at the federal courthouse in Orlando. He'd been taken from his cell at Florida State Prison at four-thirty that morning, not allowed to shower or shave, placed in the back of a van and driven to Orlando in handcuffs and shackles and without a seat belt. It was the absence of a seat belt that bothered Ted the most: "What's the point of trying to save my life on this sentence if I'm going to be killed in a car crash?!" He had bounced around the back of the van for three hours on his trip to Orlando, and now he was bouncing off the walls of the holding cell. John convinced the guards to let Ted use a razor, and we managed to talk him down, but I was afraid for a minute there that the public was going to get to see the Ted Bundy they expected to see—a raving madman. We did not need any more distraction; we already had the menacing Guardian Angels who were pacing the sidewalk in front of the courthouse, urging Ted's immediate execution. "Fry, Ted, fry."

The night before we'd had dinner with our witnesses for the day; Mike Minerva and Ed Harvey. It was one of those rare fancy dinners on the firm I'd envisioned we'd have a lot of on the litigation trail. I felt for once like we really were big law firm lawyers, graciously hosting our witnesses (although, unlike the usual corporate case, our client could not be present), who had come down from Tallahassee to testify about their experience with Ted. Jim held forth on sports and such, as we all became comfortable with each other. And then I, along with, I suspected, our guests, expected to get down to business, preview their testimony, and discuss the upcoming hearing. But that never happened. At the end of the fine meal we wished our slightly bewildered witnesses good night and that was it. See you in court. Once Jim had seen that Mike and Ed were comfortable with him, he decided not to take the freshness out of their testimony by questioning them the night before. In our previous interviews with both men, their feelings of frustrations and bafflement with Ted's conduct had been clear. Jim wanted them to tell their stories for the record in the same way they'd told us—from the heart.

So in a courtroom crowded with reporters and a busload of school-children, before Judge Sharp, on the morning of October 22, 1987, Mike Minerva testified.

JIM COLEMAN: Early in your association with Mr. Bundy, you made the following note to the file: "In my opinion, Bundy was not capable of making a decision and this has been a continuation of the vacillation he has experienced throughout the time we have been conferring with him. I believe he has a basic defect in his reasoning process which prevents him from reviewing this case in a realistic manner." What was the basis of that opinion?

MICHAEL MINERVA: It was based on what we had been experiencing in our dealings with Mr. Bundy from the time that we first had any contact with him, which was that he would say one thing and then do another. For example, in the area of whether he wanted to submit to questioning by the police, or not submit to questioning. Whether he wanted counsel to represent him or not. When he would tell us that he wanted us present, did not want to talk to law enforcement officers without us present, and then would go ahead and do it anyway without calling on us. And in the question of preparation—whether we were going to help him or whether he was going to do anything to help himself, and what strategy he was going to employ. He never seemed to settle on a course of action or theory that he would persist in. He was always changing. He never made a decision. He never said, I've decided this is what I'm going to do.

J.C.: During your representation, through the conclusion of the trial, did he ever come up with a strategy that he would pursue and stick to?

M.M.: No, sir. This was one of the fatal flaws in trying to proceed in this case. There never was—and couldn't be because of his changing his mind—a theory of the case, which is essential in my view to trying to defend anyone. You might modify it as time goes on, but by the time it gets to the trial anyway, you've got to know where you're trying to get to when you're finished. And what I was explaining here in this memorandum persisted throughout the entire time that I was associated with Mr. Bundy. Namely, that when he was confronted with the alternatives of what to do and having to come to a plan, he didn't. And if we did agree on something he would promptly change his mind about it.

J.C.: Mr. Minerva, can you tell the court please what the effect of this behavior was on Mr. Bundy's defense?

M.M.: Well, it devastated it, because we were going off in all directions at once. Here in my notes I wrote, "I do not believe that he was being ornery with us or putting on an act. He has taken the same position of ambivalence from the first time I talked with him when he was first brought to Tallahassee in February. Although he appears to have the intellectual capacity to make decisions, he lacks the mental ability to decide upon a course of action."

J.C.: Did your opinion about him and his ability to make decisions change any time during your representation of him?

M.M.: No, it did not.

J.C.: Do you believe Mr. Bundy's participation in his defense as co-counsel helped the defense?

M.M.: No.

J.C.: Did it harm the defense?

M.M.: Yes. In my view, it did.

J.C.: In what way?

M.M.: Mr. Bundy would insist on us going down a lot of rabbit trails, in a sense, pursuing evidence and leads, arguments that were wasting our time, diverting us from the main issues. And at some of the court hearings he insisted that we develop or present certain evidence that we knew would be damaging, yet he was very adamant about us doing that.

In the trial itself, he presented some questioning of one witness that brought out a whole lot of gory details that were totally unnecessary, which we had tried to keep out ourselves. During the cross-examination of Dr. [Richard] Souviron during trial, for instance, concerning the bite-mark identification, the state's evidence was bare bones, I would say, as to Dr. Souviron's direct testimony. And the cross-examination done by Mr. Harvey went to the essence of—it weakened it to some extent. We wanted to stop it at that point. We felt further questioning would only bring out more incriminating evidence against Mr. Bundy. But Mr. Bundy persisted—insisted, rather—that we do a more detailed and thorough cross-examination of Dr. Souviron, which resulted in some very damaging testimony going in.

These were the things he did in court, not to mention what he was doing to the defense team itself.

J.C.: Why don't you describe what was going on. What was he doing to the defense team during this period?

M.M.: Divisiveness is what was spawned. Plus a lack of direction. A change of direction that we were constantly undergoing. But, in addition, since there were several lawyers working on his case, Mr. Bundy wanted to control which lawyer did what. He insisted that Margaret Good, who was a female attorney in the offices who had done only appellate practice, be made a part of the defense team, and that was not our plan. But Mr. Bundy kept insisting that she participate.

He made the lawyers who were presenting the opening statements rehearse several different versions, and then he picked the lawyer who was going to make the opening statement. And he did the same thing with the closing argument. And, in effect, keeping everybody off balance, demanding to be seen at all times when we really needed to be working on the case. He would demand we come to his jail cell when it was really nonproductive to be doing that.

J.C.: During this period, up to January of 1979, what was Mr. Bundy's evaluation of the case against him?

M.M.: What he told us was, it wasn't anything to it.

J.C.: And do you have an opinion about whether that evaluation of the case accorded with the facts?

M.M.: Not to my view of the facts, it didn't.

J.C.: Did you ever discuss that with Mr. Bundy?

M.M.: Tried to. Yes, sir.

J.C.: And were you successful?

M.M.: I don't think I was able to persuade him to my view.

J.C.: Did he ever change his opinion about the quality of the state's case against him?

M.M.: Not to my knowledge.

J.C.: Did you ever discuss with Mr. Bundy the possibility of exploring competence to stand trial?

M.M.: On March twenty-second we talked about the question of competency. And Mr. Bundy at that time agreed to submit to a psychiatric examination. We had discussed also the possibility of an insanity defense, and for those two reasons I suggested, or we suggested, a psychiatric evaluation. We asked him to do that.

J.C.: Did he submit to it?

M.M.: He agreed, with certain conditions.

J.C.: What were those conditions?

M.M.: No public record of the examination, and the results would be confidential and privileged.

J.C.: Did you believe that insanity might be an issue in the case?

M.M.: Yes, I did.

J.C.: Were you able to pursue the insanity defense?

M.M.: We were not able to pursue it. No, sir.

J.C.: Why was that?

M.M.: Mr. Bundy did not want us to do that.

J.C.: Can you tell me whether in March of 1979 you believed that competency was an issue in this case?

M.M.: Yes, I did.

J.C.: Did you pursue the question of his competency?

M.M.: Yes, I did.

J.C.: Can you tell, describe to the court, how you went about doing that?

M.M.: We contacted Dr. Emanuel Tanay, a psychiatrist in Detroit, and asked him if he would be willing to do the evaluation, and he said he would, and I sent him a group of materials about the case. I sent him a letter explaining where we were in the case, and he issued a preliminary report based on those materials indicating that he thought that Mr. Bundy had—it was a probability he had—a psychiatric, or the need for psychiatric evaluation to determine both the sanity question and the competency question.

J.C.: After Dr. Tanay interviewed Mr. Bundy and conducted a psychiatric evaluation, did you receive his report prior to the May thirty-first hearing?

M.M.: Yes, I did.

J.C.: Did you take any action in light of this report to determine whether you should proceed with the plea agreement?

M.M.: Yes, sir, I did.

J.C.: Can you describe what that was?

M.M.: I called Dr. Tanay and I told him what was in the works, that there was a plea agreement contemplated, and asked him if his opinion would be different if Mr. Bundy in fact entered a plea to the charges, receiving a sentence, and then Dr. Tanay gave me his response.

J.C.: Which was?

M.M.: That if Mr. Bundy were actually to go through with the plea agreement, it would be evidence of his rationality, which would demonstrate competence to stand trial. But Dr. Tanay expressed great reservations [about whether] Mr. Bundy would actually be able to go through with the agreement because of his mental illness.

J.C.: Mr. Minerva, sometime in the spring of 1979, did you begin to discuss with the state of Florida a plea bargain in the two cases pending against Mr. Bundy?

M.M.: Yes.

J.C.: And those two cases were the Lake City case and the Leon County [Chi Omega] case?

M.M.: Yes.

J.C.: Can you tell me how those discussions developed?

M.M.: Around April 18, 1979, I had a conversation with Larry Simpson, who was the chief prosecutor in the Chi Omega case, and he said that before the next scheduled round of pretrial motions had to be heard, that he thought we should consider the possibility of plea negoti-ation. That those hearings would develop a great deal of incriminating evidence against Mr. Bundy, which might make it impossible to later conclude a plea agreement once the public was aware of, say, all the evidence. So he suggested that we explore the possibility, and he wanted to know, sort of as a last grasp before we plunged along in the full adversary proceedings, whether negotiation was going to be possi-ble, and he asked if Mr. Bundy would be receptive to that. I talked to Mr. Bundy about that, about the possibility of it, and Mr. Bundy rejected it at that time.

J.C.: Now, subsequent to this time, did the discussions resume?

M.M.: Yes they did.

J.C.: Can you tell me how that occurred?

M.M.: I talked with Joe Nursey, who was a lawyer associated with Millard Farmer [the Atlanta death penalty lawyer Ted had wanted to represent him at trial]—and Joe also had been in our offices—and I told him that the state had expressed some willingness to negotiate the case and that Mr. Bundy had declined the offer, and Mr. Nursey told me that Mr. Bundy had always wanted to—or he gave me indication that Mr. Bundy had indicated he would—accept a plea bargain for life sentences. So that was the way that began, and Millard Farmer then became involved with it, insofar as talking to Ted, because that had been a different answer than I had gotten when I spoke with Ted.

J.C.: Can you describe what the negotiations were between you and the state concerning this plea agreement?

M.M.: Basically, it was to enter a plea of guilty to all three of the pending murder charges, the two in the Chi Omega case and one in the Lake City case, plus all the affiliated charges, the burglaries and so forth that went with it. And in exchange for the plea, the state and we would join to recommend three consecutive life sentences, which carried twenty-five years each without the possibility of parole, or a real life sentence of seventy-five years with no possibility of parole, plus consecutive sentences on everything else.

J.C.: Now, can you tell me who, on the state's side, approved this agreement?

M.M.: Everybody who was involved with the case, which includes the judges [Edward Cowart and Wallace Jopling]. There were conferences with the judges in both cases telling them what the agreement was, asking if they would concur. They did concur. The state attorney's office in each of the two circuits made contact with all the law enforcement agencies that were involved and with the families of all the victims and the victims who had survived.

J.C.: Did all of them agree to the plea bargain?

M.M.: Yes.

J.C.: Mr. Minerva, did you consider this agreement to be in Mr. Bundy's interest?

M.M.: Yes, I did. I considered that the evidence that the state had, combined with the great amount of pretrial publicity, would have made it highly likely that the state would have been able to secure convictions in at least the Chi Omega case; and that the possibility was also very great, because of the nature of the offenses and in weighing the statutory aggravating and mitigating circumstances there in the Florida death penalty statute, that Mr. Bundy would very likely receive a death sentence or several death sentences. To avoid that possibility and keep him alive—with the hope that staying alive is always better than being dead—that that was definitely in his best interest. Because the alternative I saw was going to trial and being convicted anyway and getting the death sentence.

J.C.: During negotiations did you have an opinion about whether Mr. Bundy would accept such an agreement?

M.M.: Yes, I had an opinion.

J.C.: And what was that opinion?

M.M.: That he would never go through with it.

J.C.: Why did you have that opinion?

M.M.: Just from every action that he had taken during the time that I had anything to do with him. His—what I spoke of earlier, his inability to stick to a course of action. The changing nature of what he was saying to us. During the time that the negotiations were going on, right from the very outset when I approached him about it, he told me he wouldn't—didn't want to consider it.

Then [I heard] through Millard Farmer—and ultimately from Ted himself after he talked to Mr. Farmer—that he would accept it. The first day that we went to Lake City to talk to the prosecutors and the judge about the case, we went to the jail to see Mr. Bundy in the morning to get his permission to make that overture. But then, while we were gone, he called the office and left a list of instructions on what we were to do to prepare for the trial—so he had us going in two directions at once on that score. And then his continued attitude about the plea during the time that the negotiations were going on. Even when he told me he would accept it he also had some holdback question, reservation, and just from the nature of the way he had behaved the whole time, I did not think he was able to get up in court and enter a plea of guilty.

J.C.: Now, did you have an opinion about the effect of the negotiation on Mr. Bundy's subsequent trial if he did not accept the agreement?

M.M.: We were afraid that if the word got out that he was willing to enter a plea of guilty, [that] that would precondition any potential juror anywhere in the circuit—probably any place in the state, because of the widespread publicity there—into believing he was guilty, and this would make it extremely difficult, if not impossible, to get a fair trial after that.

J.C.: Did you advise Mr. Bundy of that fact?

M.M.: Yes, sir.

J.C.: And did he permit you to go forward with the negotiation?

M.M.: Yes, sir, he did.

J.C.: Mr. Minerva, would you please describe Exhibit ten.

M.M.: Exhibit ten is a memorandum that I dictated. I believe I was in my car after I left the jail and was on the way to the courthouse to meet with the prosecutors. This was in between the time that I had been at the jail talking with Mr. Bundy and others finalizing the plea agreement, getting the signed plea agreement from him, and before we met with the prosecutors later that day.

J.C.: Now, this memorandum describes the circumstance in which Mr. Bundy ultimately signed the agreement?

M.M.: Yes, it does. This is the thirtieth of May, 1979. The plea was scheduled to be entered the next day, and as of the afternoon of the thirtieth we did not have Mr. Bundy's signature. It was one of the conditions of the agreement that the prosecutors had asked that we not go forward until we had Mr. Bundy's signature on the agreement to enter the plea, and so even though there was oral agreement that he would do it, we had to get him to sign it in order to actually have a court session the next day and to get the prosecutors to sign. So there had been for several days before this a number of people, including Mr. Bundy's mother and other friends who had visited with him, as well as Millard Farmer, trying to encourage him to accept the plea offer because, again, even though he had said he would do it, he hadn't put his name on the dotted line. And I was told that he was wavering on whether to accept it even at that late date.

So we went to the jail in the afternoon of May thirtieth to get the signed agreement, and when I arrived Mr. Farmer was there talking to Mr. Bundy alone. After Mr. Farmer came out, I went in and talked to Mr. Bundy alone, and I had the agreements, and we talked. Ted and I talked for about forty-five minutes about whether he was going to sign the agreements, and he just seemed as paralyzed then as he had been on other occasions as far as going forward with the decision. And eventually I knew we were running out of time. I asked for Mr. Farmer to come in, because he seemed to have more information about Mr. Bundy's willingness to plead, had more influence over him. I think Mr. Bundy trusted him a little bit more than he did me. And I asked Mr. Harvey to come in so he could witness what was going on, because I knew the plea had to be voluntary and I didn't want this to be a coercive situation, such as it would later be said that I had done something to force him to enter a plea when he didn't want to. So, anyway, the three of us sat there and pondered it, and Millard eventually persuaded Ted we had no more time and he either had to sign it or not sign it. And with great reluctance he signed both agreements.

J.C.: Did he give you instructions about what to do with the signed agreements?

M.M.: Yes. He did not want [them] to be delivered until we went into court.

J.C.: What was Mr. Bundy required to do the next morning in court in the proceedings to enter the plea?

M.M.: He was to enter a plea of guilty and of course be subjected to the plea colloquy that each judge was going to put forth to insure the voluntariness of the plea and the factual basis of the plea, and he was to make no extraneous statements. The prosecutors were very clear on this: that if Mr. Bundy equivocated at all, if he made any comments about his lack of time to prepare or about the quality of the representation he had received, or [that] he was not allowed to have Mr. Farmer as his lawyer—in any other way to seem to hedge—the deal was off. Mr. Bundy was to answer the court's questions but was not to go into any side arguments or attempt to equivocate the plea at all.

J.C.: Was Mr. Bundy aware of those arrangements?

M.M.: Yes. We told him.

J.C.: Can you describe what was supposed to have happened in the courtroom in terms of who would be present and how the proceedings would go forward?

M.M.: We had asked the prosecutors not to disseminate this information. We were hoping that there would be very few people in the courtroom for a couple of reasons. One, it would very likely startle

Mr. Bundy or have an unsettling effect on him to see a big crowd in there, psychologically—to stand up and have to admit guilt to crimes such as these. Seemed to be a little bit easier if it was not in a big, excited atmosphere with a lot of people watching. And also, in the event that the plea didn't take, that he wanted to have as few people witness the attempt as possible.

J.C.: Were both Judge Cowart and Judge Jopling, the judges in the two cases, present for the proceedings?

M.M.: Yes.

J.C.: Can you tell us what happened on the morning of May thirty-first, 1979?

M.M.: Yes, sir. The defense lawyers met in the public defender's office, and I went over to court first, as I recall. And when I got there [I found that] Mr. Bundy had prepared a typewritten motion which he was distributing or about to distribute as court was about to start. And the content of the motion in effect was totally inconsistent with the entry of a plea because it was a request for other counsel or to fire us and, you know, just generally saying that we had not done our job and we should be removed as counsel. And when I got wind of what that was I asked for a recess so that I and the rest of the defense lawyers could talk to Mr. Bundy about what his intentions were.

J.C.: Did you have the recess?

M.M.: Yes, we did.

J.C.: Did you have an opportunity to talk with Mr. Bundy?

M.M.: Yes, I did.

J.C.: Can you describe that discussion?

M.M.: We went back into the holding cell, and at various times Millard Farmer was there, I was there, John Henry Brown, who is a lawyer and also a friend of Mr. Bundy's, I believe Ed Harvey came in. I'm not real sure what the effect of it was. We were trying to find out from Mr. Bundy what was going on and what he planned to do. And I remember Millard virtually praying over Ted, in a sense, to urge him that, and convince him, that this was in his best interest. That this was vital. This is what we had been pushing for the whole time, was to save his life and that his life was worth saving. And that the only way he could do that was to enter this plea, and that if he rejected the plea there were no more chances for plea, and that the results of trial would be disastrous for him. They would mean the death penalty. After all of that Ted said he still didn't know what he was going to do, and Millard's assessment was that there was a fifty–fifty chance that Ted would enter the plea, but we still didn't know. And so we went back into the courtroom and we sat down. The judges were pushing us to reconvene. They were cooling their heels while we were going through these discussions. They wanted to find out—they were asking us what was happening. So we went into the courtroom not knowing what was going to happen and the record will show what was said. I believe that I stood up and said Mr. Bundy has a matter to present to the court, and sat down and—

J.C.: Let me ask you, when you made that representation to the court, did you have any idea what he would do?

M.M.: I did not know what he would do. He had not told me what he would do. So it was a surprise to me.

J.C.: And what happened?

M.M.: He offered his motion to relieve us as counsel and did not offer the plea.

J.C.: And as a consequence of that, what happened to the plea agreement?

M.M.: The prosecutors waited until he finished. When he had completed his motion attacking us and asking us to be released, then he sort of looked at me and sat down. We had a little whispered discussion—he seemed to want to enter a plea now that he'd gotten this off his chest—and the prosecutors down the table said no deal, it's off.

J.C.: Can you tell me, Mr. Minerva, what was the effect of Mr. Bundy's rejection of the plea agreement?

M.M.: Well, the effect of it then was to have the matter—both cases—go forward for trial. That was the meaning of that.

J.C.: Can you tell me what the effect of the plea agreement was on the defense lawyers?

M.M.: It took all the wind out of our sails, what little wind we had left at that time. We had—we had become quite emotionally involved in the case. We were pretty well exhausted. Our expectation had been going up and down with the case for a long time. We thought we had an end to it. To a very complicated, tension-filled situation. We hoped we did, anyway. And the disappointment that this brought about psychologically was quite a blow to us and, in addition, it had thrown us completely off stride in trial preparation. We were less than two weeks, I think, away from the beginning of the trial. We had interrupted the vital trial preparation time that occurs in the weeks immediately before the trial—getting witnesses and preparing memorandums, all of the things that you do to get ready for a trial—because we had been diverted into this effort to bring about the plea agreement. And so we lost very valuable time at a very critical time in case preparation.

J.C.: What happened after the plea agreement was rejected?

M.M.: We made some motions for continuance. We also made a motion to be relieved as counsel, and then we also went forward with the psychiatric evaluation and requested a competency hearing.

J.C.: Did you represent Mr. Bundy at the competency hearing?

M.M.: No, I did not. Mr. Bundy requested other counsel.

J.C.: Were you called as a witness at the competency hearing?

M.M.: No, I was not.

J.C.: Did you personally continue to represent Mr. Bundy after the competency hearing?

M.M.: To a very limited extent only, and that was in connection with the bite-mark evidence.

J.C.: And why was that?

M.M.: Mr. Bundy had made a personal attack on me and I tried to put that aside. I explained to the court when I made the motion to withdraw that I thought that there might be some vestiges of resentment that I would never be able to get rid of, and that those might prevent me from being as zealous an advocate on his behalf as I should be, and I was worried that I would do things, even subconsciously, that might be damaging to Mr. Bundy. So that was one reason. Another reason was that Mr. Bundy, in his motion, had made statements about me professing a belief in his alleged guilt. And that statement had received widespread dissemination in the media. I was afraid that if I participated to any real substantial extent in his defense that jurors would remember that statement and, consequently, they would think that I was being hypocritical in trying to argue on his behalf when I, myself, believed he was guilty. And I think that I thought that that would be a very damaging posture for me to be in and would compromise his right to a fair trial.

J.C.: Compared to your own experience as a defense lawyer, can you tell me what the experience of the remaining attorneys was on the defense team?

M.M.: Well, none of them, as I recall, had experience, or very little experience, in capital cases, so my impression of their skill and ability to handle this case was that they were being asked to do something that they were not really qualified to do.

J.C.: Mr. Minerva, if you will return to Exhibit fifteen, page eight?

M.M.: Yes. This is Dr. Tanay's report to us.

J.C.: In the full paragraph on page eight just above the middle he says that "I would anticipate that in the unlikely event that the prosecution's case against him," meaning Mr. Bundy, "would weaken, he would through his behavior bolster the prosecution case." Now can you tell me whether your observations of Mr. Bundy were consistent with this prediction?

M.M.: Yes, they were.

J.C.: And did this type of behavior in fact occur?

M.M.: Yes, it did.

J.C.: Can you describe what that behavior was?

M.M.: Disruptive, in a word. Disruptive to the court. There were occasions during that time when I was there that Mr. Bundy refused to come out of his cell; he made demands on the defense team. He came into court sometimes dressed in a sweatshirt. Gave press interviews, badgered the defense team, calling them all hours of the day and night, making them do things that were distracting from their participation in the case. He refused, or was unable to, or didn't—I guess, was unable to—really focus on a theory of the case. We got a local attorney named Robert Haggard to assist us because he was familiar with the court structure in Miami and was familiar with the kinds of people who would be serving as jurors. We got Mr. Haggard to help us in the jury selection, and then he stayed on for awhile in the case. And after a while Mr. Bundy and Mr. Haggard had severe falling-outs, which led to Mr. Haggard's withdrawing from the case in the middle of the trial. And there was the constant—and Mr. Harvey can describe this better than I can—the constant interplay between Mr. Bundy and various counsel as to who would do what, and changing of mind as to what the strategy would be, plus the other instances I mentioned with Dr. Souviron's testimony, which I saw.

J.C.: Now, did you have an opinion about whether Mr. Bundy was doing this solely to disrupt or whether this was something that was beyond his control?

M.M.: My opinion was that he was doing it because it was beyond his control, and I base that in part on what Dr. Tanay's report had said, and the behavior of Mr. Bundy fit the predictions of Dr. Tanay.

J.C.: Do you believe that Mr. Bundy's behavior at the trial affected the outcome of his case?

M.M.: Yes, sir.

J.C.: In what way?

M.M.: Well, there were several ways to approach the case. One, you could just try to win it, hoping for a "not guilty." And another would be to—you could try to win it with affirmative evidence that he didn't do it. You could try to win it by creating reasonable doubt as to the strength of the prosecution case. Or you could decide that the best you were going to come out with was a hung jury.

You need to know that before you start the trial because you need to know what kind of jurors you're going to pick. Are you going to pick jurors who are going to be able to agree, or are you going to pick jurors who are going to hang up? There was never any agreement about that from the beginning. And all throughout the trial the question of what sort of an opening statement to present—what were you going to condition the jurors for as far as your defense? What were you going to try to show? How was that theme going to be developed through the evidence and the arguments to the conclusion of the case? And then, what do you do if there's a conviction and how has that set the stage for whatever you have to do in phase two to prevent the death penalty from being imposed? All of those things that go into the makeup of trial strategy and theory of defense were never agreed upon with Mr. Bundy.

Now the defense lawyers had a good idea of what they wanted to do, but Mr. Bundy would never allow that to be implemented by his disruption and by his changing and by his insistence that certain witnesses be called or not be called, or certain questions be asked or not be asked. And certain arguments made or not made and who was going to make them, and keeping everything in a state of total disarray. And so it turned out. I mean, I got off the case from the very beginning because I felt I had lost any hope that I had of helping him or defending him. Mr. Haggard dropped out of the case for similar reasons. We had to send other lawyers down to help with the penalty phase, because Mr. Bundy refused to let us put on certain evidence. So the whole thing was not a plan but a reaction day by day to his whims and his desires and you could not, in my opinion, conduct a complicated defense of a complicated case with that kind of activity going on.

J.C.: Did Mr. Bundy ever express to you a rational understanding of the evidence that the state had against him?

M.M.: No sir.

J.C.: Did he ever appear to appreciate the evidence, the significance of the evidence that the state had against him?

M.M.: Never.

As Mike Minerva testified, it was clear that it still bothered him after all these years that he hadn't been able to save Ted from himself and prevent his death sentence. Sitting next to me at the defense table, Ted had tears in his eyes; it was evident to him as well. Mike's compassion really got to him.

Ed Harvey took the stand after the morning break. He began by testifying that he had been present as standby counsel at the depositions Ted took in the fall of 1978, when Ted was still unable to decide whether to accept counsel.

JIM COLEMAN: And as a result of your presence at these depositions were you able to conclude what Mr. Bundy's purpose was in the various depositions?

ED HARVEY: Actually no, sir. I was not able to make that conclusion.

J.C.: Were you able to evaluate the usefulness of the depositions that were being taken?

E.H.: Well, I do know that later on, when we got actually appointed to represent him in that case, most of the depositions had to be taken over. When Mr. Bundy would question a witness he would sometimes technically ask a lot of questions and find out some of the information but not really ever make a point. Never went to any issues of the case.

J.C.: Can you tell me what your role was on the defense team after becoming counsel, not just standby counsel, in spring 1979?

E.H.: Again, a lot of my role was to go to the jail, spend time with Mr. Bundy, at his request.

J.C.: Could you describe what the nature of your contact was with Mr. Bundy during this period?

E.H.: It's hard to remember any specific one occasion, but when I was called out it was usually because Mr. Bundy had a specific request to come out and help him prepare a certain amount of the case. When we got there we would talk about baseball or running or health or something and usually the time was wasted. When I would try to get him to concentrate on these various aspects again we would basically waste time. Never able to do that.

J.C.: What you just described, is that what happened on some occasions or frequently?

E.H.: Ninety-nine percent of the occasions.

J.C.: Can you tell me what Mr. Bundy's role was in developing trial strategy in the Chi Omega case?

E.H.: Well, I'm not sure exactly when, but he had made a pro se motion to be appointed co-counsel. Judge Cowart granted that motion. At that point he became fairly active in wanting certain questions asked of witnesses, certain questions not asked, certain avenues pursued. Once we got into the actual trial in Miami, at some point during trial the court made him chief counsel, and at that point he had the authority, as I understood it from the judge, to make all the decisions.

J.C.: And did he proceed to exercise that authority?

E.H.: Yes, sir.

J.C.: Can you tell me, can you describe, based on your relationship with Mr. Bundy and your ability to observe him, whether he was able to make decisions in the process of the preparation for the trial?

E.H.: Well, he never made any decision that lasted. Didn't seem like it. And when we would get on to the issues that were very important, especially during trial, even when he supposedly made a decision, it would seem like at some crucial point he would back off the decision and put us at odds with each other.

J.C.: Were you ever able to, with Mr. Bundy, to develop a defense strategy for the Chi Omega trial?

E.H.: We thought we had. We were all in Miami and met with him, and we all discussed what each member of the team would do in terms of the trial. There were many areas of the trial, and each lawyer had specific functions that we were going to do, and we thought we had come to an agreement with everyone concerned, including Mr. Bundy. But as it turned out, those agreements were not lived up to.

J.C.: Can you explain what happened, as you say, "as it turned out?"

E.H.: I can give you an example. One example was that when it ended up that myself, Mr. Thompson, and Miss Good were down there, we realized none of us actually had gone through a capital trial. I know I had handled capital cases, but I'd never gone to trial on one, and Mr. Thompson hadn't. Mr. Haggard, however, had done approximately twenty-five capital trials. And all of us thought that since he had had that experience with the jury in capital trials that he would pick the jury, make the opening statement, make the summation, and at least have that continuity in the case. And we had a pretty good strategy at the time. But as it turned out, when we won some of the pretrial motions and [it] looked like the case was going our way a little bit, some of the evidence was kept out, that's when I started to perceive

Mr. Bundy was actually trying to sabotage our case. And by that I mean he talked one of the lawyers into getting up and trying to pick the jury while the other one was supposed to do that. He let Mr. Haggard do the opening statement, but of course he picked somebody else for the closing arguments. With the opening statement he wanted me to prepare the opening statement and Mr. Haggard to prepare an opening statement and he would make up his mind which one he wanted. He did go at the last minute with Mr. Haggard. It was those kind of issues that, once we had decided with him and with everybody, it was often changed.

J.C.: Did you discuss the state's case with Mr. Bundy?

E.H.: Yes, sir.

J.C.: And do you have an opinion about his ability to evaluate that case?

E.H.: Yes, sir.

J.C.: What is that opinion?

E.H.: I don't think he could evaluate the case. He could look at certain issues in the case and discuss them fairly rationally one at a time, but he couldn't see the whole big picture. He couldn't see how one issue fit with another.

J.C.: Now, can you tell me what was the effect of the plea negotiation, in your opinion, on the defense team's ability to prepare for trial?

E.H.: Well, it was my opinion we were within a month of the actual trial date, and either our time should have been spent preparing for trial or working this plea agreement out. Because of the fact [that] we had to spend all of our time working the plea agreement out, we were obviously not prepared for trial. And the effect, when it fell through, was devastating. We knew we had wasted all that time.

J.C.: Now, let me ask you to turn back to the plea negotiation. And can you tell me what your observation of Mr. Bundy's approach to those negotiations was?

E.H.: He—I'm not sure I can describe it much better than Mr. Minerva did. He would talk to one set of people and say one thing—I think at least to those people he said those things—and when he talked to us he would say something else to me, specifically. I don't think I ever had a doubt he would not enter the plea.

J.C.: Why did you believe he would not enter the plea?

E.H.: I didn't think, number one, he could—well, let me back up a little bit. Number one, I really think he was sincere in thinking the state did not have a case, in spite of all the evidence that they had, because, like I said, he could only look at one issue at a time.

J.C.: Did you share his opinion, by the way, that the state did not have a case?

E.H.: No, sir. No, sir.

J.C.: Do you think that his opinion was consistent with the facts?

E.H.: No, sir.

J.C.: Now, were you present at the proceeding at which the plea agreement was offered?

E.H.: Yes, sir.

J.C.: Can you just briefly describe what happened there?

E.H.: Well, my perspective was a little different. I had been there when the agreement was signed the night before. And as everybody left the room, Ted caught my eye and just kind of shook his head *no*, and I didn't know what that meant, but I had my ideas. The next day we got into court and I observed what happened. He basically got us. He had two sets of papers. He had papers with the plea that had been signed, and he had the motion against Mr. Minerva in our office. And he sat up literally for a period of time and in utter silence, going back and forth, and finally picked one, and the one was the motion.

J.C.: Now, during the time that you were involved in the defense of Mr. Bundy, did you have a question in your mind about his mental condition?

E.H.: Yes, sir.

J.C.: Can you describe in terms of your meeting with Mr. Bundy what it was that raised the question for you about his mental condition?

E.H.: His total refusal to admit that there was any evidence.

J.C.: Now, did you ever discuss his mental condition with Mr. Bundy?

E.H.: Yes, sir.

J.C.: Can you just briefly describe what happened during that meeting with Mr. Bundy?

E.H.: Well, up until that point we, each of us, had talked about some parts of the case with Mr. Bundy, and now all of us sat down and had really gone over everything. And we thought at this point he needed to know. He kept on denying there was any evidence, and we thought that he needed to understand what the significance of the state's case was. And basically we did that, and we discussed some different options that were available including the defense of insanity and incompetence, those issues which Mr. Bundy refused to discuss.

J.C.: Did you have an opinion about whether insanity was a defense that should have been at least pursued?

E.H.: Yes, sir. I have an opinion.

J.C.: What is that opinion?

E.H.: That was the only defense.

J.C.: Did you discuss that with Mr. Bundy?

E.H.: Yes, sir.

J.C.: And with what result?

E.H.: Mr. Bundy would not discuss it. He said it was not an issue. He said insanity was not a viable defense in a criminal case and insanity was not an issue in his case. He could talk to a psychiatrist, but the result would be the same as if you talked to a truck driver. He said the well-planned manner of the incidents, the charges, the prior charges, dictate against an insanity defense.

That, by the way, was one of Ted's craziest delusions—the supposed "well-planned manner of the incidents." By his own account, both the Florida crimes were completely *unplanned*. Both were chance opportunities at times when Ted was in his "Other Ted" state—a backdoor left open at the Chi Omega house; a young girl crossing the grounds of Lake City Junior High School, near the highway. But even the morning the bloody carnage at the Chi Omega house was reported on the radio, Ted remarked to a roommate that it "looks like a professional job." When, in fact, it looked like the work of a rabid animal.

J.C.: Were you aware of the competency hearing held in the Chi Omega case?

E.H.: Yes.

J.C.: Do you know what the basis for the motion filed by the defense was?

E.H.: It was in part on Dr. Tanay's opinions and part on our observation.

J.C.: Did you testify at that hearing?

E.H.: No, sir.

J.C.: Did the state's psychiatrist, who testified at that hearing, interview you?

E.H.: No, sir.

At this point, Judge Sharp interrupted Ed Harvey's testimony to ask, "You said that it was partly your observations. Yet how were they articulated if you did not testify?"

That was exactly our point: The lawyers with the actual information, the real observations, had been *excluded* from the competency hearing.

E.H.: Judge, I understood the question was why we had moved for the hearing. That's why we moved for the hearing. I did not testify.

J.C. (TO JUDGE SHARP): That's correct. The fact that the defense lawyers did not testify is the basis for our challenge in the Chi Omega case to the adequacy of the hearing. They were excluded by order of the court.

Judge Sharp nodded slightly—no doubt sorry that in trying to poke a hole in Ed's testimony he had actually *reinforced* our point—and Jim continued.

J.C.: Can you tell me the circumstance in which he became chief counsel?

E.H.: Again, I haven't been able to look at the record for seven or eight years. But at some point during the trial Mr. Bundy raised a number of issues as to the fact that we had not met with him every night, spent three hours a night. He had already gotten up and cross-examined a witness without our knowledge that it was coming. He had already tried to talk one of our lawyers into working against us. And it was obvious to me that his decision and what he was doing during his trial was hurting himself, and I was aware of Dr. Tanay's report. I thought the additional evidence was such that at this point we could put on a better competency hearing. I made a motion during the middle of the trial to have him examined. This was before he was appointed chief counsel. The court denied my motion, would not allow us to get any evidence in on that issue. At that point I felt that the relationship between Mr. Bundy and everybody on the staff was such [that] we could not ethically go on and represent him. There was no lawyer/ client relationship left. So I made a motion to withdraw as counsel on behalf of the office of the public defender, and as I remember—again, I don't have the transcript—as I remember it, the result of that was that the court appointed him as chief counsel and relegated us to the official position of being just standby counsel.

J.C.: Now you mentioned that at some point Mr. Bundy got up and cross-examined a witness without your knowledge. Could you describe that incident, please?

E.H.: It was—let me just go back and explain it in context. It's an example of what we're talking about. Early on in the discussion we had tried to find a way that Mr. Bundy could participate in the jury trial, try to make some participation, before the trial actually started. However, we decided as a team—and Mr. Bundy was in on that decision—that in front of the jury it was probably better not to let him do that. And everybody was in agreement. The state put on one of the first people to the scene in the Chi Omega house. When the state put the officer on he went through, [in] a very bare bones manner, describing the room. Didn't describe anything other than that. Didn't have any harm [on our case] whatsoever. Mr. Thompson was supposed to do the cross-examination with one or two questions. At that point Mr. Bundy, my recollection is, grabbed the file from Mr. Thompson's hand, walked up and asked the question of—I forget how he worded it. The result was that the officer had then a chance to go through every gory detail that he saw, blood and everything.

It had a tremendously bad effect on the jury. In fact, when the trial was over and they interviewed the jurors, the juror that we had picked to be our strongest person in the beginning of the trial said Mr. Bundy looked like a "beady-eyed killer" when he asked those questions. And I think it's an example of just what Dr. Tanay said, that if the defense's case got better Mr. Bundy would help the state. That was a perfect example of that prediction coming true.

J.C.: Can you tell me what the effect of Mr. Bundy's behavior was on the cohesiveness of the defense attorneys?

E.H.: It just drove us apart.

J.C.: Can you tell me in a little more detail what happened?

E.H.: Well, as an example, for instance, Mr. Bundy had convinced one of the lawyers they could do jury selection as good as all the rest of the lawyers. And even though the team made the decision to have two lawyers picking the jury, Mr. Haggard and another one, Mr. Bundy was able to convince another lawyer that she ought to get up and be able to do the same thing. That's an example of when he would hook onto one of the lawyers to try to drive wedges between them— between us—and really try to sabotage the defense theory.

J.C.: You indicated that at various times during the trial Mr. Bundy required members of the defense team to meet with him?

E.H.: Yes, sir.

J.C.: Can you tell me what happened during those meetings?

E.H.: Well, my recollection is that every morning we had to be there at nine. We went until late. It was approximately six, seven before we would get out of the courtroom at night, and he demanded not only one of us, but *all* of us, come see him every night so he would know everything that's going on in the case. And once the judge required us in fact to do that because he was chief counsel. Usually what happened is, we go there and he talked about running shoes or how much mail he got or telephone calls or something. Very rarely on the case. In effect, what he did was take up two or three hours of very valuable time—the only time we had to prepare for the next day—and systematically did it day after day. Even after we told him the effect it was having on us.

J.C.: Can you tell me whether during these meetings, during the trial, Mr. Bundy was involved in things other than his defense?

E.H.: Yes, sir. He was involved in setting up some kind of corporation, civil corporation. He was involved in all kinds of matters that didn't have anything to do with the case, and I can't remember specifically, but I know that one of them was brought to my attention about every day. I mean, that's what he would spend his time on. We were facing a jury that had the power to send him to the death penalty on two cases, and we weren't talking about that. We were talking about other things.

J.C.: Mr. Harvey, based on your observation and your contacts with Mr. Bundy during the trial, can you tell me whether his overall impact was positive or negative?

E.H.: Negative.

J.C.: And did Mr. Bundy appear to appreciate the fact that he was having a negative impact on his trial?

E.H.: No, sir.

Thus ended our first day of hearings. The state's attorney, on cross-examination of all our witnesses, attempted to suggest possible rational reasons for each of Ted's seemingly irrational actions, taken alone. But then, what was the rational basis of the entire *pattern*? It was the same flaw as in Ted's own reasoning: Imagining an alternate explanation for each piece of evidence against him, ignoring how they fit together, added up.

CHAPTER 13

When we got back to Washington we had to prepare for the four remaining days of hearings coming up in December. Jim flew to Utah and Colorado to interview the lawyers who had worked with Ted there. I took Ted's Aunt Audie up to New Haven to interview her along with Dr. Lewis. Then I did a loop of the other Florida lawyers and investigators who had worked with Ted, ending on a balmy night in the otherwise silent and deserted offices of Lynn Alan Thompson, the Robert Redford of the South. Yes, interviews were my favorite part of the case.

In November, I persuaded Ted's mother, Louise, to fly to Washington and to travel with me to see Dr. Lewis in New Haven. The law firm paid for her trip, and I made all the arrangements. Louise was not accustomed to travel, especially without her husband, Johnny. She was a diminutive woman, polite, cautious, and tightly controlled. She took an immediate dislike to Dr. Lewis and insisted that Ted was innocent and that there had never been any problems. She was impenetrable. Dr. Lewis finally called me in, and together we confronted Louise with the fact that Ted had indeed committed the crimes he was sentenced to death for. Still no break in character, no emotion, just frosting-covered steely reserve.

Louise Bundy and I spent most of the rest of that night on a polished wooden bench facing the big wall clock in New Haven's old-fashioned train station. We had missed the last plane out as Dr. Lewis and I tried to squeeze something, anything, out of Louise, so we were forced to take the train home. It was severely delayed. When finally it arrived at 3:00 A.M., we learned that it had killed two teenagers at a crossing.

On another wild trip, Jim and I went to New York to prepare Dr. Lewis for the extended evidentiary hearing in December, and ended up working so late, with so much more to do, that we rented a limousine in order to continue to work with Dr. Lewis on her way home to New Haven. And then Dr. Lewis graciously invited both Jim and me to stay overnight in her comfortable home, so we could continue to talk. During the limousine ride, we talked of our usual subjects: rage, rape, serial murder, and the manifestations of multiple personalities. As I was paying the driver outside her home, he asked, "Are you lawyers?" I said yes. "Well, I didn't catch ever'thing, but it sure was in'eresting what you all was talkin' about." Like having Geraldo Rivera's show right in the backseat of his car, I guess.

It was indeed interesting, all this high-flying investigating, each new fact leading to a new insight and a new twist in the case. You can judge lawyers by how they deal with facts in the case. At the lowest level, lawyers deal only with facts favorable to their own side and ignore the others. Better lawyers dispute or diminish the facts in opposition and emphasize that the preponderance of the evidence supports their case. But the best approach is to gladly embrace all the facts, no matter what, and show that every last one of them only reinforces the unassailable correctness of your position. As each new fact emerged Jim and I would roll it around in our minds like a loose marble on a Chinese checkers board until it fell neatly into its slot, consonant with the overall picture. Perfect.

It was so interesting, in fact, that we never had time to prepare for the trial itself. There would be no rehearsal for my first time questioning a witness for the record. We were investigating up until the last minute, placing all faith in our ability to think on our feet once we got there. This was all well and good for Jim Coleman—he was an experienced litigator and spontaneity was his forte. I, however, was a rank neophyte.

My first official task went all right, though. On Saturday, December 12, 1987, along with Mark Menser, the assistant Florida state attorney general with lead responsibility for the Lake City case, I took the deposition of Dr. Emanuel Tanay in a vintage Art Deco skyscraper in Detroit. Although Jim and I had interviewed him before, and had come away unsure of whether his observations would be helpful to us (Dr. Tanay obviously thought that Ted was a despicable psychopath, a label we were trying to avoid), he showed—at this, my first deposition—why he truly deserved the title "expert witness." Still thickly accented after some thirty years in this country, the Polish-born Dr. Tanay projected perfect Germanic confidence in his psychiatric findings, which just happened to fit our legal arguments perfectly. Yes, Dr. Tanay thought Ted was a psychopath, but he also was very clear that Ted's psychopathology had rendered him unable to assist in his defense and was a disease over which he had no control. As a bonus, Dr. Tanay manifested equally perfect disdain for the efforts of the state's attorney to throw my questioning off track or to undermine any word of his testimony, going into speeches on the record about how Mr. Menser was interrupting him, and he had never been treated so rudely, etc.

Emanuel Tanay, my hero.

POLLY NELSON: What were your impressions of Mr. Bundy when you examined him on May eighteenth, 1979?

DR. EMANUEL TANAY: My impressions were that he was an individual who was indeed rather intelligent—who was well informed about a variety of matters—but, just as I indicated in my preliminary report, based on documents only, namely April twenty-seventh, 1979, he showed a typical picture of someone who suffers from a lifelong personality disorder. Someone who was, what we would call in psychiatry, an impulse-ridden type of individual, prone to acting out and more involved with immediate gratification than any long-term concerns. He was what in the literature has been described in the past as a typical psychopathic type of personality. This is an old term that is no longer used outside of textbooks, but nevertheless, I found it quite descriptive of Mr. Bundy.

P.N.: What do you mean by the term "impulse-ridden"?

E.T.: Someone who has no control, or at least impaired control, over his or her impulses. Most people might perceive a certain impulse to act in a certain fashion, because it might gratify some kind of a need, but they will reflect about it and make choices. Impulse-ridden individuals don't have that ability. They are driven to gratify their impulse without subjecting it to reflection.

P.N.: Turning to page four of Exhibit fifteen, you state that "in the nearly three hours which I spent with Mr. Bundy I found him to be in a cheerful, even jovial, mood. He was witty but not flippant; he spoke

P.N.: This psychopathology that you note, with which he deals with the criminal justice system, was that a temporary phenomena or was it a chronic condition?

E.T It was a lifelong pattern. It was not a temporary phenomena. It was an expression of his basic personality structure.

P.N.: Would you describe Exhibit one?

E.T.: The real background of it is the fact that I told Mr. Minerva that I did not believe that Mr. Bundy would do what he was told to do, and my recollection was that Mr. Minerva was writing this to confirm that I was right, because I did—I recall Mr. Minerva expressing to some degree, I would have to say, admiration, for the fact that I had anticipated what would occur—I did not think that Mr. Bundy would cooperate.

P.N.: Cooperate in what manner?

E.T.: With the advice of his lawyers—including even Mr. Farmer, who supposedly Mr. Bundy greatly respected and admired—and that he would take the guilty plea, because it was my view that he would not, because that would terminate the show, his ability to be the celebrity would come to an end, he would be just someone who was spared from the death sentence, and the show would be over. Whereas, his need was to have the proceedings go on and on in order to gratify his pathological needs.

P.N.: If Mr. Bundy made the decision to reject the plea bargain, in your opinion would that have been a rational decision?

E.T.: No. It was, in my opinion, clearly an irrational decision, even though I anticipated it, not because it was rational but because it was consistent with the psychopathology, the mental disorder from which he suffered. In fact, had he done what his lawyers advised him to do, that would have been rational, since it was foreseeable that he would be convicted and face the death penalty.

P.N.: Was Mr. Bundy's behavior with his attorney and his actions in terms of self-representation and other defense matters, was that an integral part of his psychopathology?

E.T.: Very definitely so. He behaved like a typical psychopath with his lawyers and, for that matter, with me.

P.N.: You testified at the competency hearing of June eleventh, 1979. At that hearing, did Mr. Bundy's competency counsel, Mr. Hayes, explore your opinion to develop facts on which to make a decision as to Mr. Bundy's competency?

E.T.: No one did that. To be very simplistic about it, my feeling of that hearing was like someone who dressed up for the party and arrived and they canceled the party. I was asked very few questions, and very little information about my knowledge of Mr. Bundy or the case was placed on the record.

P.N.: In your experience as an expert witness, was this proceeding unique?

E.T.: I have testified—I believe the first time was thirty years ago, and I have testified on many occasions since—but this is the only case like that, where I have been declared an adverse witness to both parties, and where information that I had was really not developed by the means of an adversary proceeding. Normally, one side pulls in one direction, the other side pulls in the other direction, and considerable information is elicited. I always consider cross-examination to be essential to develop a point of view that I am presenting.

P.N.: Did you feel that your opinion was adequately presented in this hearing?

E.T.: Not at all. Not at all. There was no exploration—that was my impression, I made some notes of it—that was my impression of what happened, and when I read it now that just confirms that my considerable work invested in the case was not utilized in that hearing. I mean, I did not develop my opinion and explain my opinion in this case. An expert witness, unlike a lecturer in a classroom, cannot function on his or her own. He or she is completely, say, at the mercy of whoever takes the testimony.

P.N.: Did you have an opinion at the time of the hearing on June eleventh whether or not Mr. Bundy was able to assist his counsel?

E.T.: Considering the nature of the functions that he was to perform as a defendant claiming innocence, it was my opinion that he was not able to stand trial. When you say assist his counsel, he was his own counsel.

P.N.: Was he capable of changing that behavior and not becoming his own counsel?

E.T.: In my opinion, he was not. He was predictably unpredictable. What I mean by that is that one could anticipate that he would be guided more by showmanship than prudence.

P.N.: Was Mr. Bundy able meaningfully to assist his counsel at that time?

E.T.: He was not.

P.N.: Referring to the first factor in the Florida rules of criminal procedure governing competency to stand trial, do you have an opinion as to whether Mr. Bundy was able to appreciate the charges?

E.T.: Yes, I do have an opinion that he was able to appreciate the charges intellectually.

P.N.: When you say "intellectually," do you mean that there was some way in which he was not able to appreciate the charges?

E.T.: That's true. I'm of the opinion that he did not appreciate the seriousness of the charges. He could intellectually tell you what the charges were, but he just dismissed them as real insignificant—based on his rich imagination of law enforcement—which was not the case. Clearly the charges were based upon solid evidence, but that was not his view.

P.N.: Dr. Tanay, when you say that Mr. Bundy dismissed the weight of the evidence against him, was that merely carelessness on his part or was that due to an emotional or mental factor?

E.T.: It was part of the illness, his attitude was the product, the outcome, of the nature of his illness.

P.N.: Looking to the second factor of the Florida standards, was Mr. Bundy able to appreciate the range and the nature of the possible penalty?

E.T.: Again, intellectually he was. As I pointed out in my report, he said that he would cross that bridge when he came to it, when I was asking him, Do you know that you are facing a death sentence? He could intellectually acknowledge it, but he sure didn't act like a man who was facing a death sentence. He was acting like a man who did not have a care in the world. I think I commented upon it in my report, that he was cheerful and acted more like a man who was not in jail but onstage.

P.N.: Was that fact psychiatrically significant?

E.T.: Yes. It's consistent with the diagnosis that I have previously described, of someone who is typical psychopath or suffers from a personality disorder.

P.N.: Dr. Tanay, did you ever observe Mr. Bundy with Mr. Minerva?

E.T.: Yes. As I indicated in my report, Mr. Bundy was acting as if Mr. Minerva was his third assistant and not a lawyer representing him.

P.N.: Did you in June of 1979 have an opinion as to Mr. Bundy's ability to assist his attorneys in planning his defense?

E.T.: I did have an opinion.

P.N.: And what was that opinion?

E.T.: That he was unable to assist in planning his defense. To the contrary, he was interfering with whatever meaningful plans the defense made. He sabotaged pretty consistently what the defense lawyers had worked out. His conduct was symptomatic of his illness, and it was outside of his control.

P.N.: What was your opinion as to Mr. Bundy's motivation to help himself in the legal process?

E.T.: He was not motivated by a need to help himself. He was motivated by the need to be the star of the show, as I pointed out in my report. He was the producer of a play in which he was playing a big role. The defense and his future were of secondary importance to him.

P.N.: Was he competent to perform the functions of cocounsel?

E.T.: Definitely not. I have absolutely no doubt that he was a disaster as cocounsel or chief counsel of his own defense and that was clearly foreseeable.

When the deposition ended, Dr. Tanay took me to lunch with characteristically continental flair, and sent me off to the airport, where I celebrated taking my first deposition with a manicure and pedicure before the flight. Unfortunately, there was not time for the polish to dry completely, so I had to wear paper slippers onto the plane.

Jim, John Sandage, our legal assistant Linda Williams, and I flew to Orlando the next day to set up for the four days of continued evidentiary hearings before Judge Sharp. There were several frantic messages waiting at our hotel from Diana Weiner—whom I had still never laid eyes on, and whose continuing prison visits Ted generally still did not discuss with me. She was saying that Ted was very upset about the hearing, so upset that he might disrupt it, and that the best thing for us would be to authorize the sheriff's department to let her visit him at the jail.

I called her back and told her I did not think that would be necessary.

It was true, though, that Ted was no more happy about having to appear in court in December than he had been in October. I had received several letters from him on the subject. Not only the matter of seat belts and grooming supplies (we brought him clothes and a shaving kit this time), but Ted also thought it was unfair that the law enforcement officers escorting him wore bullet-proof vests, while he— the likely target—was not provided with one. For this second hearing, he wanted a bullet-proof vest, too. But most striking was how Ted had been "terrified," as he put it, on his way to that first hearing, to see people on the streets for the first time in nearly eight years. It looked so strange, so uncontrolled to him. People just walking, shopping, oblivious to the passing unmarked van and its contents, one Ted Bundy. I was surprised that the sight did not make him want to join the pedestrians in their freedom, that it frightened him so. All he longed for right then was to return to his circumspect, regimented, and predictable life at Florida State Prison.

Early in the first day of hearings Linda Williams told us she had been approached by a woman who asked her to pass a note to Ted, but she had refused. It was not until the end of that day, when she introduced herself to us—to Jim, primarily—that I realized that the raven-haired, dark-eyed young woman whose long legs emerged from a slinky blue wrap dress and dangled in the aisle of the spectator section was none other than Diana Weiner.

The December hearings were a long ride on a bumpy roller coaster, but we got everything on the record that we wanted to get in. Just before her testimony, as we drove up to the courthouse, Dr. Lewis panicked and blanked out on all the facts. Jim fled the car in terror, and Dr. Lewis and I stayed in the backseat, in the parking lot, going back over the basics:

"Okay, Dorothy, I know you remember this. We have the four documented episodes were Ted went through some altered state: twice with Joe Aloi . . ."

"Who's that?! I don't know who that is!"

"Mike Minerva's investigator. You know, you talked to him on the phone last night."

"Yes, yes, yes, okay, okay, I remember."

"Then there was Aunt Emily at the train station, and the episode noted by the Tallahassee jail nurse . . . ," etc.

Soon she regained her confidence and, once on the stand, Dr. Dorothy Lewis was brilliant—clear, convincing, articulate. Resplendent in a deep purple suit, she illuminated the courtroom. The state's witnesses, on the other hand, made a mockery of the proceedings with their baseless, nonsensical, and hyperbolic "psychiatric evaluations." I am not exaggerating. The dips in the ride came mostly in my arena. My two witnesses, Don Kennedy, the defense investigator in the Lake City case, and Lynn Thompson, the Robert Redford of the South, were nowhere to be found when it came time for me to call them. Just asked to sit down. Shaking and holding back tears, I spoke my mind. I was shocked to hear this audience willing to see Ted die. In my mind the very point of this work was that *all* human life was sacred, without judgment or distinction, and that it was the truly heinous cases that tested whether we as people and as a society really meant that. Furthermore, Ted Bundy was not a symbol, a metaphor, a cardboard cutout. He was a real man, captive and rendered harmless at present, made of flesh and blood.

I also pointed out something no one ever seemed to take into account about Ted: Even in the absence of any mitigating evidence in his behalf, the jury that convicted him of the Chi Omega sorority house murders had been hung at six to six for life or death, until Judge Cowart erroneously instructed them that they were required to break the tie. Without that instruction Ted would have gotten a life sentence. And no death penalty opponent would be saying now he should have been executed instead.

The room was silent for a moment, then the meeting picked up where it had left off. A few anonymous notes of support were passed to me. For a brief moment, I was one of them.

At the end of August, back at the office, I heard for the first time the name of the woman who would provide the critical missing link in our case: a recognized mental illness that had rendered Ted incompetent to assist his attorneys at trial. CCR called to say that a prominent psychiatrist, Dr. Dorothy Lewis, was going to be conducting an exhaustive evaluation of condemned adolescents at Florida State Prison and that we should try to get Ted tested while her team was there. I asked CCR to do what they could to make that happen. At least it would be a beginning. Another law firm, Sherman & Sterling in New York, was footing the bill for the juvenile study as part of their pro bono commitment. I jumped at the chance to get some free psychiatric assistance.

Immediately after the stay in July, Ted had sent his thank-you letter, along with a card he had written the day before the execution date in case it was his last chance. Both expressed "my profound gratitude" for our work. He had asked for a list of all the people who had worked on the case so that he could send them thank-you cards as well—and he did, in care of the firm. Dara was ambivalent at best about receiving hers. I guess it's not every day a letter arrives from a serial killer, addressed to you personally.

*   *   *

My brand-name client attracted the attention of a *Life* magazine reporter who was especially persistent. Linda Gomez called frequently after the July stay, wanting to do a story on him. She said she might be able to funnel some money to Carole Boone by calling her a legal assistant to the project or something like that, if Ted would agree to an interview. Florida had a "Son of Sam" law preventing inmates from profiting from the stories of their crimes.

Ted was very anxious for me to explore this possibility. He was always trying to find a way to earn money for Carole and Tina. I was very cool to the idea of *anyone* interviewing Ted, for several reasons. First of all, I knew from firsthand experience that the final story can come out with a very different slant than you had thought it would. Second, nothing Ted could say could help our case, but he could certainly say things that could hurt it. Ted was scrupulously honest in his own way, and his honest opinion, of course, was that our competency claim was hogwash. Heaven forbid someone should ask him that question in an interview. Finally, although Ted's current mental competency was not yet an issue, it wouldn't help to have rational-sounding statements by him in the press or to have a reporter able to testify as to how very mentally competent Ted seemed during their interview. Ted, of course, thought it was quite impossible he would ever say anything that would be damaging to his case—he was far too clever for that. But history had shown him wrong. Nonetheless, he was the client, and I didn't feel I had a right to dismiss the idea out of hand when it meant so much to him, so I eventually agreed to meet Ms. Gomez for lunch.

When Jim left on vacation he told me—as usual—to follow my own judgment on this. I felt very uncomfortable with the prospect of even meeting with a reporter, much less granting access to Ted. So I sought the advice of other partners at my high-powered, high-profile law firm of highly experienced and highly opinionated lawyers. But no one would give me advice. No one. The partner I worked with the most outside the Bundy case told me he did not want to interfere with another partner's case, so he would not venture an opinion. A communications partner who represented major TV networks on press issues told me he had no opinion on what I should do. "I really can't help you," he said, as he reached for the phone by way of dismissing me. Finally I asked a venerated senior partner at Wilmer: Is this ethical? Should I be negotiating with a reporter? Am I exposing the firm here

B.L.: As they presented it to him, he just stood there and listened to them read it, and I remember him smiling a little bit. After they left, he said that he expected this, that now that I'm here this is probably opening the floodgates. But he said he wasn't worried about it, that it was really nothing, that they didn't have anything, there was no case against him, and he was looking forward to going to Colorado, and he wasn't worried about it. I told him he ought to be worried about it.

After Ted was extradited to Colorado, he wrote Lubek a letter, expressing concerns about his public defender, noting that he didn't "act" much like a lawyer, and "he did not give me the standard—and I believe essential—warnings not to speak or write anything about the case to anyone without his consent." In January 1977, Ted asked Lubek to help him draft a request for withdrawal of court-appointed counsel, including a request to represent himself. Most telling, Ted also asked Lubek to draft a motion "for an order directing the administrator of the jail or to whoever's custody I am in to receive my expressed written consent before a law enforcement officer or prosecution investigator would be allowed access to me. And consent must be specific as to time, date, and officers. To be signed. Without such an expressed written consent no one would be allowed to talk to me."
B.L.: I told him, if he didn't want to talk to anyone just not talk to anyone.

Ted also sent Lubek a "statement for the media" which claimed that an "investigation that confirmed that Mr. Bundy was in no way involved in the death of the young woman in Aspen tends to show that I was not even in the state of Colorado at the time of her death." Lubek knew of no such investigation.

Next to testify was Joe Nursey, an attorney in the Leon County public defender's office at the time of Ted's arrest in Pensacola, Florida. He was working now in the offices of Millard Farmer in Atlanta.
JOE NURSEY: From February 1978 until October 1978, I saw Ted very, very frequently, probably at least two times a week. I think very soon after I began representing him I got the impression that I was dealing with a person who was not mentally healthy. What I personally observed was at times his moods were okay and other times he was extremely depressed. And I saw that when he was under periods of

stress, like getting close to a court hearing or something, he became much more agitated and his moods became much more depressed, and he was—at times he became much less rational.

JIM COLEMAN: Was Mr. Bundy able to focus on a discussion of his cases with you during that period?

J.N.: No.

J.C.: Can you describe the process of trying to get him to do so?

J.N.: I would go out to see Ted at the jail very, very frequently, and generally what would happen is, we would end up having discussions about movies that I had been to see, about current events, about all sorts of things other than the case. I don't think Ted was capable of focusing on his case.

J.C.: With respect to the decisions that you presented to Mr. Bundy, was he able to make decisions?

J.N.: No. Whenever I tried to discuss decisions that had to be made, we would end up discussing it, discussing it, and discussing it. But Ted was incapable of making any kind of decision. I would end up making all the decisions, what had to be done.

J.C.: Did you during the period that you represented him have an opportunity to observe his ability to evaluate the significance of the evidence?

J.N.: Yes. The one incident that sticks out most strongly in my mind, and I can't be sure of a specific date—it was during the summer of 1978, I think it was in May—and the state had obtained a search warrant for a blue blazer that Ted wore to court. They wanted to search it for hair and fiber. And it was through the affidavit to get this search warrant [that] I also became aware of some evidence in Lake City, that the state was saying there was a person who could identify Ted as being the driver of a van in the Lake City vicinity. And feeling that I should tell Ted this, rather than have it presented to him by a police officer, I went out to the jail to discuss this with Ted. I considered that to be an extremely significant piece of evidence in the Lake City case. And I went out to discuss this with Ted, and explained it to him, and at the end of the conversation it was like he didn't comprehend what I told him. It was like, the only way I could really describe it is the impression I had when I was walking out of the jail going back to my car. I was just shaking my head, like wondering if I had been speaking the English language. He didn't seem to be able to comprehend what I was telling him.

Ted was indicted for murder in both cases in July 1978 and represented himself for several months. He did nothing, however, to prepare. Joe was present on the October date scheduled for the trial,
and after requesting a continuance, Minerva and Nursey and another
lawyer met with Ted in his cell.

J.N.: Ted was pacing back and forth in the little area you could move
in in the isolation cell they had him in the whole time. Every time I
visited him Ted always did this, paced back and forth, it was almost
compulsively racing back and forth in the cell. And on this particular
day he was doing it in an extremely agitated manner, pacing back and
forth, back and forth, very rapidly, for a couple of hours that afternoon.
Ted was talking in a very agitated, very hurried manner, and it was
almost completely incoherent what he was saying, it made no sense
whatsoever. The few phrases that were comprehensible from what he
was talking about [were] something about people being out to get him
or conspiracy or something like that, but [it was] almost completely
incomprehensible what he was saying. I went back to the office and
signed an affidavit saying I thought he was not competent to stand trial.

Then it was my turn to present my two witnesses. Donald Kennedy
was the investigator for the Lake City public defender and had been
assigned to work with Vic Africano on the Bundy case. Kennedy had
not been particularly gracious or forthcoming when I'd interviewed
him in his office the month before—he apparently despised Ted and
was looking forward to his execution—and he was also not the most
eloquent of witnesses. Mark Menser's frequent objections didn't help
any. As I said, not my shining hour.

I did manage to get Kennedy to repeat some of what he'd told me
about his assignment to "babysit" Ted.

DONALD KENNEDY: I was aware that some of his actions were agitating
the attorneys, and I would talk to him at times when he, to keep him
relaxed, to keep him, more or less try to subdue him, to keep from
doing what he was doing as far as agitating them. I don't know whether
maybe the word agitated is the right word to use, but bothering them
while they were trying to listen to the voir dire going on there in
Live Oak.

POLLY NELSON: Mr. Kennedy, would you describe the substance of
your conversations with Mr. Bundy during the trial?

D.K.: Yes, ma'am. We talked about what we were going to have to eat that day. Discussed the weather, people sitting in the courtroom. Just passing-the-time-of-day type of comments.

After many attempts, I got Kennedy to testify about the drugs and alcohol Ted was receiving daily during the Lake City trial in the "bag of goodies," supposedly health foods, from the outside.

P.N.: Mr. Kennedy, once you discovered the drugs and alcohol in Mr. Bundy's lunches, as you've described, did you continue to provide these lunches to Mr. Bundy?

D.K.: Well, first of all, I didn't provide them to begin with. I wasn't the provider, so to say, I'm sort of the in-between type, the go-fer, so to say, but let's clarify that matter. No, I did not, not after that, after what I discovered. And after I had brought it out to the attention of the attorneys, my request was, is, that I not be involved anymore in transporting the lunches to and from.

P.N.: Mr. Kennedy, you testified earlier that you had knowledge that Mr. Bundy had access to drugs and alcohol because of his behavior on certain occasions. Could you describe those occasions?

D.K.: Yes, ma'am. This was in the first week of the proceedings here in Orlando at the courthouse during jury selection, which lasted at least a week, seven days, six days, seven, eight days, and during that first week I had observed Ted on more than one occasion, thick-tongued, with slurred speech and unusual behavior. And those occasions, one in particular I remember, was during jury selection, where Ted became upset, outraged, belligerent, whatever term you want to attach to it, regarding a specific juror by the name of, I believe his name was Patrick Wolsky, Wolfsky, ski, something like that.

After the particular motion was denied by the court, he became upset, approached the bench shaking his finger, shaking his finger at Mr. [Jerry] Blair [the prosecutor], and informing Mr. Blair that he would "rain on his parade" and yanking his jacket off, jerking away from one of the bailiffs. All this time with thick tongue and slurred speech.

Kennedy testified that Ted had not been concerned about the verdict. Instead, he was concerned about his marriage, his appearance, his diet—"more so than the proceedings itself."

After Ted had been found guilty of kidnapping and murdering Kimberly Leach, and before the penalty phase, Vic Africano passed a copy of Dr. Tanay's report to Judge Jopling, as a hint that Ted may have had a mental disorder that would mitigate against imposition of the death penalty. He did not argue the point, however. Instead, the penalty phase of the Lake City trial was given over to Ted, so that he could recite his wedding vows with Carole Boone on the stand.

Ted and Carole had been trying to get married behind the scenes during the trial, but Judge Jopling had put a stop to it. Ted, then, was going to use his opportunity to call witnesses in the penalty phase to marry in the presence of the judge himself, supposedly validating the marriage. No other witnesses were called, and no evidence was put on against Ted receiving the death sentence. This was wrong. If it was worthwhile to put on a defense in the Lake City case even though Ted already had a death sentence in the Chi Omega case, it was worthwhile putting on a case against the imposition of a second death penalty. Were the Chi Omega conviction to be reversed on appeal, the Lake City sentence would make the difference between Ted's life or death.

P.N.: Mr. Kennedy, you mentioned earlier what you referred to as a marriage ceremony. When did this occur?

D.K.: Actual ceremony itself?

P.N.: That's right.

D.K.: The day of the penalty phase, on Saturday, January, or excuse me, February eighth or ninth, somewhere around there.

P.N.: Do you recall?

D.K.: Ninth, I believe.

P.N.: Do you recall Mr. Bundy's conduct immediately before the proceeding?

D.K.: Yes, ma'am. He was real uptight. Real nervous, I guess, very similar to one's big wedding day. But he was real concerned about the way he was dressed, with his cute little bow tie. You could tell he was real nervous about having Carole take the stand, and whatever he had to properly say to complete the ceremony, very concerned about that.

P.N.: Did you do anything extraordinary on that date?

D.K.: Myself?

P.N.: Yes.

D.K.: I guess I was the photographer for the wedding. I guess you could say.

P.N.: What manner?

D.K.: I just, I had my own camera there at the courthouse. And took some photos of the groom.

P.N.: This was during the penalty phase?

D.K.: Yes, this was the day of the penalty phase.

P.N.: Were you aware whether or not there were preparations leading up to this marriage ceremony?

D.K.: Aware and involved.

P.N.: Would you describe the first time you were aware of such a ceremony?

D.K.: Yes, ma'am. When Vic instructed me to notarize the marriage license. Had to be, I guess, at least two weeks before the actual ceremony itself, probably three weeks, back in the middle of the trial.

On cross-examination, the state attempted to suggest that maybe the pills were vitamins, not Valium; maybe Ted hadn't gotten *that* drunk; and maybe he had married Carole Boone on the stand to win the sympathy of the jury. Maybe, but that was not how anyone remembered it.

Then I questioned Lynn Thompson, who had been cocounsel in both the Chi Omega and Lake City cases.

P.N.: Mr. Thompson, what role did Mr. Bundy play in the Lake City proceedings in relation to you as his counsel?

LYNN THOMPSON: He did not participate very much at all in that case.

P.N.: Can you describe Mr. Bundy's conduct?

L.T.: He more than anything else appeared to be disinterested in the proceedings.

P.N.: What was he doing outside of the courtroom?

L.T.: In the anteroom that served as our office, there was a telephone which had a WATS line or some similar type service. He would use the phone, call people around the country. He would answer the phone if he could get to it first, saying "Bundy defense team, defendant speaking" or "Crisis Center." That's outside of the courtroom. Talked a significant amount, in my opinion, about this pending marriage ceremony to Miss Boone. Again, there were a lot of conversations extraneous to the proceedings, about running shoes and athletic events and snow skiing out West, that kind of stuff.

P.N.: Did Mr. Bundy assist you in preparation for the Lake City trial?

L.T.: No.

P.N.: Did Mr. Bundy assist you during the jury selection phase of the proceedings?

L.T.: He did not assist that process. He was seated beside me throughout the fifteen days, however long that took. Upon occasion I would talk to him about whether he thought a particular juror would be satisfactory, but as far as any input into how to question people or what questions to ask, he had no input at all.

P.N.: Was Mr. Bundy engaged in any other activities at this time in the courtroom?

L.T.: He would frequently take in a file folder and inside the file folder would be a magazine or some other reading material. He would peruse that throughout the day. He'd write—I don't know what was being written, but he wrote a lot.

In fact, Ted was spending his days and nights during the Lake City trial working on his memoirs.

P.N.: How did Mr. Bundy's demeanor during the Lake City trial compare to other criminal defendants in your experience?

L.T.: There is really no standard defendant. There is a tremendous range in a person's actions during trials. Mr. Bundy in that case I think was unique in his seeming disinterest in the proceedings.

P.N.: Did you believe there might be grounds to explore the issue of Bundy's competence to stand trial in the Lake City case?

L.T.: Yes. But there was no particular effort on my part to encourage a discussion of competency in Lake City. Basically, I felt that it could have been very disruptive in the proceedings in the Lake City case. I believed Mr. Bundy's reaction would have been negative, that he would forbid that to occur and could lead to a rift between Mr. Africano, myself, and Mr. Bundy.

P.N.: Did Mr. Bundy seem concerned about receiving a death penalty in the Lake City case?

L.T.: No.

P.N.: Do you know what he was concerned about in the case?

L.T.: As events approached the hearing on the penalty phase, his attention was directed to this marriage ceremony to Miss Carole Boone.

P.N.: Did Mr. Bundy, in fact, meaningfully assist you in preparing a defense in the Lake City case?

L.T.: No.

Next up was Michael Korin, who had been the assistant public defender called in from Tallahassee to assist with the penalty phase in Lake City. He arrived on the scene on a Friday afternoon, the day after Ted had been found guilty. The penalty phase was to begin the next day.

JIM COLEMAN: Did you discuss with Mr. Bundy the penalty phase of his trial?

MICHAEL KORIN: Yes, sir.

J.C.: Can you tell me what the substance of that discussion was?

M.K.: Well, I can tell you that when Mr. Kennedy picked me up at the airport he acted sort of like the cat that ate the canary and like there was something up. And when I asked him, well, what is going on, he indicated, well, you'll have to talk to Ted or Vic or Lynn. I then recall I met with Mr. Bundy, I asked him about any witnesses he wanted to call at the penalty phase, if there were any, and at that time he indicated that he desired to call Carole Boone.

J.C.: And did he tell you why he wanted to call Miss Boone?

M.K.: My recollection is unclear as to whether he would specifically tell me why he wanted to call her. I want to believe that he didn't tell me exactly why, and that I did not find out why he wanted to call her until I had thereafter seen Mr. Thompson and Mr. Africano.

J.C.: Now, you say you want to believe that. Why do you want to believe that?

M.K.: Because at one point I was very, I guess, upset. I felt duped, I guess, is the way to—you know, it was not the type of thing that—I would not, I wouldn't want to intentionally participate in something like that.

J.C.: And what is the something like that you refer to?

M.K.: The marriage.

J.C.: Did Mr. Bundy provide you with other information that could be used in the penalty phase?

M.K.: No, sir.

J.C.: What was your reaction when you discovered that Mr. Bundy intended to get married at the penalty phase?

M.K.: Well, he was, like, co-counsel, so I wouldn't have anything to do with calling her as a witness. He called her. Of course, it wouldn't have done any good for me to have called her as a witness if the purpose was to exchange vows. I wasn't about to exchange vows with her, so—

J.C.: Did you discuss your—I think you testified earlier that you felt duped?

M.K.: Yes, sir.

J.C.: Did you discuss that with the other attorneys in the case?

M.K.: I'm sure I expressed my—well, I wasn't a happy camper, that's the only way I can put it, at that time.

One of the concerns of the state's attorney was that we not have the opportunity at this hearing to build on our case against Vic Africano for ineffective assistance of counsel. Two possible grounds for ineffectiveness were Vic's failure to raise the possibility of Ted's incompetency when he had Dr. Tanay's report and knowledge of some of what had happened to the Chi Omega defense team; and his failure to put on any kind of case during the penalty phase, instead allowing Ted to play with it, use it for some purpose other than avoiding the death penalty. We had made the ineffectiveness claim in our habeas corpus petition, which Judge Sharp had rejected in November 1986, and it was still, theoretically, pending in the Eleventh Circuit, which would decide on it after the competency claim had been resolved. Judge Sharp certainly did not want anything in his courtroom to trigger another evidentiary hearing in this case, this time on the ineffectiveness claim, so he cut off all questioning on what Vic knew or was told about Ted's conduct.

Given that concern, it's not surprising that the state didn't call Vic to testify at this hearing. But we were holding our breaths for those four days. He was potentially the state's strongest witness—Ted's lead counsel in the Lake City trial, who believed that Ted was perfectly competent, "more than competent, even."

J.C.: Were you aware of psychiatric reports that had been prepared on Mr. Bundy?

M.K.: No, sir.

J.C.: Can you tell me what appeared to be Mr. Bundy's attitude about the penalty phase?

M.K.: He was very interested in calling Miss Boone. I don't recall any participation by Mr. Bundy in my preparation of any jury instructions or legal arguments that I would be making in his behalf.

J.C.: Did he show any concern about the death penalty?

M.K.: No, sir.

Korin testified that he had been aware when he got there that Ted was still receiving alcohol in juice cans. He verified that the only witness called for the defense was Carole, and that Ted did the questioning. He said that when Ted sat down, Vic told him he'd done it wrong, they weren't legally married, he hadn't done the vows right. So on redirect, he did it again.

Dr. Lewis testified on Tuesday. She began by describing the violence and bizarreness of Ted's grandfather and his grandmother's hospitalizations for manic depression. She told Aunt Audie's story of how at three years old Ted had placed knives in his sister's bed and stood there staring at her and explained how that indicated he had already been exposed to violence. Dr. Lewis told how Ted could not remember any of this.

She described initially finding symptoms in Ted of major mental illness in the course of her study. As she grew comfortable on the stand, Dr. Lewis's meticulous evaluation of our thousands of facts, documents, and personal interviews came together as a seamless story of one man's bipolar mood disorder.

JIM COLEMAN: Dr. Lewis, did you find evidence of a mood disorder in Mr. Bundy's background?

DOROTHY OTNOW LEWIS: Yes, I did.

Well, first of all there is evidence that Mr. Bundy's mood and that his functioning fluctuate widely, and that [they] fluctuated widely, I would say, from at least 1967 until the present. The first evidence of severe mood disorder, to the best of my knowledge, occurred in, I think it was 1967. After Mr. Bundy had spent a year at college and had apparently done adequately, he took a summer course at Stanford University in Chinese language. However, at that time he became extremely depressed, and he was unable to function, and he did not attend his classes. On occasion he returned home and, according to his mother, he was disheveled and he was not himself, and she noted that he was extremely depressed. I believe he was also tearful at times and, as I said, doing very badly.

Let me give you a few quotes from him also. By the way, I should say that, when I first interviewed Mr. Bundy, he was, as far as I could tell, sublimely unaware of these fluctuations, and it was in the course of talking with him, of asking him about particular periods, that he could give information about these times, but he had absolutely no insight into these wide fluctuations until we, you know, had kind of documented the ups and downs.

He said that at the time when he went to Stanford he was unable to focus on his schoolwork. He said, quote, "I didn't go to classes, it became a nightmare. It's like being disconnected, a panicky feeling, being lost and alone." He went on and described it as a time when he felt despondent, he felt fearful.

And I asked him if he cried and he said "I cried lots. There was a chapel. I would go in and weep." I asked about his appetite, but he interrupted there and said "I was smoking, and I'm not a smoker." He did say that he skipped meals, which is often characteristic. Sometimes during a depression people eat and eat and eat and sometimes they lose their appetite.

And according to him he did not take the final examination at summer school. But, equally important, when he attempted to return to classes the next fall at the University of Washington, he was unable to attend the classes, and he says that he did not take his final examinations there as well. And he then, for a period of time, I believe he dropped out of school.

J.C.: Let me ask to you look at plaintiff's Exhibit number thirty-two, which is the transcript of Mr. Bundy's enrollment at the University of Washington. And let me direct your attention to the autumn quarter '67, winter quarter '68, and can you tell me whether his performance during those periods was consistent with what he told you?

D.L.: Yes. What is interesting, actually, is the juxtaposition of this period against the other periods in his academic life.

Prior to the spring of '67, he had gotten B's and C's and an A here and there. Then in the autumn of '67, he was failing and withdrawing from courses. And when he attempted winter of '68, he simply, I guess, withdrew. He was unable to function there, so that there is a period of time that is in marked contrast to his performance prior to that and subsequent.

J.C.: Did you find evidence of any mood changes after that?

D.L.: Yes. He subsequent to this had severe depression.

I should add, by the way, that it's rare that one can get such nice objective documentation of impaired functioning. Usually it's just told to you and it's kind of interesting that you have it here in black and white.

But subsequent to that, he said that around May of 1968 his depression began to lift, and then he could document what sounded like a fairly clear manic episode that lasted from about May '68 to November '68. And at that time he became extremely involved in politics. He got involved in the campaign for the lieutenant governor of the state of Washington. Got involved in the Rockefeller for President campaign. He attended a national convention. He apparently worked eighteen-hour days. I believe this was also a period of time that he got into kind of a dirty tricks type of behavior in this kind of political work that he did. And he described himself at that time as saying that he met, quote, "great people," and he felt connected, and he just said he was more sociable, he was more excited, he was more gregarious. He felt "on top of the world."

And I asked him about relationships at the time, and he said he was more socially adventurous. He said he was able to make connections with anyone and impress them just by, as he put it, "the force of positive vibrations." And he talked about himself being "charismatic" at that time. And I asked him whether he was ever outspoken or opinionated, because that is often characteristic of a manic type of phase, and he said that this was a time when he was more opinionated, sometimes in disagreeable ways. He said, "I rubbed people the wrong way."

He said that he remembered, actually that he could remember times before that when he was in states like this. So this may well have antedated '67, but I wasn't able to document previous dates. But he would have episodes where he would be debating people, made his opinions known, felt compelled to get his point across. He said he would become contentious, critical. And he would become intolerant, he could become insensitive. But also, he was, during times like this— and he recalled previous times, so my guess is there were episodes that antedated that depression—that he also was extremely academically successful, which is, by the way, not that unusual in a hypomanic state. When you are not completely out of control, you spin your wheels, and you do a lot of work.

So anyway, it looks as though he went into this manic or hypomanic state, it's hard to tell, during 1968, during that campaign. It was fairly short-lived.

Then, subsequent to that, there was another down, and he tried to pull himself together. As I recall, he wrote to his grandfather and he said that he was really getting his act together, and he went to Temple University. And according to him he had a lot of trouble there, he had trouble concentrating on his work, felt lonely, unmotivated. He said he felt removed from whatever was going on around him. My recollection, though, is that he did do the work at Temple, so that it was far from this severe depression. He recalls it as a down, but I believe, I don't recall, I might have the transcript here, but I believe that he did pass his courses there, so that it was not. I think he was functioning a whole lot better than he had been in, what was it, '67.

J.C.: Now, was there additional evidence, following the period that he was in Philadelphia, of mood changes?

D.L.: Let me find this again. Apparently he then went back, according to him, but I believe it's confirmed in part by the transcripts, he felt that he could at the end of this period go back to the University of Washington, and there his recollection was that he did better. Let me just look, because we have that transcript here.

Right. He clearly was doing a whole lot better in '70, '71, when he returned to Washington.

J.C.: And how long did this period last?

D.L.: Well, let me see.

By the way, as far as I could tell, this was not just a "doing better," but it sounds as if he had started to go into a sort of high again. And he said that he worked well, he got A's and B's, he could work all night long. He also could have a part-time job when he delivered for a medical supply company. And he also said he was not only doing very well academically, he was extremely sexually active with a girlfriend of his. And he started a new major in psychology. But, as I've noted here, I said that this high was fairly short-lived, and during the last semester at the University of Washington, he began to become depressed again.

Let me look at this and see.

Now, at the very end he gets a withdrawal from his undergraduate research, and he mentioned to me he was having a lot of trouble at that time concentrating on his own research. So this was, again, the beginning of a down.

J.C.: Now, Dr. Lewis, at the time that you interviewed Mr. Bundy, and the report that you were referring to, did you have the transcripts of his college performance?

D.L.: No, I didn't. In fact, I think I just saw these maybe a few weeks ago.

J.C.: Now, following his graduation from the University of Washington, did you find evidence of subsequent mood changes?

D.L.: Yeah. After his graduation he got a job in a psychiatric hospital, and he said he lost interest in psychology, and he said, quote, he "felt uncomfortable in some of my relationships." And he had planned to go to graduate school in psychology and his plans changed. He decided he would try law school. And he enrolled in a night program at the University of Puget Sound.

And again, he became—but it looks as if he's been sliding into this for a while—extremely depressed. And again, he did not attend classes, did not go to his final examination, and seemed to be in a significant depression at that time. Indeed, he did realize that he was functioning very badly and so he applied to the University of Utah Law School at that time. I guess hoping that he would come out of this. And he concealed the fact that he was flunking out of the University of Puget Sound Law School.

J.C.: Now, what was his mood like once he enrolled at the University of Utah Law School?

D.L.: My recollection is that at first he had not yet come out of his depression and that he did badly. But he was starting to come out of the depression, and he managed to convince his professors not to kick him out. He was able to improve to some extent, and by spring he was getting C's and a B, and I think he had an incomplete there. And then what is interesting is, by summer, he has brought up his grades, he's only taking two courses, but he's getting B's. So clearly something then picked up again.

J.C.: You said that initially he was having problems, and then he seemed, towards the summer of the school year 1975–76, I believe, to come out of that. But could you describe what the problems were initially that you identified?

D.L.: Well, according to him, he said that he could not attend. He became very depressed. He said that he couldn't attend classes, said he stayed home, he watched television, and he had never been interested in television before, didn't care about it. And he said [that] even at that time he smoked pot, which he didn't usually do. And he said, quote, "I just couldn't bring myself to go to class. I would sleep late, I stayed in the house, I cut the grass. I was manager of the house I was in."

I mentioned that subsequently, during the second semester, his mood lifted, and apparently fairly dramatically, and he said that he had started to enjoy going to class, that "I met a lot of kids, I got into a clique," and he said that actually it was about a month after the beginning of his second year at the University of Utah that he was picked out of the lineup and he was arrested. But he was on an upswing, I guess, at that point and doing better.

J.C.: Now following his arrest in Utah, did you find evidence of mood changes?

D.L.: There I would have to look at my notes. Well, again, this is as I understand what occurred in terms of what his lawyers described. That initially when he first was arrested, and he met his lawyers, originally he seemed like a perfectly normal client, which by the way is characteristic of a manic-depressive illness. There are stages where a person is absolutely coherent, functioning well, doing okay, kind of remission, and then. However, in the course of his trial something changed, and he started to become flippant. He was, as I understand it, inappropriate in court, would call the prosecutor by his first name, would write letters to the judge. And, apparently, even when he was confronted with an arrest warrant for murder in the state of Colorado, he brushed it off, thought it was nothing, and then threw himself into becoming an expert in the laws of Colorado. So he at this point really didn't seem to appreciate the jeopardy that he was in, what the evidence was like, but was kind of high as a kite.

J.C.: Following that, did you continue to find evidence of moods?

D.L.: Well, again, when he was in Colorado, as far as I can reconstruct it, this high kind of continued, and there he spent his time writing motions, writing briefs. He even, I believe, filed a motion to attend a conference for defense lawyers. This kind of a grandiose, flippant, just a total lack of appreciation of what his circumstances were like. As I understand it or I can reconstruct it, he, you know, planned kind of daring sorts of escapes, and indeed he did escape on two occasions.

Now, the one that I asked most about and know most about was the second escape, and I could tell you about that, because there was a dramatic kind of series of events, and a dramatic change in mood that occurred. I would have to again look at my notes.

J.C.: Why don't you do that and let's turn then to the period following his second escape.

D.L.: Well, when he was on the run, when he had left Colorado, he apparently felt terrific. He traveled from—I forget the whole route, but I think he flew to Chicago, took the train to Michigan, I forget where he went, and then took the car down to Atlanta, was going and going and going, and let's see, what did he tell me?

He said he had gone from Colorado Springs to Denver, from Denver by plane to Chicago, from Chicago to Ann Arbor, I guess by plane from Chicago to Ann Arbor, then by stolen car to Atlanta, Georgia. He described himself as being, quote, "high as a kite." And I said to him, well, did you have any drugs during this period of time, because that could create a high, and he said he had not. He said that he only had beer while he was in Ann Arbor.

And I asked him whether there was any time when this kind of high ended, and he said, "I can tell you the precise moment that it ended." He said that it ended while he was waiting for a bus at the Omni Center in Atlanta, and he said, "All of the sudden I could feel it drain out," and at that point he felt depressed and felt lonely, he felt lost. This was around January third or fourth, I think. And it was at that time that he went into a down, and I believe he was probably in that state when he arrived in Florida.

J.C.: This is January of 1978?

D.L.: Right.

J.C.: Now, following that, were there other, was there other evidence of moods once he arrived in Florida?

D.L.: Apparently at the time he was arrested he was still in one of these downs, he was rambling. He was not coherent. He was disheveled. He was quite a different Ted Bundy from the previous one who had been in campaigns, whatever. He would also at that time stay up late and talk with police, and just go on and on. I have listened to some of the tapes, and he just seems to have a need to be with people, and to talk with people. And they are not always the most coherent or the most concise things, but he seemed to have some kind of need to keep something going. Maybe he couldn't sleep—it's very possible that was one of the issues. But apparently he had been warned and had been told by his attorneys to not talk with anybody and not talk with police, at least not unless they were around. He was absolutely unable to do this during that time.

Then he was apparently indicted in July of '78, and at that time I think there was a brief period when he became overconfident. He said he was ready to go to trial, didn't understand why the state was waiting. However, between August and October, when he was to go to trial, he, to the best of my knowledge, was unable to work on his case at all. That he really did nothing of any usefulness. In October he had to ask for a continuance.

Then in October again there was a period that was fairly dramatic. Where he again went into one of his highs. But this time he was working and working and working, but he was really accomplishing nothing. It was at that time, I think between October and November of '78, that he actually took ninety depositions. And, as I understand it, he was busy. He was ravenously eating chocolates and candy and stuff like that—by the way, appetite changes often occur during highs and lows. And again, I reviewed some of the depositions, and I am not an attorney, but they certainly don't seem to go anywhere. They seem to be words, words, but nothing that is extraordinarily useful to his case. I understand that his attorneys did not find many of them useful and had to retake them. But he's going and going and going, and he's his own lawyer then. Apparently he filed a flurry of motions, but he could not comprehend what the evidence was, which happens during highs.

And this must have gone on for quite a period of time.

In May he was evaluated by Dr. Tanay, and at that time Dr. Tanay describes him as grandiose, as kind of orchestrating where the sheriff's deputies sit, kind of taking over, and certainly being inappropriate.

Then, apparently in May of 1979, he was offered a plea that, if he confessed to the murders of which he was accused, his life would be spared. And, as I tried to reconstruct that, it's not that easy to reconstruct, that period of time. It sounds as if he was very confused. That he was in a sort of agitated state, where one time he thought and saw one thing, another time he thought another. As I understand it, he signed one agreement to plea, and then suddenly changed his mind, stayed up all night the night before he was to accept the plea, and then fired his lawyer, Mr. Minerva, and decided to take over his case.

So here again you get this kind, these wild fluctuations, and this kind of inability to function effectively.

Then I saw some of the tapes of the actual Chi Omega trial and, you know, read some of the transcripts, and he talked and talked at least on some of the tapes I saw, and seemed unable to sort of give up the floor. He was not terribly effective counsel for himself, and he apparently, even at that time, would cross-examine witnesses, and he would elicit very damaging kinds of evidence. There was one time, I don't remember who the officer was, but I think he was interviewing an officer who had found the bodies, and he couldn't stop himself, he went on asking about the details and the blood and where bodies were, and these sorts of things. So clearly he was not in a state where he could handle this in a judicious manner that was helpful to himself.

He apparently also would be kind of glib, he would wave and say "Hi" to a juror. He was very eager to talk to the press, and as I understand it his lawyers just felt they had absolutely no control over it, what was going on, and he couldn't be reasoned with, could not be focused.

J.C.: Let me interrupt you for a second to go back to something. You indicated that at the time Mr. Bundy was involved in trying to decide whether to accept a plea agreement, that he appeared to be in an agitated state, and you said you couldn't tell whether, what the mood was. Was there any evidence reflected in nurse's notes or prison records that would suggest one way or the other?

D.L.: Well, I don't recall the exact timing of the notes. I did review notes from the jail, and there was a period of time when I believe he was suicidal, and he was put on suicide watch. There was a period of time when—I am not sure if that was when he flooded his cell, I can't recall the date of that—when he acted out quite peculiarly. If you could show me.

J.C.: I am going to hand Dr. Lewis an entry from the Leon County sheriff's office, but I believe the date is October sixth, 1978.

D.L.: Let me just see. From Janice Turner, R.N., yes. This is the note that was more interesting to me. It's dated October sixth, 1978, and says that date he had flooded his cell, and when Mr. Golden—I guess the director of that prison—arrived, they said "Mr. Bundy's voice was loud as he was speaking to Mr. Golden's question, exact repetition of Mr. Golden." That's called echolalia, and it's a puzzle because you often see this kind of echolalia in extremely disturbed psychotic individuals. Sometimes children repeat exactly what is said to them, but this kind of loudness and repetition suggests he was in a very excited kind of state here.

Let's see. There was a request here that he stand in the hall at a certain place, and then—apparently this person thought his behavior was peculiar—he stood with his right shoulder against the wall, he'd had a rolled-up magazine in his left hand, wouldn't communicate verbally. And then, subsequent to that last report, that his cell door vibrated and there was loud banging on the cell door, once they got him back into his cell. And so I assume he was in this very excited state. And then apparently it ended, and at five P.M. he was just calm and relaxed. That's what I recall, and apparently his moods and his functioning fluctuated tremendously during that period of time.

J.C.: Anything else of significance in the jail medical records?

D.L.: On 5-17-79, there is a note that says "Sergeant Wade was concerned and asked me if Mr. Bundy was on medication because he apparently had unsteady gait when leaving the slammer"—I like that— "this P.M. and Sergeant Wade and myself entered the slammer and found Ativan tablets, two, still in the medicine cup on the top of" whatever it was. "Medication to be given tonight."

So it's interesting that he was ataxic [unable to coordinate voluntary muscle movements] then, and assuming this is not something like a brain tumor, this kind of not being able to walk straight or whatever suggests that he had been taking some kind of drugs or medication and couldn't walk straight. And then there is another notation later that day that his speech is slurred and his pupils are dilated and reactive. And he says he admits saving Ativan from last night and taking the same before noon that day. So, and then they make a note there to "observe closely."

And then there is a note that he's—let's see—he's alert the next day. Then they decide to increase his Ativan in the morning—there is a puzzle—on 5-25, so something was concerning them. They don't say what it was, but on 5-25, shortly before this other entry, they give him *more* of what caused the ataxia. And then it's shortly thereafter, on the thirty-first, that he is depressed, and that he apparently on 5-31-79 had taken the medication in the morning, and though he was told not to do that, and they were quite concerned about him. So he's depressed on 5-31. I thought that was the date that he actually made the plea. I could be mistaken. Or I mean rejected the plea. And then on 6-1-79 he's placed on suicide precaution.

So at least from these data it looks as if he was in a down and people were concerned about him and they were concerned about suicide during the weeks prior to his rejecting the plea. And certainly on the day as well. It's interesting that they continued with the Ativan, because with a depressive person, things like Ativan or Valium and this kind of thing will increase depression, so it's about the last thing you want to do with a depressed individual.

J.C.: Now Dr. Lewis, I believe we had gone up to the time of the plea agreement in your description of Mr. Bundy's behavior. Could you continue from there, please?

D.L.: Well, we have gone beyond that. We have gone to during the Chi Omega trial itself, and at which time he was his own attorney, he felt competent, sort of on top of the world and capable of doing the cross-examination and whatever—he kind of took the role of defendant and defense attorney. And would say "Hi" to the jury. He was just inappropriate, and according to his lawyers, not effective, unable to focus on the issues of the trial, and more concerned with these other peripheral kinds of things.

Also at that time there was an episode where he broke a light in his cell, where he refused to come to court. And I saw a tape of his talking with the judge, and in this kind of very flippant fashion, and pointing his finger at the judge, and what I recall is his saying "Whoa" or something of that sort, and the judge kind of took him up on that and tried to kind of put him down, at least control him a bit. At which point he kind of pointed at his attorney instead of the judge, but he was—I would say he was feeling no pain.

What is interesting is that apparently even when he was found guilty, even when sentenced to death, there was no evidence that he was chastened by this or frightened by it or depressed by it. This high seemed to continue, this inability to quite appreciate what was going on.

Again, the Lake City proceedings: I can tell you what it looks like to me. It looks as if he was still in a high. Although he was at this point not being his own attorney. But he apparently was not cooperating with his attorney either. He again couldn't seem to appreciate what the issues were, what the jeopardy was that he was in, but he was into a book deal, and he was on the phone, sometimes several times a day, with a writer named Michaud, and at nights I think he made dozens of tapes, some of which I have heard, some of them rambling, some not terribly coherent. And also he was very focused on a wish to get married, and this was something that he kept pushing his lawyers to help him with, and pushing other people to help him with.

And what, the other thing that I think is very interesting, and which I have only talked with him about briefly, is that he was taking alcohol and drugs at this time. Certainly a portion of it. He was apparently being brought alcohol by somebody who was visiting him. I think in his lunch. And he was also being given Valium, and he would take somewhere between four, five, six Valiums a day, and when I asked him, you know, why this was, apparently this helped him to be calm and bring him down a bit. So that he clearly must have sensed that he was not in good control and so was taking these drugs and this alcohol to try to control himself.

J.C.: Now Dr. Lewis, in June of 1979, there was a hearing into Mr. Bundy's competence. And he objected to having any participation. Was there any significance to that type of behavior?

D.L.: Well, Mr. Bundy doesn't think there's anything wrong with him. I think that—I'm not sure, but he may have objections to me being here today. He feels that his behavior has always been reasonable and rational, and that he—his insight into his own psychiatric condition is nil.

My recognition is that it was also during a high that he felt that Dr. Tanay was wrong, that he was not in any way impaired, and that he was going to run the show. So it would be consistent—by the way, I should mention that when people with bipolar illness are either experiencing a high or even a depressional low, their judgment is often severely impaired. You know, with a high, a person would be more likely to not appreciate what was, what the dangers were, and to be more glib and just euphoric. During a low I have known individuals who really would not participate at all in their defense. They felt hopeless and unable to function.

So during either one of these kinds of phases an individual would certainly not be competent to be of really good assistance to himself.
J.C.: Now, Dr. Lewis, there are references in the record of this case to Mr. Bundy appearing to have more than one personality. Did you find any evidence in his background that he experienced altered states?
D.L.: Yes. That he experienced altered states, yes. The nature of these I don't claim to understand, I'm not sure what they are. I can tell you what my differential diagnosis would be, but there are some reports from different people. There is a report from a family member, from Virginia Bristol, of an episode, and I think this was when he was at Temple, when he had gone back to Philadelphia, where she was on a platform with him, I guess waiting for a train or something, and suddenly he had changed and she felt suddenly he was a different kind of person, that he frightened her. Let me see if I have notes on that. I may not.
J.C.: Dr. Lewis, apparently at page five of Exhibit thirty.
D.L.: Right. Here, according to Mrs. Bristol, because I've also spoken with her and I wish I remembered verbatim exactly what she had said. Apparently after a very pleasant evening at a concert, as they waited in a train station, Mr. Bundy suddenly started to ramble, and she said he made no sense and he looked crazy and she felt that he was not in touch with her. And she said, "I was afraid to be alone with him." So this was one of the episodes that occurred.
J.C.: And this was in 196—
D.L.: I think it was '68, if I'm not mistaken. I also spoke with one of the investigators on the case there, Mr. Aloi, and he described a couple of episodes. I think I have notes about that—Oh, I found it. Mr. Aloi said that he was in Mr. Bundy's cell, and this, he said, occurred about five months after he was incarcerated in Tallahassee. And he said they were talking, he said, not about anything important, and he said, quote, "He became weird on me." He did a metamorphosis, a bit of a body and facial change, and he felt there was almost an odor emitted from him. He said, "Almost a complete change of personality" with extreme tension. And he said, "That was the day I was afraid of him."

Mr. Aloi said it lasted for about twenty minutes, and said he knew that [Mr. Bundy] was not approachable because [Mr. Bundy] said he was afraid that he might hurt somebody and [Mr. Aloi] just waited until it stopped. And he described it as very scary. And then he also described an episode that was somewhat different when, and I think that was on the day that Kimberly Leach's body had been found, and at this time he said that Mr. Bundy flew into a rage, that he was pacing, that he was muttering things, that he was hyperventilating, and apparently, I'm not sure who, but somebody gave him a bag to put over his face.

This, by the way, does not sound as peculiar as his first episode with Mr. Aloi, this sort of sudden metamorphosis and the episode with his aunt.

There is also another interesting thing, that at least to my mind perhaps sheds some insight into this. I reviewed sort of a log or a diary or some papers that Mr. Bundy had written and I think they were around the time of, around the time that he was in college, and before these episodes, and there is a drawing that he did, and there is an interesting kind of metamorphosis in the drawing and also in the writing on the page.

Let me see, I think I have it. Do you have a copy of it?

J.C.: Your Honor, I'll mark this petitioner's Exhibit forty-one.

D.L.: And this, when I asked Mr. Bundy about it, first of all, he said, "Did I do this?" He said, "This is my writing," which I think is quite interesting, because certain individuals, when they are in an altered state or whatever, write differently from the way they do at other times. And here is a picture where, first of all, there is a head, a person of some sort, and then the head enlarges and the head has teeth like Dracula. And there also seems to be a change in the writing right within the page itself. It looks as if he becomes less organized or whatever on the page.

And, by the way, when I showed this to Mr. Bundy, his first reaction was, "Did I do that?" He didn't remember it, and then he said, "Was I on drugs?" I don't know, but this was at college, and as far as we know he was not into drugs. And this seems to be a sort of visual representation of perhaps what happens with him when he goes into these states.

What causes them would require a lot more time, a lot more evaluation. It could be any number of possibilities.

J.C.: But what is the significance of these types of episodes? What may be the significance of them?

D.L.: Well, you wonder, when you see dramatic changes in an individual, where they are not themselves, where a person cannot reach them, you wonder about a possible seizure disorder, where there is a very brief episode where a person is just not with it. Though this is not a grand mal seizure, but another kind of seizure, you wonder about abnormal activity in the brain for a short period of time. You wonder about the diagnosis of a disassociative state, which would be a kind of state similar to a fugue state or a hysterical state, where again these are times when sometimes individuals go off and don't even know who they are for a period of time, and wind up somewhere else in the country, don't know how they got there.

That's one of the differentials. Another would be a hysterical kind of state. I'm trying to think, because there are certainly other possibilities. There are episodic psychoses, and we don't know the causes of those. My guess is there is abnormal brain activity, but we don't, we just don't know what causes them. Certainly there is something episodically going on that is aberrant and abnormal.

J.C.: Dr. Lewis, I asked you earlier whether you had formed an opinion about whether Mr. Bundy suffered from a mental illness at the time of the two trials in 1979 and 1980 and I believe you said that you had?

D.L.: Yes.

J.C.: Can you tell me what that opinion is?

D.L.: Yes. I believe he was suffering from a bipolar mood disorder, otherwise known as manic-depressive illness.

Dr. Lewis went on to describe how Ted's symptoms matched the criteria for the illness in the psychiatrist's reference book, the Diagnostic and Statistical Manual III (DSM III). Then Jim continued his questioning.

J.C.: Dr. Lewis, do you have an opinion whether his mental illness substantially impaired the ability either to represent himself or to assist his attorneys to represent him in the Lake City trial?

D.L.: Yes. I believe that it did. As I understand it, according to his attorneys, he was unable to focus on the issues that they were presenting, he was unable to comprehend the evidence that was before him. He didn't appreciate, I don't think he appreciated the nature of the evidence or charges against him.

And, in addition, at this time he was, he was involved in these kind of peripheral but very all-consuming activities, like writing a book, making tape after tape, dictating these tapes, some of which, by the way, are rambling and are not logical. And then it varied into getting married. The only piece I've seen of that trial, by the way, was his attempt to get married and the kind of inappropriate affect that he had there.

So given this state that he was in, I believe that he was not competent to assist his attorneys.

J.C.: Dr. Lewis, there is a reference in the record of this case to an opinion by Dr. Tanay at the time of Mr. Bundy's plea agreement, that if he accepted the plea agreement it would indicate that he was competent, but if he rejected it, it would indicate that he was incompetent. Are you familiar with that opinion?

D.L.: Yes, I am.

J.C.: And do you agree with that opinion?

D.L.: No, I don't. I don't even think Mr. Bundy was competent to accept or reject a plea at that time. I think that he was high as a kite, he was grandiose, his judgment was impaired. And whether at the moment he had decided yes or whether at the moment he had decided no, he was still experiencing a manic psychotic episode and he would not have [been competent], I don't care what he answered.

Dr. Lewis's testimony concluded our case. We had Ted's attorneys' testimony that he did not seem to comprehend the evidence against him and *in fact* did not assist (to say the least) in his defense. We had Dr. Tanay's and Dr. Lewis's testimonies that his behavior in that regard was a product of a lifelong mental illness over which he had no control. Dr. Tanay ascribed it to psychopathology; Dr. Lewis identified a bipolar mood disorder and a suggestion of multiple personality.

CHAPTER 14

The next day the state put on Judge Wallace Jopling, who had presided over the Lake City trial. He was questioned by Assistant State Attorney Richard Doran.

RICHARD DORAN: Mr. Bundy presented argument to you during the penalty phase after the jury returned a recommendation?

WALLACE JOPLING: Yes.

R.D.: What type of argument did he present you?

W.J.: It was much the same as he presented to the jury, that testimony was not sufficient to justify the verdict in the first instance, and that he was being persecuted, that sort of thing.

R.D.: Judge Jopling, did you ever conduct a formal competency hearing regarding Mr. Bundy's ability to assist his counsel or to assist himself in his trial?

W.J.: No, I didn't.

R.D.: Could you explain for the Court why you did not?

W.J.: Three main reasons. First, there had been a competency hearing conducted before Judge Cowart, eminent jurist in the Chi Omega case, in determining of that case only six months before the case I was presiding over, and he had been found competent in that. Secondly, that the issue of competency was never raised before me by him or his counsel. And third, and probably most importantly, was because I was convinced from the word go that he was eminently competent and capable of rational understanding and conferring with his lawyer, knew fully well the consequences of the proceedings.

R.D.: Do you have an opinion as to Theodore Robert Bundy's competency to stand trial?

W.J.: I would say, considering, Mr. Bundy was one of the most intelligent, articulate, coherent defendants I have ever seen.

R.D.: Do you feel that Mr. Bundy had an appreciation of the charges he was facing and the penalty he was facing?

W.J.: Most definitely.

R.D.: Could you give me a factual example for your reason?

W.J.: His statements in the penalty phase to the jury, surely, the way he cited the crucifix of Christ, and other things [that] certainly apply in the death penalty to himself, and realizing that he was facing that, certainly indicated to me that he understood all along.

R.D.: Did you have an occasion prior to trial to convene for the purposes of a plea, accepting a plea of guilty on Mr. Bundy's behalf?

W.J.: Yes, I did.

I and Judge Cowart met in Tallahassee; we convened court jointly. Mr. Bundy came in and we were in expectation of the plea being entered and the usual dialogue be engaged in between the court and Mr. Bundy. But he, at the moment when that was starting, he arose and began to read from a paper attacking Mr. Minerva, his counsel, and claiming that Mr. Minerva was not convinced of his innocence and was not strongly enough contesting it for him. When that was done, the state attorney for the Third Judicial Circuit, I understand— I did not hear this—but withdrew the offer of a plea and the hearing was very summarily terminated.

R.D.: Judge Jopling, how would you compare Theodore Robert Bundy's incompetency to stand trial to all the other defendants who appeared before you over your many years on the bench?

W.J.: I would say I never seen a young man that was more intelligent, coherent, articulate than he was.

Just as there were no bad facts, facts that could not be folded into our theory of the case, there were no bad witnesses. Jim cross-examined Judge Jopling.

JIM COLEMAN: Now, Judge Jopling, you were present at the time that Mr. Bundy was supposed to enter the plea in the two cases. Is that correct?

W.J.: Yes, sir, I was.

J.C.: And you testified about what you observed at that hearing?

W.J.: Yes.

J.C.: And I believe you testified that Mr. Bundy got up and started to attack Mr. Minerva. That was unexpected?

W.J.: On my part it was.

J.C.: What was your reaction to that?

W.J.: Well, I would probably say some surprise on my part, and some disappointment that the whole matter was being aborted. Seemed to me that it was working toward a reasonable solution of all of these problems and charges, and I can't help to say I was somewhat disappointed.

J.C.: Now, you indicated that there are three reasons that you didn't raise the issue of competency at your trial.

W.J.: Yes.

J.C.: You said the first was because there had been a competency hearing in Chi Omega case. Is that correct?

W.J.: That's, that was one.

J.C.: Could you tell me why that was significant?

W.J.: Well, number one, as I alluded to, I had a very high respect for Judge Cowart, presiding judge who made that ruling. And I felt that the ruling, his ruling was entitled to respect from me.

J.C.: So is it fair to say that you felt somewhat bound by Judge Cowart's ruling?

W.J.: No, I didn't feel bound by it, but I felt it was reasonable and that I would accept it.

J.C.: Were you aware of the proceedings that had preceded Judge Cowart's determination that Mr. Bundy was competent?

W.J.: I don't know exactly what time it was. I saw that proceeding, I mean I heard all of the, read the various reports. It was sometime later that I learned about what went on there.

J.C.: Now tell me what you learned about what went on there?

W.J.: Well, I learned Mr. Brian Hayes was appointed to represent Mr. Bundy in that proceeding, Mr. Bundy not being willing to—Mr. Bundy contending he was entirely competent and Mr. Hayes was presenting that contention on his behalf. And that he did make such a contention, that they had the testimony or reports of Dr. Cleckley, who declared him to be competent, and of Dr. Tanay who conceded Dr. Cleckley's eminence in the field of psychiatry of this type, and of Dr. Tanay's testimony, all of which was considered by Judge Cowart.

J.C.: Now you said that you became aware of this at some point following the proceedings. Would that have been following the proceedings in Chi Omega, but before the trial in Lake City?

W.J.: Really, I can't tell you exactly when it was. I just can't say [at] what point I learned more of the details I just recited about that competency hearing.

J.C.: Can you tell me from whom you learned the details of the competency hearing?

W.J.: Probably from the state, the state attorney's office.

J.C.: And can you tell me the circumstances under which you learned the details of the competency hearing from the state?

W.J.: I am trying to recollect. May have been after the verdict, after the guilty verdict, and may have been after that.

J.C.: In Chi Omega?

W.J.: No, after the guilty verdict in the Leach case.

J.C.: Is it possible that it was before the guilty verdict?

W.J.: Could have been before that.

J.C.: And can you, do you recall whether this was a meeting of all counsel or was this just a meeting between you and the representative from the state attorney's office?

W.J.: I don't recollect any of the details of that being furnished. I remember that, I remember seeing the reports that, some time during the latter part of this trial.

J.C.: My question is, whether Mr. Africano or any of the lawyers representing Mr. Bundy were aware that you had been presented with this material?

W.J.: I am not certain. I couldn't stand here and say I know if he did.

J.C.: So it's possible that Mr. Africano was not even aware of that?

W.J.: That's possible.

J.C.: Now, did you read Dr. Tanay's report when the state presented it to you?

W.J.: Yes, I did.

J.C.: And that report raised questions about whether Mr. Bundy was competent to stand trial. Is that correct?

W.J.: Well, the report suggested that.

J.C.: Suggested that he was not competent to stand trial. Is that correct?

W.J.: Yes, I would say, say so.

J.C.: Suggested that he would act in a way to jeopardize his own case. Is that correct?

w.j.: I don't recall that specifically.

j.c.: Let me ask you, you have indicated that you also learned that Mr. Hayes had been appointed to represent Mr. Bundy at the competency hearing.

w.j.: Yes.

j.c.: And did you also learn that Mr. Bundy had refused to have the issue of his competency advanced by his lawyers?

w.j.: Yes, sir. Yes, I knew that.

j.c.: And did you know that Mr. Minerva and the other lawyers who represented Mr. Bundy did not testify at the competency hearing before Judge Cowart?

w.j.: I didn't know whether they did or did not.

j.c.: You had no knowledge?

w.j.: No.

j.c.: Did you know that both parties in the competency hearing argued to Judge Cowart that Mr. Bundy ought to be found competent. Were you aware of that?

w.j.: Yes.

j.c.: Have you ever seen a competency hearing where three motions have been filed to challenge, to raise questions about whether a defendant is competent, and no party appears at the hearing to argue in favor of the motions?

w.j.: No, I haven't.

j.c.: When you say you had heard of Judge Cowart's ruling as to competency, could you explain why it was that you found that was significant?

w.j.: Well, because I understood that there had been a competency hearing, like I say. I knew Judge Cowart and knew his ability and knew that he would have required a proper hearing and that his ruling, in my opinion, would be persuasive on me. Not binding, but persuasive.

j.c.: So based upon what you knew about Judge Cowart as a jurist, it was your opinion that that hearing had been thorough and complete and explored all the legal possibilities?

w.j.: That was my assumption.

Assistant State Attorney Richard Doran called Brian Hayes to the stand, the attorney who had represented Ted at the competency hearing and again, briefly, just after the Chi Omega trial, on a motion for a new trial. John Sandage and Andy Munro had interviewed Brian Hayes a few months earlier and had found him to be a cordial and thoughtful lawyer who believed his assigned job had been to urge Ted's competence, not question it. He also acknowledged that by the time he had seen Ted again at the end of the trial, he had seemed strangely unconcerned about the outcome. We did not consider Brian Hayes to be an adverse witness.

RICHARD DORAN: Would you describe your appointment as special counsel to Mr. Bundy at the Leon County competency hearing?

BRIAN HAYES: This was a unique appointment, one I had never quite had before. According to my time records, I was called by Judge Cowart on June fourth, 1979, and he advised me that he would appreciate it very much—and of course we as lawyers know what that means, when he says he would appreciate it very much, that meant change your calendar—if I would represent Ted Bundy for one hearing, and he indicated at the time that the hearing was going to be a competency hearing and that he, Judge Cowart, had raised the issue because the defendant in this case was disinclined to do so and he was fussing with Mike Minerva, his lawyer, and apparently there was a pending motion for Mr. Minerva either to get out or to be authorized to get out, and maybe a motion by Mr. Bundy to let him proceed pro se [on his own].

Hayes admitted that he had not been privy to the conduct of Bundy with Minerva because Minerva had filed what Hayes called only a "bare bones" competency motion, since Ted had not waived the attorney-client privilege. He testified that he interviewed Bundy for an hour and a half one day and then forty-five minutes before the hearing.

R.D.: What was your role during the hearing on the competency issue?

B.H.: I was appointed to represent the defendant, and my role in that case is no different than my role in any case. I was to serve his interest. And that means, among other things, of course, doing what he wanted me to do within, of course, the ethics of what I could do, and I think I did it.

R.D.: What was the basis of your argument in support of the idea that Mr. Bundy was competent to stand trial?

B.H.: As indicated, I spent some time with Mr. Bundy at the Leon County jail advising him of who I was, what I perceived my function to be. He was aware of the hearing coming up and we conferred at some length. He was very, very insistent that he did not wish the defense raised, did not go along with Mr. Minerva raising it, and was upset with Mike Minerva, and proceeded to give me, referring to my notes, the names of five lawyers who could testify not only to his legal skill, but his knowledge of the legal system and his ability to go forward.

And based on that, my discussion with him, I cranked up for the hearing accordingly. And as the record I'm sure reflects, he was aware of what Dr. Tanay said. In fact, when he called me at home he imitated the voice of Dr. Tanay in sort of an Eastern European type voice—very good imitation by the way. But he didn't have much regard for Dr. Tanay or Dr. Cleckley [the state's appointed psychiatrist at the competency hearing]. Didn't have much regard for Mike Minerva. He felt the P.D. office wasn't doing their job. He had wanted Millard Farmer from Atlanta to represent him.

R.D.: Let me ask you, in terms of, you say you cranked up for your motion, when you cranked up for your motion, did you refer to the criteria that are set out in the rules to discuss competency?

B.H.: Absolutely. But bear in mind I was representing him and he did not want to assert that as a defense—at all. Either insanity at the time or insanity or incompetence to proceed to stand trial.

R.D.: Could you give us your personal observations of Mr. Bundy when you first met him?

B.H.: When I met Mr. Bundy at the jail it was approximately one P.M., according to my notes. He was well dressed, well groomed, his shoes appeared to be shined. He was very affable—that word has been used today, but he certainly was. He was smiling, we chatted.

R.D.: Was he able to share with you certain facts to this particular motion that you felt were helpful?

B.H.: No, not really. The only thing that he indicated—he was insistent that he was competent now, that he had various people that could corroborate his competency, and that he seemingly indicated he was given these medical exams or these psychiatric exams largely without his consent. It was Minerva's idea. And he thought it was a bad tactic and bad judgment and, most of all, it wasn't true. He was competent as the day was long and he wanted to go to trial.

R.D.: Did Mr. Bundy appear to you to understand the concept of competency to go to trial?

B.H.: That's a—you know, he appeared to me to understand what I was saying and he appeared to understand the purpose of the hearing. He did not want to be adjudged incompetent to stand trial. He wanted his trial to be had. His only fuss was that he didn't think his lawyers were ready to try it right then. He had filed, I think the day before, a motion for continuance. But nothing was raised, I mean he didn't indicate to me that he was unfamiliar with the tests for incompetency.

And I indicated to him I'm sure what I tell every defendant who wants to represent himself. I don't have it in my notes, but I oftentimes come across defendants that want to represent themselves. It just happens in our practice that, especially repeat offenders, they come back and they—I don't know if they've read some law books in the state prison system, but they want to represent themselves. And I have a very standard little talk I give them and I've been giving it for years and I would guess I probably told Mr. Bundy the same thing, but I can't be sure.

It's generally against, I almost invariably advise against anybody representing themselves, and I tell them a story connected with that, and I usually say I'm not competent to represent myself. And I tell them a story where I was involved in a small civil case and hired a lawyer, and I kept badgering my lawyer the whole time, until he finally told me to shut up and sit down and let him try the case, which he did and which he won, a fuss over some investment.

I realized after that, that, you know, I don't think hardly anybody does a very good job of representing themselves. I think it's almost a physical impossibility. That's from a wisdom standpoint, that's not from a, from the actual ability to go through the motions. I just don't think it's a very smart idea and I'm sure I told Mr. Bundy that.

Brian Hayes was cross-examined by Jim Coleman.

JIM COLEMAN: Now, when you talked to Mr. Bundy, did he express any concern at all about the charges against him and about the consequences if he were convicted?

B.H.: No.

J.C.: Did he ever during the time that you saw him, either for the competency hearing or the appeal and the motion for a new trial, express any concern?

B.H.: No. And I found that—not necessarily at the competency hearing, but at the motion for a new trial, when I saw him in court—here was a man who was convicted and sentenced to the chair, and I did remark that I found it unusual that he wasn't extremely anxious and upset by that, because in my experience all defendants can talk about at that point is when, how much time have I got. To that extent, I would consider that out of the norm, unusual.

J.C.: And in fact, he basically dismissed the whole thing and thought that there were some legal problems that would be taken care of on appeal. Isn't that correct?

B.H.: The adjective that comes to mind is "blasé" about the conviction which, as I indicated, I found unusual.

J.C.: Now isn't it also correct that during the time that you represented him in connection with the competency matter he had no interest in addressing the merits of that issue?

B.H.: His interest and his instructions to me were to not address, not get into the facts, for instance, of Dr. Cleckley's finding of sociopathy but competent, and Dr. Tanay's findings, I believe, of personality disorder. He did not want me to explore it, lest it be interpreted to be an admission that he was somehow incompetent.

J.C.: Right. And you abided by that wish on his part?

B.H.: Yes. I felt I had no choice. I was appointed to represent him, and that's what he wanted to do. Unless he was asking me to do something that bothered me so much I would have to go to the judge to adhere to his wishes, I was going to follow what he told me.

J.C.: Now didn't you also get the impression that Mr. Bundy's real interest in these proceedings was to appear to be "a sophisticated lawyer in a high-profile case"?

B.H.: I formed that judgment, I think, at the motion for a new trial, after talking to him and reading in the newspapers—and I do admit I read all the newspaper accounts of it—and I formed a subjective personal judgment that he was interested in being a high-profile lawyer.

The state called Dr. Peter Macaluso, physician for Leon County jail in 1978–79. He testified that he had prescribed Ativan for Ted for anxiety and Limbitrol for agitated depression and had also diagnosed Ted as suffering from "acute anxiety neurosis." He had ordered the tablets crushed because Ted had been caught hoarding pills, and pills had also been intercepted on their way into the jail. He said he had not seen any symptoms of a major mental illness.

Again, even though Dr. Macaluso was the state's witness, even his direct testimony was very valuable to us. First, his records and the nurse's notes were independent confirmation that Ted was having *some* kind of mental problem at the time of the plea bargain and competency hearing—and even six months earlier. Second, he treated Ted with psychoactive medication, was unable to control his condition, recommended a psychiatric consultation, and *no one else knew about any of it.* Not Ted's lawyers, not Dr. Tanay, not Judge Cowart, not Brian Hayes—none of the people who were involved in evaluating his mental competency at that very same time.

On cross-examination, Dr. Macaluso was nearly as unresponsive as he had been on the day I'd seen him in Tallahassee. He clearly did not want to be here.

JIM COLEMAN: Did you advise anybody that you were prescribing these drugs for Mr. Bundy?

PETER MACALUSO: I don't follow your question.

J.C.: Well, did you advise anybody that you were prescribing the drugs for Mr. Bundy?

P.M.: The nurse and Mr. Bundy.

J.C.: Do you know if Mr. Bundy's attorneys are aware you were prescribing these drugs?

P.M.: I am not aware.

Jim reviewed for Dr. Macaluso the contents of the 1979 jail records. Starting on the fourteenth of May, Ted was receiving one tablet of Ativan at night. Then, on the twenty-eighth he began receiving two milligrams during the morning—including on May 31, the morning of the plea agreement hearing. A nurse's note that day states: "He was depressed and needed to talk with someone." Ted was placed on suicide watch. On June 1, he was displaying $+4$ anxiety—the top of the scale. The notes state, "He was extremely agitated with symptoms of depression." The plan of action was to stop the Ativan, a tranquilizer, and try other medication. On June 8, Dr. Macaluso's notes stated that Bundy was "slightly better," his anxiety reduced to $+2$, but with $+4$ repressed anger and despair. The plan of action was psychiatric consultation for any psychotropic drugs. He was given chlorhydrate, a psychoactive sedative, only until psychiatric consultation could be obtained. It was ordered that day, but there was no indication it ever occurred. Dr. Macaluso claimed absolutely no recollection independent of the records.

Finally, the state put on its two star witnesses—their psychiatrists. Neither had conducted an examination or interview with Ted or interviewed his family or his attorneys, other than Vic Africano, who was interviewed by only one of the doctors, Dr. Umesh Mahtre. Both had reviewed written records provided to them by the state. Their testimony was simply incredible. The first to testify was Dr. Charles Mutter who, by his own count, had testified "approximately a thousand times." He appeared to be a great admirer of Ted.

RICHARD DORAN: Did you see evidence [in the record] that Mr. Bundy was able to appreciate the nature of the charges against him and the seriousness of the penalties that were possible?

CHARLES MUTTER: Yes.

R.D.: Where did you see this?

C.M.: Everywhere. I think what this man did was brilliant. And I think that he was able to, in his very detailed, organized, meticulous research of the facts and the issues, certainly knew the gravity of the charges. This is evidenced in his word-by-word argument when he asked Mr. Minerva to be discharged as counsel [at the aborted plea hearing]. And this is his words and testimony, which is extremely compelling. Very specifically, he did not want this man to be his counsel because his belief was, how can a man who does not believe in me represent me. I think, I don't think you can beat that. This is compelling. This is lucid. This is rational. Even a man who sells a car or sells a product must be convinced about his product.

   This man certainly was aware of the nature of his charges and gravity of the implications, and his requesting [the] type of representation [of] somebody who believes in him, supports him, is very lucid. If I were a defendant I wouldn't want to have somebody that thought I was a loser represent me. I don't think there's anything illogical about that. I don't think you have to be a psychiatrist to figure that out.

   Of course, that was one of reasons that Ted's ranting motion at the plea hearing was so *crazy*: Ted himself had admitted his guilt when he authorized plea negotiations in the first place. The real malfeasance would have been if Minerva had *not* believed Ted was guilty yet had still pursued a guilty plea. Dr. Mutter continued singing Ted's praises.

C.M.: I am also aware that Mr. Bundy had legal training, because this is part of his history, and I think that the brilliance of Mr. Bundy speaks for itself in another way, in the record, and that, that during the trial there were very few times that the judge sustained any objections by opposing counsel. Now, the judge certainly is in control of the court, he knows what is going on, and his arguments at times were brilliant, very logical, and very lucid. They didn't win, but they were still compelling and they were more important. The issue is mental status examination. Everything he did was organized. It was goal directed. It was reasonable to a fault, practically.

R.D.: What were your impressions of Mr. Bundy's presentation, vis-à-vis a factual understanding of the case?

C.M.: Well, there was no doubt that what he said was very compelling. I think it was designed to elicit sympathy, to have somebody reflect upon what was going on, [a] recap of the facts of the case, [including] his being upset why an individual [was] picked as a juror when he lost options to—I guess [defendants] have [only] so many options to—exclude jurors. I am not a lawyer, but he certainly knows a lot more about this than I do, and an individual might possibly be biased against himself, which was one of the segments of this argument.

The idea of his belief about the press, the power of the press, and that [the press] really tried him and convicted him. His compelling argument that the only living individual, or the only person, who could really exculpate him was the victim. I think this is a very compelling argument.

See, if we have a person who is manic or bipolar or psychotic or insane, it means, by definition, that these people are out of touch with reality. That means they don't know what is real and what is not real. If Mr. Bundy gave an argument in sentencing that was totally irrelevant, and out of context with everything that happened, his talk about somebody way out in left field, tangential, not coherent, then certainly there would be a good reason for anyone to question this man's mental state.

This man's arguments were brilliant. This man is brilliant. He has beat two death warrants. Is that insanity?

Jim and I liked to think we had something to do with those death warrants being beaten.

R.D.: Doctor, let me talk to you a moment about Mr. Bundy's relationship with his attorney Michael Minerva. You reviewed the documents, affidavits of Mr. Minerva regarding his situation representing Mr. Bundy?

C.M.: Yes, I did.

R.D.: How do you explain Mr. Minerva's attitudes in dealings with Mr. Bundy?

C.M.: Ego. Here is an attorney who is trying to defend his client, and client will not help him. Maybe client is smarter than the attorney, and in this case, or has better mythological organization, and what else is the man going to say?

R.D.: In your review of the record, did you see any red flags that might call into question Mr. Bundy's mental competence?

C.M.: In my opinion—my judgment was based on what I saw—no. There was nothing here that showed this man was showing signs of [being] out of touch with reality, out of the scope of reality testing, or doing things unreasonable.

The state then called Dr. Umesh Mahtre to the stand. He, too, claimed to have seen no evidence in the record that suggested Ted may have been incompetent at trial.

R.D.: How about any evidence regarding whether or not Mr. Bundy was able to relate to his attorneys?

UMESH MAHTRE: No. In fact, they related very well. Mr. Africano indicated an incident, which, to get a point across, Mr. Bundy and he were getting ready for the closing arguments, and Mr. Bundy told him that he was wrong. Mr. Africano promptly got very upset and angry and thought that, Gee, nobody is going to tell me I'm wrong. He argued with Mr. Bundy for about an hour and finally considered that Mr. Bundy was correct and changed his oral argument. That shows that even though they disagreed and had some differences, they were able to patch it up and get on with the main track again and provide a united front.

R.D.: How about Mr. Bundy's ability to respond to the challenge of the prosecution's witnesses?

U.M.: I think he has done an extremely good job of it. You know, he has deposed a lot of people. Dr. Lipkovic [the medical examiner] testified how Mr. Bundy asked him several questions about maggots and things like that, and he was really impressed during my conversation with him, that he was surprised that he knew so much about things that most even lawyers don't know.

R.D.: Did you review any of the records of the Orange County jail regarding the time prior to the Lake City trial?

U.M.: Yes, sir, I did, and I didn't find anything of any seriousness in that. Going back to Leon County, I had extensive conversation with the two nurses, just to let the court understand what shape Mr. Bundy was in. He has written a letter to Jane [sic] Turner that she read to me on the phone in which Bundy had made several requests. The requests for dental floss even specified that he wanted one unwaxed because in

his opinion unwaxed dental floss does a better job than the waxed one.
He asked for nail files to manicure his nails. He asked for body lotion
to keep his skin intact. Asked for vitamins.

I talked to Dorothy Johnson, who said that Bundy was always very
friendly. Every time anybody passed by he spent some time talking to
you and carrying on conversations, and she used the word that he was
jovial, did not indicate he was excessively happy, but just always very
jovial and more friendly person.

R.D.: What about Mr. Lubek's observation regarding Mr. Bundy's
appearance?

U.M.: Well, Mr. Lubek also very emphatically stated and thought
something bad about [the fact that] Mr. Bundy was well dressed. He
has been very well dressed throughout the trial here. Being well dressed
is not something bad. It's something good. We all raise our children
to, say, get dressed properly. Being well dressed indicates that he
was not depressed, indicates that he had motivation to keep up his
appearance. If you reviewed the notes and evaluations done in the past
by several people, one of the things that everybody was very observant
and impressed about is his need for personal appearance. Even in the
Leon County jail he was concerned about dental floss and his dental
care, his body cream, his skin condition. I think that's great, shows
that Mr. Bundy definitely is not depressed.

R.D.: Mr. Kennedy testified in detail about arrangements regarding the
marriage to Carole Boone?

U.M.: Yes, I have sat here just amazed that people are so upset that
Mr. Bundy got married in the courtroom. Whether people should get
married in the courtroom or somewhere else is their prerogative. I have
seen people dropping with parachutes ten thousand feet from the air
marrying on the way down. I was myself involved in a marriage where
people were being flown in a plane getting married and everybody else
sat on the ground. And I have known of people with scuba gear in
their mouth taking vows underneath the water.

In conclusion, Dr. Mahtre testified, "I have no doubt that Mr.
Bundy was more competent than any other person I have examined
so far." No doubt Ted enjoyed the state's evidence much more than
ours. Jim asked Dr. Mahtre only a few questions.

JIM COLEMAN: Dr. Lewis related in her testimony an incident from
Mr. Bundy's childhood involving knives. Do you recall that?

U.M.: Well, are we talking about the cats and dogs?

J.C.: No. We're talking about the knives.

U.M.: Knives, yes.

J.C.: Did you find that significant, that kind of behavior?

U.M.: Well, I come from a town where it's not unusual for kids to carry guns and knives.

J.C.: At three?

U.M.: At three I have seen people carry knives.

With the conclusion of Dr. Mahtre's testimony, the state had finished putting on its evidence. Still to come were final arguments to tie all the testimony together, and then an opportunity—according to Judge Sharp during the hearing—to respond to the audiotapes and videotapes of Ted that the state had presented and that we had not had time to review or to have Dr. Lewis evaluate. That's what we thought was still to come. Instead, as soon as the last witness had spoken, Judge Sharp said that final arguments would not be necessary and he was ready to issue his decision immediately:

> Gentlemen, the Court will submit a written finding of facts and conclusions in this case. Of course, everyone realizes that this is the second time that this Court has had this case. The Court reviewed this case last year and after having received boxes and boxes of transcripts and reviewed hundreds of pages of testimony, trial testimony, the court concluded that Mr. Bundy was competent to stand trial in the Kimberly Leach case.
>
> This is a very narrow hearing in which the Court was ordered to have an evidentiary hearing to specifically determine the competency of Mr. Bundy to stand trial in the Leach case.
>
> After hearing all of the testimony, the Court now concludes that he probably is the most competent serial killer in the country at this time.
>
> The evidence shows that he was a graduate in psychology with distinction. The Court notes that two of the courses in which he received A's in were in deviant behavior. The letters and the writings that are in evidence, the videotape, the exhibits by the witnesses point out very clearly that he is a most intelligent, articulate, complex individual. This Court views him as a diabolical genius. Certainly he was able to understand the proceedings and was able to assist in the preparation of his trial.
>
> I would like to particularly commend the team representing Mr. Bundy, they did a most commendable job, but I think it was merely an exercise in sophistry, because I don't really feel that anybody that was in this courtroom seriously, seriously, questions Mr. Bundy's competency.

The psychiatrists that testified in these several days, the Court was most interested in listening to the psychiatric testimony. Psychiatrists present most compelling testimony in that they are intelligent, they're very believable. I tend to believe everything a psychiatrist says because their presentations are so orderly. That's why it's important for both sides to buy a psychiatrist and have them come in here and testify.

This case has the most eminent psychiatrists in the country, and even in the world, and that's why it's necessary for eminent psychiatrists to come up and say why the other side's conclusions are incompetent. Psychiatrists are like NFL tackles, you have to get the best tackle you can to run over the opposition, and if you can't do that, you at least have to cancel them out. I think that's what was done in this case.

Judge Sharp also said that this case was not about a serious question of Bundy's competence but a case about the death penalty, in that the issue never would have been raised so vigorously if it were not for the death penalty. If his sentence had been life, the judge said, this case would not have been brought. He said that death cases were clogging his court, and the legislature should either abolish the death penalty altogether or find a way to prevent this endless litigation. He favored the latter.

Despite Diana's earlier warning, Ted was well behaved during the entire week, even detached. He sat between Jim and me, with his hands in his lap, never speaking unless I spoke to him, passively passing on the notes between Jim and me. He remained calm, even peaceful, in the face of all the work that had been done on his behalf, all the witnesses willing to come testify even though he had been so difficult. Judge Sharp's decision—although surprisingly sudden, vitriolic, and, again, so aggrandizing of Ted—was not unexpected, so neither Ted nor the rest of us suffered much disappointment. We had made our case for the Eleventh Circuit.

Ted relinquished the summery sports clothes we had bought for him, as well as the nifty shaving kit, and was taken back to the prison. Jim, John, Linda, and I spent the day at Disney World, where we bought Ted a Mickey Mouse watch as a memento, and rode the real roller coasters, the kind that come to a happy ending.

PART V

CHAPTER 15

On the first of January 1988, I moved out of Tatyana's Skin Care Salon. I wish I could say that it was because I finally found it intolerably ridiculous to be living in a beauty parlor, sharing my stove with a pot of simmering leg wax and my sofa with ladies in mud masks. But, in fact, the building was being torn down. I was pleasantly surprised at how nice it was to have my own apartment again—what a luxury to come home and not find strangers in my living room.

Once we'd had our competency hearing, and I'd filed our appeal of Judge Sharp's decision in the Eleventh Circuit Court of Appeals, I told Jim that was it. I really meant it this time. I told him I wanted off the case. My career was going down the tubes, and although I probably couldn't repair my relationship with the law firm, at least I could learn some skills other than death penalty law, which I intended never to practice again. Jim said he understood, he could see how I would feel that way, it made perfect sense. But, no deal. The case could not be done without me, it would be malpractice for the firm to assign it to someone else, he said. I had to stay on. Secretly, that was what I had wanted to hear: I was indispensable.

Ted was feeling antsy, too, probably for the same reason that I was, underneath all my protest. The bets were in, the horses were running, there would be only one winner at the end. If the Eleventh Circuit ruled in our favor, Ted's conviction in the Lake City case would be overturned (and, in effect, the Chi Omega case along with it, since the competency facts there were essentially the same—better, even). If they ruled against us, affirming Judge Sharp's judgment, all hope was lost—no subsequent court would take us seriously. Although Judge Godbold had retired from the bench since the panel had last heard our case; he had been replaced by Shirley Kravitz, another respected member of the court. With our blue-ribbon panel, whatever their decision was would stick. We expected a win. We had proven everything we had told them we could prove—and more. Our case looked as good, if not better, than it had a year ago, when the Eleventh Circuit had found it so compelling.

Certainly it would not be easy for them to rule in our favor, overturn Ted Bundy's conviction, and order a new trial. But they must have been prepared to do that when they sent the case back for a hearing. And it was hard to imagine how they could word an opinion affirming Judge Sharp's decision when our evidence was uncontradicted by any credible testimony. Judge Sharp and the state had merely speculated that there could have been a rational basis for Ted's behavior each time he had seemed to be acting irrationally. But, then, toward what end was he rationally directing that behavior? The state had suggested that Ted was purposefully seeking his own death—sabotaging the plea agreement and ruining his defense lawyers' efforts at trial in order to make sure he was executed. Judge Sharp had implied Ted had been rationally directing his behavior toward an eventual appeal by masterfully setting devious traps so as to appear, in hindsight, to have been incompetent. Neither scenario stood up against all the undisputed facts in evidence—*as demonstrated by the fact that they directly contradicted each other.* So, except for the public pressure, our case looked very good. Losing Judge Godbold, who obviously understood our position clearly, presumably would not make that much difference—Judge Johnson, at least, would know what needed to be done and have the courage to do it. But, there was always the Bundy Exception to worry about.

Ted was hit with another DR when he returned to FSP from Orlando, an unearned deprivation of his visiting and outdoor exercise privileges. Among the items in his file folder of legal materials on the Lake City case was a map of the Lake City area that had been used at his original trial. Prison officials charged him with possession of contraband escape matter, even though it was years out of date. Ted was furious. On January 18, 1988, he wrote me:

> When I first came to FSP I feared that the notoriety surrounding me would result in me being subjected to treatment harsher than my comrades. It never happened. Then after three warrants in 1986 I encountered in the prison personnel a kind of tension and animosity that I hadn't sensed in the previous seven years. Whether or not I have become some kind of lightning rod for frustration over the death penalty I don't know, but I do know that the officials here have demonstrated that they now intend to make life miserable for me.
>
> I must protect myself. This trend will only continue if something isn't done to stop it. The formal grievance process is a charade, controlled as it is by the very people [who] conspired to harass me in the first place. The logical place for me to go now is in the courts.

That meant the prison-conditions lawsuit he had ginned up with Diana Weiner as a way to justify to prison officials their continued "legal" visits. Ted's letters started taking an officious tone, asking me to communicate through "Ms. Weiner" whenever I needed to get something to him quickly, because she was his trusted confidante. On a visit, I confronted him: "Ted, quit giving me this 'Ms. Weiner' stuff. I know why you see her, and it has nothing to do with any lawsuit. She's beautiful, she's interested, she can come during lawyers' visiting hours, and you can have unsupervised legal visits with her."

Ted paused, and then grinned bashfully.

"That about sums it up," he said.

But later that spring I received a startling letter from Ted. We were still waiting on the decision from the Eleventh Circuit. In his letter, Ted said that he wanted to begin developing a strategy for cutting a deal with the governor for some specific amount of time, say, three more years, to live. In exchange, Ted would provide a full, descriptive confession of all of his crimes and agree not to fight his execution at the end of that time period. Ted's rationale for the three years was that it would take at least a year to reconstruct the crimes, because they had been so long repressed in his mind and it would be so emotionally draining to do so; the next two years of life would be his reward.

Even putting aside our feelings about the morality of such an exchange, Jim and I believed Ted's plan had no chance of success. Ted's execution was too great a political asset. Newly elected Governor Bob

were large and bony. I looked at his face. Ted's skin was darkening as he spoke. He was on a roll now, in a sort of trance, recalling every detail as he reviewed the fifteen-some-year-old film in his head, frame by frame. No detail was too small to recall, everything was important, everything had meaning. He was like a reverent disciple describing a spiritual revelation.

Ted was no longer censoring himself; he had slipped into a warm wave of memory and was transported. For the first time ever, I was afraid of him, acutely aware of how swiftly he could reach me with his hands if he wanted to, of how it would be too late by the time the guards on the other side of the glass reacted. It was the absolute misogyny of his crime that stunned me, his manifest rage against women, that left me no place to retreat to. He had no compassion for this victim at all. It wasn't that Ted took sadistic pleasure in telling his story, it was just that he was totally engrossed in the details. His murders were his life's accomplishments. To him, each recollection was a profound illustration of his skill, his willingness to go forward, his good luck. There had been no guarantees—to Ted, each completed murder had seemed like a small miracle.

He drove across the state line to a secluded place in the woods that he was already familiar with. He led the girl out of the car, assuring her that no harm would come to her. He made her strip and kneel on her hands and knees while he took Polaroid pictures of her. (For Ted, another small miracle had been that when his apartment had been searched upon his first arrest in Utah, the investigators had failed to check the building's utility room. When he was released on bail for the attempted abduction of Carole DeRonch he retrieved the shoebox of photos he'd hidden there and destroyed the most graphic and conclusive evidence of the true depth of his depravity.)

She cried.

He could see the look of terror in her eyes, her eyes begging for mercy. He kept reassuring her. He didn't like to see their hurt, he said, he didn't like to see his victim as a person—he wasn't the kind of person who would harm another. On several occasions, Ted had told me, "Believe me, Polly, I am not the kind of person who would hurt a fly. I never even hit a man. Except once, on the playground at grade school, and I didn't even want to do that, but the other kid forced me. I felt terrible afterward, disgusted with myself."

Then he got behind her, slung a noose around her neck, and strangled her as he raped her. He'd continued to reassure her he would let her go, and she had seemed to believe him. He said he'd felt a little sad that he could not let her go, that he had to kill her, but she would be able to identify him, of course. Afterward, he pulled her body deeper into the woods and, the next day, drove back to take more pictures and to cut her body into pieces.

When I got back to Washington, Jim's first words were, "You've changed."

Changed? Why should I be changed? Just because my client was, without a doubt, the Devil Incarnate, a killing machine set loose on society to do the will of a diabolical power?

I sat in the chair across from Jim's desk, unable to speak.

The Eleventh Circuit was taking forever to issue its decision following our competency hearing. My initial confidence that the court had seen that we had proved our case and was again reversing Judge Sharp was fading. Increasing anxiety took its place. Were they taking so long in order to nail down a decision in our favor so that it would be clear why they had to rule that way, or—and this was hard to believe—were they blowing us away on every single issue? We hadn't had a hearing on anything other than competency, and there were other important issues that could not be disposed of easily, such as Andy Anderson's hypnotically altered testimony and Vic Africano's failure to explore the issue of Ted's competency.

Nevertheless, we lost. We lost in an opinion written by the most liberal member of the panel, Frank Johnson, that made no logical sense whatever. But it was politically correct. In order to save the system, our panel ignored the law and relinquished the despicable Ted Bundy to the mob. The decision came out on July 7, 1988, when the court was already in summer recess. Incredibly, Judge Johnson wrote that he and his colleagues agreed with Judge Sharp that the testimony of Drs. Mutter and Mahtre "better accorded with the testimony of other witnesses and the associated exhibits" than did the testimony of Dr. Lewis and Dr. Tanay. Judge Johnson cited as evidence of Ted's ability to assist his counsel the tapes he was recording for the book about him. He noted that, on a tape Ted made immediately after the guilty verdict he'd said, "I can remember throughout the course of the trial, my counsel, myself, speculating on the reactions of jurors to state witnesses, the reactions of jurors to defense witnesses, speculating on the ineffectiveness of certain state witnesses, and the convincing qualities of our witnesses." But Ted's pompous ramblings on those tapes only reinforced the testimony of almost everyone who had ever worked with or examined him that he was more concerned about "playing lawyer," acting like "Perry Mason," than he was about the possibility of being sentenced to death. As usual, taken out of context, specific instances could be interpreted as something else—but not in the context of all that really happened. What about the plea bargain lost while he was secretly being treated with psychoactive drugs by the jails' physician? What about choosing to forgo a chance to plead for his life in order to perform a farcical marriage ceremony?

Now Ted was very hot to confess. Although we would appeal to the U.S. Supreme Court, and although new issues had arisen in the course of the evidentiary hearing that we could base new claims on, Ted knew as well as we that Jim and I had lost our best shot—but he didn't think it had been *his* last shot. All along, Ted had secretly thought that he was sitting on a gold mine—the true account of three dozen murders, the final answers to unsolved crimes, invaluable insight into the true mind of a killer. That's what he had meant during the last death warrant, when, in the final hours, he had pleaded with me to tell him as soon as it looked as if we might not get a stay. "There are some things I need to do," he'd said.

At last, he was going to bring out the gold, and barter for his life.

I was really dragging now. We had been robbed. We had proved our case and had still lost. Ted now was almost surely going to be executed—it was only a matter of time. Yet, I'd still have to keep going through the motions: a cert petition to the U.S. Supreme Court; then all new collateral proceedings. Before Judge Jopling testified at the competency hearing we'd had no way of knowing that he'd had discussions with the prosecutors, ex parte, without defense counsel present, about Ted's mental state and competency, and that he had relied in part on Judge Cowart's one-sided competency hearing in the Chi Omega case. We also, of course, had the entire Chi Omega case still pending before Judge Zloch. With the Eleventh Circuit decision against us, the die was cast; but even though ultimate success was virtually hopeless now, the case could well drag on for years, pulling me behind it like a spent nag.

The court did, at least, agree to extend its stay of execution to allow us to file a cert. petition asking the U.S. Supreme Court to review the decision. They gave us until November 15. I plodded through its preparation that fall of 1988 and, as usual, filed at the last minute, with the heart-stopping excitement of the usual last-minute word-processing breakdown. Again, the governor was poised with his hand above the death warrant, hoping I would miss the deadline. His office called the U.S. Supreme Court clerk every hour. When I ran in with the single copy that I had cut and pasted from earlier drafts, the guard in the clerk's office smiled kindly and said, "You made it."

With no other Bundy work pending, I began contentedly sorting roomfuls of documents in response to a discovery request in another huge products liability case. Ted sent his Christmas card early that year. His handwriting looked a little weak, a little shaky, and his spelling was off. There was a weariness, a resignation in his sign-off, "Thank you for all you've done for me. peace ted."

In mid December Judge Zloch awoke from his deep sleep. Sensing the direction of the wind, after the Eleventh Circuit had flatly rejected our evidence of Ted's incompetency and all our other issues in the Lake City case, Judge Zloch finally dared to respond to the summary judgment motion he'd required us to file (on an expedited schedule) fifteen months before. He set a full evidentiary hearing on all the issues in the Chi Omega case, to take place on January 23. Even Jim was not ready for this one. We were going to have to go through all that effort and tremendous expense again? With less than a month to pull the evidence together on all twenty-one issues? I started going through the motions, but it was like trying to run in a nightmare.

The news clippings I received weekly from Florida showed the media were predicting a quick decision by the Supreme Court and an execution in the next few months. My phone started ringing with calls again, asking if it was true that Ted was going to be executed soon and how was I going to stop it. As I began to make arrangements for Judge Zloch's hearing, the prison warned me that they had received death threats against Ted, and that we should take extra precautions ourselves if he was going to have to appear in Ft. Lauderdale. There was, again, no reason to have Ted at the hearing, but this time when I suggested to Ted that we ask to have him excluded, he balked. He couldn't decide. This time he thought that we were up to something, to be so eager for him to stay away. Ted was taking back control.

To keep human beings fully occupied yet completely unproductive, you need only present them with two dire but opposing possibilities to prepare for. Then, every time they start preparing for one eventuality, the anxiety mounts—and then suddenly the other one seems the more

December 13, 1988

Dear Polly,

How are you?
Going home for christmas?
Wherever your as, I hope you
have the best Christmas
Thank you for all you've done
for me.

Peace

ted

Season's Greetings

Christmas, 1988

likely and demands their immediate attention. The result is, nothing gets done. Judge Zloch's bombshell—scheduling a full evidentiary hearing in the Chi Omega case for January 23, while I was at the same time anticipating at any moment a Supreme Court decision in the Lake City case that would probably be swiftly followed by a fourth death warrant with a tight deadline—had just that result.

I was paralyzed. I had to prepare for the hearing, but it seemed so wasteful, so useless, so redundant. I had to call Dr. Lewis to start preparing her again; I had to prepare Ted's former attorneys to testify again. We would ask that the record of Judge Sharp's competency hearing be entered instead of presenting all these witnesses again, but there were no guarantees. We had to be prepared to put on a full hearing that day. It would be another great expense for the law firm. If only the two cases had remained consolidated, if only Judge Zloch had acted soon enough for that to happen. Still, I went through the motions. I struggled with Ted, and the court, to get him excused from the hearing; I worked out a security protocol with the sheriff's department; I filed preliminary briefs to establish the parameters of the hearing. I proceeded as if it were going to happen.

On Friday, January 13, I got a tip. The Supreme Court would be issuing its decision on Tuesday—Monday was a holiday, Martin Luther King's birthday. Somehow, I knew what that meant. Forget Judge Zloch's redundant evidentiary hearing; there was going to be a death warrant. I spent the weekend beginning to prepare for that, and promptly at 10:00 A.M. on Tuesday the Supreme Court announced that cert. was denied in the Lake City case—the Court had chosen not to review the Eleventh Circuit's cowardly and feebleminded decision denying every one of our claims. By noon, Governor Martinez had signed a death warrant, the second in the Lake City case, and set the execution for an unprecedented seven days later.

This was the first time that, on receiving an unfavorable decision, Jim was unable to come up with some way in which it was "Perfect! We have them just where we want them now!" Instead, for a few minutes, Jim and I sat facing each other in leaden silence. It was a rare shared moment between us: Our Ted was lost.

I spent the night throwing together whatever documents I could. I tried to anticipate all the dozens of different filings we would have to make in each of the four courts we would be addressing starting tomorrow. Mark Menser refused my request that the state join us in asking Judge Zloch to postpone his hearing, and Judge Zloch refused my motion to postpone. Perhaps he thought that we had engineered this execution date as a clever trick to throw him off track.

Around midnight a radio talk show producer in Seattle called me at the office, asking if I'd go on the air to explain what was happening with the case. I usually said no to these kind of requests, because all anyone wanted to know was "what about the victims?", for which I had no answer. But the producer assured me that the host wanted to talk about the death warrant and what we would do to try to stop it. I wanted a break from the frantic preparations, and it was a Seattle station, not one in Florida—I figured I wouldn't be doing the case any harm—so I agreed to go on. A few seconds later, I was on the radio, being introduced by the host, and his very first question was: "Miss Nelson, I know you're Ted Bundy's lawyer, but *what about the victims?*"

Around 4:00 A.M., I realized we were going to need help. Once we got to Florida, we would be sprinting—Jim would be arguing and drafting, I would be drafting and dealing with Ted and the court clerks. We needed someone to take care of us. I called Mike Ollen, our law clerk, at home and told him he was going to Florida at 7:30 A.M., and to bring his American Express card.

The three blurry-eyed members of the final Bundy team met at National airport at seven Wednesday morning, Jim looking expectantly at my document carriers, hoping they contained the key to stopping this execution. We flew to Gainesville, where we met with Ted and Diana Weiner. Diana had tried to reserve all the attorney time remaining until the execution for herself and had taken a hotel room near the prison so that she could keep as close contact with Ted as possible. Diana had already approached Governor Martinez with the idea of postponing the execution to give Ted time to confess. They believed that the next best step was an all-out media campaign to create a groundswell of public support for delaying Ted's execution. After some discussion, Ted at least agreed to hold off any public announcement on the confessions until Monday, until we had had a chance to try to get the execution stayed through the courts.

In Lake City we filed our motion for a stay of execution, based on Judge Jopling's admitted ex parte communication with the prosecution about Ted's competence to stand trial. We had our last sit-down supper together in Jacksonville that night.

There was a sense of dread on this warrant that I'd never had to face before. Before I had always believed the execution would be stayed.

This time I knew there was very little chance. Our best issue had been competency, and now that was dead. Besides, capital defendants nearly always are allowed one run through the federal system. We'd had ours. Most capital defendants go through more than once; new issues arise and are given a hearing. Jim and Jeff had saved Booker on his third warrant, and this was only Ted's second in the Lake City case. But we knew that Ted was not going to get any leeway. It was the general perception that we'd had our shot, and that now it was time to let the inevitable happen. As if it all had been only a game, or a performance. But just to make it interesting, the press now speculated that we'd win.

Thursday started out with a bang. I went down to breakfast only to find that Jim had gotten an idea for yet another legal motion during the night and had driven himself to the airport to put the documents on a plane to Tallahassee. It unnerved me to have him gone. We had a hearing at nine in Lake City, and Jim did not know the roads of Jacksonville. Mike Ollen hadn't insisted on driving when Jim had knocked at his door and asked for the keys to the rental car. Mike did not make that mistake again. He stayed close to Jim from then on— we had to keep our fighter in the ring.

Starting that morning I had the feeling of time slipping away like blood dripping from a fresh wound. There was only a limited supply; each minute of time lost was lost forever.

At the Lake City hearing, Judge Jopling disqualified himself from presiding because he was a material witness to our claim. Judge Peach immediately took his place and, after allowing us thirty minutes to read the state's brief in response to ours, heard oral argument and ruled against us. He also informed us that Judge Zloch had canceled his evidentiary hearing in the Chi Omega case. Not, we suspected, for judicial economy; not because our client was in litigation over his imminent execution. Judge Zloch most likely canceled his hearing to prevent any claim that it entitled Ted to a stay of execution. Then we were off to Tallahassee, where the Florida Supreme Court had already scheduled a hearing, anticipating our loss in Lake City, for 1:00 Friday afternoon.

When we got there, however, we learned that it had been moved up to 8:00 A.M. We also learned that the court, *and the attorneys for the state,* already had copies of the briefs we hadn't even filed yet, because the U.S. Supreme Court clerk had supplied them from the copies we had lodged with him as a courtesy, so that the Court could monitor the case. Everything was skewed because of the governor's arbitrarily set execution date. Courts sharing information with prosecutors, hearings scheduled one after the other, with no time for deliberation by the court, no time to prepare the required papers, just because the governor decided to allow only seven days in the warrant period. Just because no court wanted to be the one to delay, for even one day, this highly anticipated public killing.

We checked into the hotel in Tallahassee on Friday afternoon, all under Mike's name, and prepared to work overnight at CCR to create the briefs and other papers to be filed in the Florida Supreme Court the next day. I talked to Ted on the phone twice that day—as I did all that week. He was extremely distracted by the meetings he was having with law enforcement officers from the western states, and it was hard to hold his attention. He reiterated, however, his promise not to go public until Monday.

At 2:00 A.M., I caught fire. My usual on-the-road writing block burst and I told Jim and Mike to go get some sleep. Jim strode out confidently, but Mike lagged behind, bewildered and more than a little concerned.

"Trust me," I said. "I've got it under control."

I had a sudden, firm sense that I was going to be able to complete the fifty-page brief and that I was going to do it by six-thirty, in time to complete the word-processing and copying by 8:00 A.M. And Jim knew it too. I wrote furiously, nonstop, almost autonomically, for four hours. There's nothing like a real deadline for focusing the mind.

Friday morning I had to sit in the audience rather than at counsel table because I was still in my sweat pants from the night before, but the Florida Supreme Court had the briefs. And their questions to Jim and the state's attorney showed they'd read them. In fact, at the end of the hearing, we began to allow ourselves a glint of an optimism we had never expected to feel in state court. By lunch we were practically giddy. Maybe, miraculously, our quest for a stay was over. But five minutes into my nap, the word came: We had lost. Time to call Ted, time to prepare for the proceedings in Judge Sharp's courtroom tomorrow. His law clerk kept calling, demanding our brief in advance. When could we have prepared it? It seemed possible we were actually *aiding* in Ted's execution by meeting all these ridiculous deadlines. Shouldn't we just throw up our hands and say that we cannot argue the case in a different court every day and prepare a dozen pleadings every night? It was so obviously a charade, and our participation and ability to produce in this manner only gave it the appearance of justice that allowed it to continue. But we dared not risk Ted's life by calling the bluff.

Pat called from Washington to warn me that threatening phone calls had come into the firm. It was Inauguration Day, but Ted pushed George Bush and his promise of a "kinder, gentler America" off the headlines in Florida. Once again, I was able to read about my own case, my own activities, standing arm's length from the news rack.

On Saturday we flew from Tallahassee to Orlando before dawn in a darkened prop plane, like terrorists. The headline in the airport newsstand sealed our fate even before the hearing began: BUNDY ADMITS TO 12 SLAYINGS. Ted had broken his promise to wait until Monday; he and Diana had released the terms of Ted's offer believing it would cause a ground swell of public support, despite our warning that it would have the opposite effect. No court would ever stick its neck out to save him now; there could be no pretense of lingering doubt about guilt; the public would never stand for a stay of execution after such a provocative warm-up.

We arrived at the hearing to find that Judge Sharp had taken it upon himself to identify and call all the potential witnesses to be there. Had he interviewed them to see what their testimony would be, too? Did he have another twenty-page reasoned opinion already in the word-processor? One of those called this time was Vic Africano. He looked extremely nervous in the courtroom—he was not comfortable with the possibility of testifying against a former client (and friend), and he knew we would have to try to destroy his credibility if he did—but, always the Southern gentleman, he called me "Darlin'" when I shook his shaking hand.

The star witness, however, was Judge Jopling, who had come up with an explanation of how he had happened to receive a copy of the Chi Omega competency hearing transcript from the prosecutors without the knowledge of defense counsel. He had been mistaken, he said, when he'd testified at the evidentiary hearing. He had not received those documents at the trial in 1980, as he had thought, but had only seen them a few days before the hearing in 1987, as part of his preparation. He was a busy judge, and apparently it was difficult for him to remember whether he had read something seven days or seven years before. In the course of this incredible retraction, however, the hapless judge backed into another helpful revelation: He had called Judge Cowart during the Lake City trial and talked to him, or his secretary, or maybe he had just left a message (he started backpedaling as soon as he saw where Jim was going with it), but, anyway, what he had asked for and what he had gotten was a copy of Judge Cowart's opinion in the Chi Omega case *to use as a guide to his own opinion in the Lake City case*! So much for an independent judgment of Ted's guilt and punishment.

In the briefs we filed that morning we had slipped in an issue that neither Judge Sharp nor the state's attorneys had anticipated. And because this hearing was not being conducted for the purpose of *hearing* us, but to get *rid* of us, this unanticipated claim slipped right on through. It was an issue that currently was pending in the Supreme Court, and the Court had been staying executions in cases in which the issue had been raised, to allow them time to rule. At issue was whether the death penalty is valid when imposed by a jury whose responsibility for making that decision has been diminished by the judge or the prosecutor; i.e., "You, the jury, will vote for life in prison or death by electrocution, but, of course, the judge has the final responsibility for imposing that sentence" or "Your decision on life or death is merely advisory; the judge will make the final decision." In other words, don't let your reluctance to kill stand in the way of voting for the death penalty, because it is really the judge who decides; it is really the judge whose conscience bears the burden—not yours. Under Florida law the jury's decision is final and only may be overridden by the judge for specific cause, so any implication to the contrary is false. Because the state hadn't anticipated that claim, they were not prepared to argue that it was procedurally barred, that is, ineligible even to be considered because it should have been raised the last time around. As a result, Judge Sharp dismissed it on the merits—thus making it eligible for appeal—along with our claim that Judge Jopling had denied Ted the requisite individualized judgment by copying Judge Cowart's opinion and death sentence. Another significant, useless victory.

At noon, Jim, Mike, and I retreated to the hotel near the courthouse in Orlando for lunch and arranged to fly back to Tallahassee along with the state's attorneys in the state plane. The state attorney now in charge of the case was Carolyn Snurkowski, who was especially courteous, particularly in contrast to some of the death penalty zealots we'd had to deal with before. (One of them had told a newspaper reporter a few years back that he had firsthand knowledge that the death penalty was a deterrent: One time he had been so mad at his wife, he said, that only the thought of his own execution had held him back from the brink.)

We expected to prepare our request to the Eleventh Circuit for permission to appeal Judge Sharp's ruling (he had denied a certificate of probable cause again) back at CCR that evening. In calls to the Eleventh Circuit clerk from pay phones in the lobby, however, we learned that if we wanted to file an appeal brief, we had to do it by three that afternoon. We immediately checked into a room and litigated in outer space—trapped in Orlando with two hours to file an appeal, we were without a typewriter, a library, our files, or the evidence. Susie Muro and Mark Leimkuhler—a legal assistant and an associate at Wilmer—rushed into the law firm that Saturday afternoon to search through the fifteen-thousand-page trial record for examples of Judge Jopling or the state attorneys diminishing the jurors' responsibility in sentencing. I sat on the phone selecting among the frantically called out possibilities—"Nope, nope. Yes! That's perfect! Send it! What's next? Nope, nope. Try the examination of the next juror!"—which they then faxed to the Eleventh Circuit. As Jim drafted pages of the brief, Mike Ollen called them in to a secretary at CCR from the phone in the bathroom so they could be typed and faxed to the court. At 2:30 the court clerk called to say *stop*, we were jamming their fax machine; they had enough. By 5:00, the Eleventh Circuit had ruled—request for permission to file an appeal DENIED. The applicable legal standard for such a denial is that the claims are so frivolous that there is no chance that any reasonable jurist would find that any had merit. They were wrong about that.

We took a commercial flight to Tallahassee that evening—the state's attorneys had gone on home hours earlier without bothering to try to file a brief at all. When we got in, Jim crashed, but Mike and I chose to live life a little instead. We sat in an Italian restaurant, savoring the respite, the normality of the surroundings: families eating together, couples on dates. We went to a Kmart to buy some fresh clothes and lingered there, roaming the aisles. It felt like such a safe spot, well lit, carefree. I spotted an outrageously sleazy dance skirt—black netting and neon ruffles—and stood in front of it, wistfully, for the longest time. Mike bought underwear for Jim as a surprise.

The next day was Super Bowl Sunday, and apparently the courts were not going to let Ted Bundy's pesky lawyers ruin the game for them. The clerks for the Eleventh Circuit and the U.S. Supreme Court refused to take our calls all day; the justices of the Florida Supreme Court left town for a convention. Jim and Mike spent the day writing the two U.S. Supreme Court briefs, a Florida Supreme Court brief on the juror responsibility issue (in case the U.S. Supreme Court thought it was a problem that we hadn't filed that claim in a state court before), and a whole new collateral petition for the court in Lake City, claiming that Judge Jopling had simply copied Judge Cowart's opinion rather than making an independent judgment. For each of these, of course, there were the half-dozen auxiliary documents that always had to accompany them. I served as expediter, keeping track of what was needed, organizing it, placating CCR's word-processing staff—who were getting sick of us. Dr. Lewis called to offer to come down to Florida, to help Ted if she could, to be with us. "I feel so helpless up here, thinking of what you are going through there," she said. I gladly accepted. "And don't worry about me," she said. "I'll call the airlines myself."

But mostly that Sunday I talked to Ted. He was depressed. He had come down from the excitement of planning the confession deal and beginning to talk with law enforcement, and now he could see that it had come to nothing. He had expected that it would at least feel good, that he would be talking to people who understood. But it hadn't felt good; it had felt dirty. The law enforcement officers hadn't wanted to understand, they just wanted the facts—and they did not want to give him any satisfaction for providing them. He had wasted the last week of his life, undone the dignity and serenity he had built up over his years in prison in preparation for this time. I suggested he cancel the big press interview he had scheduled for the next day, and his law enforcement interviews, and instead meet with Dr. Lewis and I. He readily agreed.

That evening, I flew to Jacksonville to meet Dr. Lewis. (Imagine this case without a rich law firm's credit cards. A solo practitioner would have had to throw up her hands long before this point.) Her plane had been delayed in New York, and she called me from Atlanta, where she was stranded for the night, but determinedly poised to take the first flight out in the morning. When I called Superintendent Turner at the prison to tell him we'd be late in the morning, he told me gruffly that he would not extend Dr. Lewis's time beyond one o'clock in any case, and, by the way, I would not be allowed to attend because Ted was on phase II of death watch and was not allowed any further contact visits with his attorneys. I argued that Dr. Lewis could not interview Ted without my assistance, that I knew the facts necessary for her work. Mr. Turner was noncommittal.

Lying heavily on the king-size bed in the airport hotel, I just kept dialing the phone. I called Susan Carey, a lawyer who had worked with other inmates in the last days before their execution, and asked her what we should be thinking about. She told me to have Ted ask that his final legal visit and final personal visit be combined into one four-hour visit. Most inmates were granted permission to do this, which allowed them to have more people around them for a longer time on the night before their execution. After that four-hour period of "noncontact" visits across the glass barrier, the inmate was allowed an hour-long "contact" visit with the person closest to him. I also called Jim, and asked him to attend the execution. I did not want Ted to be alone at his execution, and something might happen during the process that would require an advocate. But I couldn't go—I was afraid I wouldn't be able to take it. I called Ted's wife and mother to tell them that we were going to lose him. Jim was still pursuing a stay but, in fact, there was no hope. They were furious with Ted and felt deeply betrayed that he had publicly confessed without telling them first. They had maintained their love for him on the basis of his innocence—or at least on his steadfast assertion of innocence, however incredible. Both women were bitter now, to have had that blanket of protection stripped away from them so harshly—by reading it in the newspapers and hearing it from reporters who wanted to know their reaction.

Neither Carole nor Louise came to Florida for the execution. Ted told them they didn't have to, but I don't think they were inclined to come, either.

It was as silent as a tomb in the hotel dining room Monday morning. No one was up yet, except for the airline employees breakfasting in their burgundy uniforms. The windows looked out onto a still-dark

asked. "I understand from Polly you told a lot of the law enforcement people about some of the murders."

"I have, and it doesn't feel any better. Not yet, 'cause I haven't really told anybody, I don't think, the whole story. Because all they're going to do is explain it for their own purposes and this is a serious statement on my part."

Ted was sitting crouched over, mumbling into his handcuffed hands on the small table. I was sitting directly across from him; Dorothy sat off to the side. Now Ted raised his eyes and steadily peered into mine. He seemed torn about continuing on the way he was. He had started to speak coherently and seemed to want to continue, but something was holding him back. He motioned for me to lean in closer, and when I did he cupped his hands around my ear and whispered,

"Are you going to go for incompetency?"

He meant incompetency to be executed and he knew better than that. He knew the only purpose of our visit was to allow him a sympathetic ear and a hope of greater understanding. But when Ted had abruptly canceled the big press conference he'd scheduled for today, and then I had arranged for Dr. Lewis and me to see him instead, the state and the press were certain we were going to claim that Ted was not competent to be executed, that he was not presently in a mental state capable of understanding what was happening and why. Although Ted knew this had not been my intention when I last talked to him, apparently he had begun to consider the possibility himself. That was why he was acting so strange, so uncommunicative: He was planning to fake incompetence.

"No." I whispered back. "You know why we're here. Incompetency is not a viable claim here." Things had certainly changed. Ted was feeling the reality of his death sentence—at last. Now *he* was the one who wanted to raise incompetency—and in this context it truly would be a false claim. In this, the most humble supplication Ted had ever made in his life, he seemed for once an integrated person, without hidden subtext or reserve. He grabbed my hands and said, "Please."

I thought my heart would break. I had always wanted to see this Ted, this Ted that I had thought I was going to help when I first took the case, this Ted that was helpless and vulnerable and in fear for his life. But I had never seen him until this moment. Until this moment I was never really important to Ted, not in the way I had thought I'd be. All along he'd thought he'd held the ultimate key to saving his life—his confession. The legal remedies that I'd pursued had, to him, been long shots, delaying mechanisms to put off as long as possible the need to play his trump card. But his well-guarded treasure had turned out to be fool's gold.

I asked Dorothy to step out of the room.

"Please," he'd said. On the last day of his life, Ted was sincerely asking for help for the first time. I searched my heart for the right response. I had come down to Starke with Dorothy to help Ted give meaning to his last hours. To allow him to explore who he really was, what had really happened to his life. To allow him spiritual grace after all his frantic gamesmanship, dignity in his final hours. A false claim of incompetence to be executed would destroy all that. I would have to lie, Ted would have to lie, Dorothy would have to be persuaded to go along—and I had no expectation that she would go along. Then there would be more court action, filings, the state would have their psychiatrists examine him. Their examination would be brutal and their results predetermined. The execution would be put off another day, or two at the most, while the courts dealt swiftly with the claim, their decisions predetermined as well. Ted was going to die that week in either case.

"I don't think it's the way to go, Ted," I said. His hands still grasped mine, we were still looking straight into each other's eyes, inches apart. I felt him holding on to me, holding on to my words. I felt him trusting me to guide him through this. "It will never fly," I said. "It would only disturb your dignity. I don't think you want to go that way." After a moment he nodded and relaxed his grip. I looked for signs of despair, but he seemed at peace with the decision. His eyes softened and his faced eased. I called Dorothy back into the room.

I told Dorothy that Ted and I had discussed the possibility of claiming incompetency to be executed. She expressed the firm opinion that it would not be a good use of the rest of his time. He needed to be real now, not waste his time performing a charade. It was important that he spend the time remaining on what really mattered. This interview meant a lot to Ted, so much that, when it was finished, he asked us to make certain portions of it available to others so that they would better understand him. Dr. Lewis recorded the session on a tape recorder, as was her usual practice.

Dorothy asked Ted if there was something he thought she should know that he hadn't told her before.

TED BUNDY: Well, it's not so much that I held something back from you or tried to conceal myself from you. But there should, there's a lot you should know.

DOROTHY OTNOW LEWIS: Like what?

T.B.: I don't know specifically. It was an evolutionary process.

D.L.: Evolutionary process?

T.B.: Well, you see, I don't dispute your feeling, your belief, that there's some kind of precursors, environmental precursors, to this violent behavior in my early years.

Ted had always been very uncomfortable talking about his childhood and family. He was always on guard that something he said would be interpreted to reflect badly on his family.

T.B.: But I must tell you that I did not begin to detect anything consciously until, you know, I was twelve, fourteen, fifteen, and even then there wasn't anything that involved acting out aggression.

D.L.: It was more fantasy? Let me tell you why I'm asking. Before I came down here, on the plane, I reread Michaud's book, and from my talking with you and from what he talked about, you talked about "another Ted," you talked about another entity. So what I was wondering, when do you think this second entity began? That's why I asked about an imaginary companion.

T.B.: Okay. Well, this is—"imaginary companion" I interpreted as some childhood fantasy, but the entity that Michaud talks about is somewhat different. And that's the word I used, I didn't want to use another person or personality. Just yesterday I was trying to explain it, and it cautions my consciousness—that's the best I can describe. A portion of my personality was not fully—it began to emerge . . .

D.L.: How did you conceptualize it?

T.B.: It was unobtrusive at first. It was something that was just something that kind of grew on me. It became—by the time I realized how powerful it was, I was in big trouble. . . .

Ted paused here for several moments, then began again.

T.B.: In my high school years I was really out of touch with my peers—really out of touch. I mean, my old neighborhood friends went on to groups, and high school, being [part of] a bigger community—and I was sort of just stuck. I spent a lot of time with myself.

D.L.: Why were you out of touch?

T.B.: I don't know. The summer—something happened, something, I'm not sure what it was . . . Well, I would think that, at the time I wasn't thinking about anything illegal or criminal or aggressive necessarily. I would fantasize about coming up to some girl sunbathing in the woods, or something innocuous like that.

D.L.: And what, and you're doing what?

T.B.: I'm just watching her . . . It was basically voyeuristic. I mean, among my sexual activities was to look out of my bedroom window, which looked down into the neighbor's bathroom . . . Nothing really harmful or threatening, but things which, because I was totally on my own and wasn't sharing this with anybody—nobody could say, "Gee, that's weird, don't do that," you see. I mean, for instance, over a two- or three-year period, I would go out at night, a warm night—we had some woods in back of our house—I would take off all my clothes and run around the woods.

D.L.: When you were thirteen, fourteen?

T.B.: Yeah, again, I wasn't flashing on anybody or trying to imagine me stalking anybody, but it was just an innocent kind of sport. So there's nothing at this point that's bad, but I see what was happening. I was beginning to get involved in what they would call, developed a preference for what they call, autoerotic sexual activity. And that's exactly what it was.

D.L.: Would you ever then go out and look through people's windows?

T.B.: No, I never, I never did that.

D.L.: Just looking in your neighbor's bathroom?

T.B.: Again, this is something that a lot of young boys would do and without intending any harm, and that was basically where I was at the time. But I see how it later formed the basis for the so-called entity, that part of me that began to visualize and fantasize more violent things and have a desire for the material of the environment—a violent nature.

Here's an example, I can begin to see it coalescing. In my mid and late teenager years there were these two sets of currents—at various levels of existence, of course, like school and family and church—but among them was one current with its interest in some more morbid material. It wasn't necessarily a sexual interest—I didn't masturbate—but it was detective magazines, books on crime in the library.

D.L.: What were you looking for?

T.B.: I was looking for basically violence in books in the library, but it was more than that. I was also looking for books that had descriptions of sexual activity and such as one could find in the library and so . . .

All through the morning, Ted would concentrate and focus for a while on the topics Dr. Lewis was exploring, remembering the past, looking inside himself, then the realization of his present circumstances would creep back in and wash over him, breaking his train of thought. When this would happen he would shudder and stop speaking. Ted would be at a loss; I would be at a loss. Dorothy seemed to interpret these lapses as Ted avoiding a painful subject—exhibiting a defense mechanism against the pain of the past. I thought it was amazing he could think about anything *but* his present situation.

D.L.: It's clear its very hard to talk about. You must be aware of that.

T.B.: It's hard to talk about right now because I'm going through some other things. I'm having a hard time articulating—we're talking about something that happened a long time ago.

D.L.: Something that you felt was the beginning of the entity. Go on and tell me a little more about how you feel your entity developed.

T.B.: On the one hand it developed, you might say, not an obsession necessarily, but a very intense interest in this kind of material and maybe who I was. Even more inflammatory was my interest in the detective magazines which I've told you about. Very potent material, the imagery, the photographs on the cover, pictures of dead bodies in the book.

Ted paused again here, looking away, looking through the glass walls of the interview room to the activities of the prison staff moving about outside the warden's office.

T.B.: Excuse me. It's just this other stuff, not related to this, what we're talking about. This—what's happening with me here. Every once in a while it crashes in on me. Here I am kind of absorbed in our conversation and memories of the past, and all of a sudden reality will flip in on me and there will be a rush . . . The only reason I was able to sleep is because of what Polly and Jim are doing, and then I would say to myself, well, there's still hope.

D.L.: But I certainly know what that wave of terror is like.

T.B.: Yeah.

D.L.: We'll stop every so often and . . .

T.B.: Take a deep breath.

D.L.: Cross our fingers.

T.B.: Take a deep breath. I'll be all right.

When Dorothy's tape ran out, Ted stopped and changed it himself. He had become very proficient at managing tape recorders over the last couple of days, as he spent hours and hours recounting minute details of his crimes to law enforcement officials from Utah and Washington, with Diana by his side.

Ted talked to us about the fallout of what was probably the pivotal time in his development. He had been reaching a high that summer during college—in fact he was on the high end of a bipolar mood swing, although he could never see himself that way. He had registered for a summer class in Chinese at Stanford University, and he was dating a young woman named Diane, whom he greatly admired for her beauty and social stature. But both endeavors ended in utter failure. He was immediately lost in a class that was way over his head, and he failed in his attempt to make love to this young woman who was so important to him—he was unable to perform.

T.B.: What I did was, after the incident at Stanford and with Diane that summer, I began to turn more to the fantasy life and pornography than ever before. It was like I just ran for cover emotionally and, of course, that was the only thing that made sense. Nothing was giving me great satisfaction now, not even school, and at least masturbating gave a temporary kind of gratification and all that. I think that was like an opening of a door on a chaotic situation that allowed these interests to mold, and at that time my sexual preoccupation was becoming more tinged with violent fantasy.

D.L.: Would the fantasy be of Diane?

Ted took some time to search his memory.

T.B.: Yes. I think it changed over and I began to, she began to appear in fantasies where I was not the perpetrator, actor in the fantasy. These would be fantasies based on things I had read.

D.L.: Who was the perpetrator?

T.B.: Whoever—somebody else, but not me . . . Some faceless character, but it was not me. What is significant is that later, when it does become me, I think that's another step, that's another breakthrough. Taking the next step down the road.

D.L.: What did he do to her?

T.B.: Well, it was . . . I think he raped her, . . . but he didn't, . . . he didn't . . . I didn't, I didn't take it . . . he didn't kill her or anything like that.

D.L.: And when did they become actions?

T.B.: Oh . . .

Ted paused for a long time. Each time he was forced to make an actual confession he had to leap a steep barrier he had built inside himself long ago.

T.B.: In the course of the next year, my life continued in this highly chaotic state, this very sad state, and I eventually fled the Pacific Northwest again and went back to Philadelphia, which is where my family's from. Looking for some sort of roots, some way to stabilize myself. You can understand that, 'cause there was so much unhappiness. I had dropped out of school, and nothing was right. So I stayed in Philadelphia for a while but still didn't find what I was looking for— I didn't just go looking for my father, per se. I mean, it was just going back to be where I was from. Just looking for something that made sense. And I couldn't stay there for long. I didn't go back there to be in school. I was just going back more or less just to get away.

It's in early '68. I went back to Philadelphia, made my way back to Seattle, and worked in politics—that was a presidential year—all summer long. Got a job after the campaigns were over in November of '68, and I decided I was going to go back to school, which seemed like an important decision, but I couldn't go to school in the Pacific Northwest, so I decided, well, I'm going to go to Temple, which is in Philadelphia, again going back to Philadelphia. And so in early '69 I did go to Philadelphia for the second semester at Temple. It's at that point that I think again that I reached the point of acting out. In part because it was quickly apparent to me that this place, just a change of place, wasn't going to solve anything, and I was hoping it would and school was just . . .

D.L.: Aunt Audie talked of times you would go off.

T.B.: Yeah, well, she was probably referring to that time. There were many times like that in, let's say, the late winter, early spring of '69. It's when we're starting to see this entity begin to reach the point where it's necessary to act out. No longer just to read books, or to masturbate, or fantasize, but to actually begin to stalk, to look. I was still very heavily . . . I think what really got me to that point, what pushed me over the edge from thought into action, was often times I would take the commuter train from Philadelphia to New York to Forty-second Street. I mean, where you have the hardest of the hard core, and this feeling was you just can't get any more graphic than this, but it just isn't enough.

D.L.: You actually saw live porno there?

T.B.: Mostly magazines and books and things. I wasn't analyzing this way, in the sense of what was going on, I thought, "Gee, this is great!" But I just kept coming up to it and I'd wonder what it was really like. And that began the lack of satisfaction, gratification, from any other part of my life, including school. It began to become more appealing because it offered something, even short term, a . . . a sense of excitement, sense of control, a sense of domination, a sense of adventure, all that. It became very appealing. In addition, it was all out of sight. Nobody knew about this but me. Nobody could say, "Straighten up, you're getting pretty bizarre here. You ought to see somebody." I held it so closely that nobody could tell what was going on, so I wasn't susceptible to any kind of modification. It was entirely, basically independent. It was a time bomb.

And what happened was, for instance, I found myself at least on one occasion . . . I remember coming into New York this time, this very first time I was going to try something, you know, of course it was very . . . amateurish, because with most any activity you learn by doing. And you learn, you can read books, but reading books and doing the real thing is something else. Right. Rationally, I knew that this is not one of the cases where a lot of trial and error was allowed. I mean, if you made a mistake, that was the end of the game—you went to jail. So this was something where I knew I had to be very tentative, because a real blunder would mean the end of the learning experience, so to speak. So I remember, in the late winter of '69, going to New York, and I'd done all those things. Like I bought a fake mustache and bought hair stuff—some hair dye. Oh, I registered in some seedy hotel-motel under a false name and all these things. I had this horribly inept plan in mind, and I wasn't sure exactly where it was going to go.

D.L.: What was the plan?

T.B.: Following some woman in some hotel to her room and rushing in on her and doing . . . I wasn't sure what . . . I think sexually assaulting her. But beyond that I really didn't . . . it was really some half-cocked effort.

D.L.: What were you thinking? Did you have any ambivalence?

T.B.: Ambivalence? You mean indecisiveness?

I was still trying to pull some sense of remorse or at least moral hesitation from Ted, as I prompted, "Or, as you were proceeding, the feeling that you shouldn't proceed?"

T.B.: Well, yes. There was still a very, there was still, in essence, a barrier there to that kind of conduct. That's another thing we haven't discussed is how, in essence, my other erotic behavior—masturbation, fantasy—was a way of deconditioning feelings of inhibition against engaging in conduct. At the same time it was a way of dealing with remorse, I mean, repressing any kind of remorse or guilt because the fantasy became more graphic cach time it was aroused.

D.L.: When was the first time that you actually acted?

"All right," Ted said, and then paused.

D.L.: You don't have to tell me if you don't want to.

T.B.: Well, later on that same year, in the spring, I went to Ocean City. Ocean City, New Jersey. And just hanging out at the beach, and looking at the young women, trailing them around. And my plan again was—I had never done anything like this before—I was, it was very confusing, kind of, and fearful, and yet I felt compelled to continue to, sort of, act out this vision . . .

D.L.: Was the vision still of Diane?

T.B.: No, this time it was just someone, some attractive woman.

D.L.: Was it now you in the vision?

T.B.: Oh, absolutely. By now that had taken place and that had started—I think it's safe to say in early 1969, maybe not long after I arrived in Philadelphia. I don't have a clear recollection of one time or how this happened for the first time, although I do have a vision similar to that. Okay, so I was just stalking around the downtown area of this small resort community and I saw a young woman walking along. And the reason I paused the first time—I think I may have misled you and wanted to straighten that out—I didn't actually kill someone this time, but I really, for the first time, approached a victim, spoke to her, tried to abduct her, and she escaped. But that was frightening in its own way. But that was the first—the kind of step that you just—that you don't—that I couldn't ever return from.

D.L.: Did you ever think about talking to a psychiatrist or someone about this?

T.B.: No. I always . . . felt . . . even though several years later, in 1972, I was going back to school and I felt I had my life back together and I had a purpose, and I was going out with a nice young woman,

Liz Kloepfer, and things seemed to be good. I felt like I had myself
back together. I was disturbed about what I was doing during 1969 in
Philadelphia. And, yet, I figured that it was in control, really. It wasn't,
I wasn't, and I probably . . .

D.L.: Do you remember the first time you actually killed someone?

Again, Ted's strong inner barrier against revealing the truth of his
crimes rose up. He paused, sighed.

T.B.: Look . . . I'll . . .

D.L.: Are you frightened that that will jeopardize your situation now?

T.B.: Not really, I shouldn't be, not at this late stage.

D.L.: How do you feel it might? I don't think it would, but I'll respect
your fears.

T.B.: You see, none of this makes a difference . . . Let me deal with
it on this level. We'll talk about . . . it was a couple years later, but
can I just talk about the difference between that one incident at Ocean
City and the first time?

D.L.: Yes.

T.B.: The difference was that it was sort of half-hearted, sort of confused, sort of, there's a lack of—it was a serious, serious, manifestation.
But it wasn't a complete, total, focused kind of aggression when I knew
what I was doing, I knew what I wanted and was going to do it, and I
had the experience and skill to carry it off. Several years later this
process continued. The acting out, getting closer and closer. I know
that I, in Ocean City, I realized just how inept I was. And so that
made me more cautious, and so I didn't do that again for a long time.
It scared me. It really scared me. And when I stopped doing it I would
get the feeling, you know, like a person who's on a diet, get the feeling
I've lost five pounds.: "I'm great, I'm going to be okay now." And then
something happens and you start eating. Well, I was feeling that I was
on top of this, I'm okay. I'm not going to do this anymore. I got scared
straight, no problem. And then I did put my life together in 1972.

D.L.: Did you continue to stalk women in Philadelphia?

T.B.: No, that was that.

D.L.: Just in '69 in Ocean City, and you then stopped everything.

T.B.: Right, right. And that's the pattern that you would see for the
next several years. There would be acting out and then, let's say, this
first incident in '69, it was two years later before I did another one,
and then six months later before I tried another one, and then finally
the first.

D.L.: Actual murder.

T.B.: Yeah.

D.L.: Which was when?

Ted didn't answer, so Dorothy prompted him.

D.L.: It would be '71 before another kind of attempt and then '71 again another attempt, and . . . who was the first? Where?

T.B.: Seattle. It was in Seattle.

D.L.: Is that one of the ones you've told them about?

T.B.: I really hadn't talked about them in detail. In fact, I didn't think they mentioned the name, even though the name of the girl is on their list.

D.L.: Who is it? Do you think that it's not important because you told them about lots of other stuff?

T.B.: Oh, no. I know it is. This would be 1974.

D.L.: So that's quite a few years later. And all those years . . .

T.B.: There were . . . for instance, on one occasion, it may have been in '72 or so, I noticed that this young woman, a waitress who worked at a cafeteria near campus, would get off at midnight and walk home and I would—she lived in a basement apartment—and I would look in her bedroom window. And so I started to formulate a plan of what I would do. I noticed sometimes she left the door open to the basement area which led to her bedroom. So . . . for instance, I . . .

D.L.: Did you make any move towards her?

T.B.: I ran, I went down there late one night, very drunk—we haven't gotten into this, of how I used alcohol to really liberate, really disinhibit myself to the point where . . .

D.L.: You know you have told Mr. Michaud about this.

T.B.: This is true, the effect of alcohol. You mean about this incident?

D.L.: I think so.

T.B.: Well, anyway . . . I rushed in there, still somewhat inept, dealing with images that came out of the movies, and movies are not real, so I ran in there and hopped on top of the bed and tried to put a pillow on top of the girl's face. She struggled and started to scream and I ran away. End of story. Even this is a step further. I mean, going to somebody's house is really . . .

D.L.: Did you ever have a sense of another Ted, or another person? Did you ever actually talk to the other?

T.B.: Oh, yes. In fact—oh, yes—I'd have this dialogue.

D.L.: I don't mean thinking, "Gee, you're nuts to do this." I mean, did you ever feel like another person?

T.B.: It reached a point, I would say in '74, where . . . it would have conversations. And I'm not saying that I was a multiple personality. I don't know. All I know is that this other part of myself seemed to have a voice, and seemed to have a need.

D.L.: What was the voice like?

T.B.: It was . . . I can sort of remember it was just very low, kind of cruel and demanding.

D.L.: What would it say?

T.B.: Oh, it would walk down the street . . .

D.L.: Pardon?

T.B.: I'd walk down the street and literally hear it talking about women I'd seen.

D.L.: What would it say?

T.B.: Oh, it had this category, system of categorizing young women, you know, I can't, I used to, it's been so long since that I can't remember.

D.L.: It's very, very important to understand how this evolved, the voice.

T.B.: Well, it seemed, the more, especially in '74 particularly, the more deeply I got into this, the stronger, the more dominant and stronger this voice became. I felt captive of this whole part of myself.

D.L.: When did it talk to you?

T.B.: Most clearly when I was very much aroused. And certainly when I was intoxicated.

D.L.: Then you would hear it.

T.B.: Yes.

D.L.: Did it ever frighten you?

T.B.: When it frightened me it scared me to death and made me just cry out to stop.

D.L.: You would?

T.B.: Oh, yes. Like the next day after something happened. After the first time, I felt like a captive. I felt . . . I can't . . . I felt like, up 'till that point, I said, "Okay, you haven't gone too far yet. It's okay. You're going to stop now." And I'd stop for a month, two months, or three or six months, and then all of a sudden, it'd be back. The day after the first time this happened I was in a panic. In hysteria of fear and sorrow and horror over what had happened and said, "What in God's name has, have I done here?" And then remembering—in the clear light of day with my rational, essentially whole, mind—I was at risk. And then, my remembering that I may have left some evidence at the crime scene. Then I found myself to have become, more or less, a hostage.

"What do you mean?" I asked. I never stopped looking for signs that Ted had been powerless to control what he did.

T.B.: In essence, that morning-after syndrome. That state of mind when I was now clear and rational—and not harmful—and remorseful, realized of course what I had done. It made me distressed beyond explanation, beyond description about it. But realizing my survival depended on my normal self covering up. Because this other . . . the force which energized, this entity, had been expended. One thing that happened, it would just sort of recede. It was like all this force was expended, all this lust or desire had been vented, sort of receded, and my other part of myself could take the forefront. And yet, now this essentially, basically, decent part of myself was faced with the dilemma of dealing with my survival, covering up.

D.L.: Could this entity have disappeared or would it talk to you or what?

T.B.: Not at this particular time, not immediately after, but over time it seemed like it would just simply begin to reemerge.

D.L.: How about during, did the voice come during?

T.B.: I don't want to begin—I want to make sure you understand that I'm not saying that this voice . . . I wish there was a way of reproducing the clear memory of what it was like then. I know that there was this kind of dialogue going on, not just talking to myself innocently. Really a *"Give in to me"* kind of thing.

D.L.: You said it sounded cruel, sounded demanding. Did it ever sound like anyone you knew?

T.B.: No, I don't think so. Not like any other person, not like anything else.

D.L.: What would it say?

Ted hesitated before answering.

T.B.: You know, it's so hard to retrace that now. I would talk about . . . this, this . . . it would be this comprehension of a voice. And I say voice. And it advises me about women, women that I would see in the streets, in a very hateful manner, in a very angry, in a very

malicious manner. "Look at that bitch there. Do this and this and
this," or whatever.

D.L.: Do what and what and what?

I saw Ted's pain at this recounting. I wanted to assure him he hadn't
lost me, that it was safe to express himself this last day of his life. Still
holding his handcuffed hands, I said, "As you describe it, right now,
this is not you, because it's very hard for you to say what it said."

T.B.: I always maintained, whenever possible . . . I told the police that
if they really wanted to know what was in my mind—I say this in all
honesty, to any law enforcement researchers and to you . . . I have—
I'd be willing to bet that under the right circumstances, I'm not so sure
now because I know that I have changed. I know I have been able to
do a lot to heal myself, basically heal myself, which was what was
wrong before. But years ago, when I was first arrested, I know that if
the police had sat me down in a room, let me get drunk on, say,
bourbon—a drink that really made me more vicious—hard liquor and
7-Up or something, and showed me some really hard-core pornography, I could have talked to them in that voice. I could have talked to
them from that perspective. It would have come out of me just, it
would have blossomed right out of me.

D.L.: It sounds as if you feel you then became that voice.

T.B.: Well, yeah. More or less, it takes over the whole, it takes over
the basic consciousness mechanism, and more or less dictates what's
going to be done.

D.L.: It says, like "Now you're going to do? . . ."

T.B.: Dictates just like you would dictate to yourself that you are going
to do something, you know.

D.L.: Have you ever been told that you did something you don't remember? The reason I'm asking is that I am wondering, because you
raised the issue of multiple personality, to what extent are you, who
I'm talking with now, really separate from the other entity, and to what
extent it's just a variant of a mood you get.

T.B.: Yeah. I hear what you're saying. I think that there's more, an
integration there, an interrelationship, which when the malignant
portion of my personality or consciousness, call it what you will—the
entity—is more or less directing the mood and the action. I'm still on
another level conscious of this, I'm not totally unconscious of, or
unaware of it.

D.L.: It's just that you're in a slightly altered state.

certainly a real down, a sequence of disappointments and stresses would precipitate it more—I'm glad you mentioned it—would more likely precipitate it than practically anything else. In fact, what would happen would be a series of downs and disappointments together with one of these triggers that I mentioned, with the alcohol or some particular visual stimuli, would start to . . . There are times, where later on, after—this is more true in the beginning than later, you see, because once it, this way of being and acting, gained a foothold it didn't depend so much on moods.

D.L.: Then what did it depend on?

T.B.: It seemed to depend on something less, something, some kind of cyclical thing that I don't even now completely understand. I mean, why sometimes and not others?

D.L.: Tell about the state of mind you were in and how, what was going on with Chi Omega.

T.B.: I got in town, got a place to stay, felt a little bit comfortable, and, yet, as I've explained—I think I said this in the Michaud book, but I've told people before—I left Colorado, went to Chicago, then Ann Arbor, and drove down to Atlanta. There was a shift. I mean, I felt very high and on top of everything, but something happened in Atlanta. I didn't . . . all of a sudden I felt some old feeling come back, like obsessive, not long, in the sense that I'm standing in this big convention center watching everybody walk by and all of a sudden a feeling of being alienated. And that was on me, that was with me when I arrived in Tallahassee. Feeling somewhat—obviously I was alone— but just not . . . Feeling that I'd lost that initiative and feeling some of these old senses of being, of lack of self worth and lack of . . .

D.L.: You told me before you remembered the exact moment it happened.

T.B.: Well, I just, my memory is that I was seeing, leaning on the railing in the civic center, and all of a sudden a feeling coming over me like, "God. Nothing's different."

D.L.: So there's a real change there?

T.B.: But still, I, I don't want to make it more profound than it was— even though it was somewhat profound. So that first night in Tallahas- see I felt that sort of sense of the old excitement come back. I mean, it was a warm, wet, steamy night, and even though it was winter time, it reminded me—because I'm from the Pacific Northwest, and it was not any kind of weather I had been in before—and it had a, I can't blame it on the weather—I felt if I went out into the dark, and at that time Tallahassee was not, parts of Tallahassee weren't all that well lit, and I loved the darkness, the darkness would excite me, it really was sort of my ally, because I could sort of creep around in the darkness. And so, there weren't many streetlights, there were a lot of trees and brush around the houses, all of the things, as a boy, I used to really pay attention to it. And so I found myself back, very quickly, just creeping around, doing all of the old things. Building up, building up that energy to a fever pitch over a period of a few days. With, you know, the night stalking and the shopping around on the college campus during the daytime, that kind of thing. And I had nothing else to do—you see, here's the problem—nothing else to anchor me again. Nobody to say, don't you have a job to go to, or what are you thinking of right now, or no other kind of gratification to fill the void.

D.L.: No reality, really.

T.B.: So this inner reality, such as it was, started to reassert itself. After a few nights, I located this one house where I'd seen some young women, and watched them through the bedroom window. And I came back to that house, let's say, like the next night, or a couple of nights later, and I saw another girl on the inside, I started to think about what I'd like to do to her. Started planning, getting excited about planning, doing something, building up to it, building up to the point where I would actually do it. I remember on a particular night going down there, decided to do something, . . . watching her through the window, she was getting . . . ready to go out. Her leaving and leaving the door open. And going in, going in and setting things up so that I could get in later on. And then waiting, going home and drinking some more, drinking heavily. Of course I'd been in jail for a year or two, so the alcohol was particularly potent. And then going back at midnight or so and seeing that she'd just got home, but the light was still on, and then saying I'll wait 'till she goes to sleep, I'll go back and drink some more.

D.L.: So twice you went back there.

T.B.: Yes, but between the place where I lived and this house, I was walking back, just happening to be walking along the road, and I was just all aroused, full of energy, you know, peaked for this. I happened to look over across the street casually and I saw a door open to the sorority house. And I just turned and walked right for the door. That's what happened.

D.L.: So you had been planning one thing, and the sorority house just was there.

T.B.: It just was there. I mean, it was just coincidental. If I hadn't turned my head to the side . . .

D.L.: What happened? How did you manage so quietly?

T.B.: It's not that—sadly enough—it's not hard to harm people, especially at one in the morning, people asleep in their beds. So I just walked in. There was nobody. Everybody was asleep. I mean, I wasn't thinking. My degree of reason, ability to reason and think was impaired, certainly by the alcohol, and by my state of arousal, and emotion, and yet I did things which clearly were dangerous in terms of getting apprehended. I just walked upstairs and went down to the end of the corridor and went into the first room I saw. Well, I'd picked up a log from this wood pile and . . .

"Where?" I asked, trying to reinforce that the Chi Omega murders, at least, had not been premeditated.

T.B.: Just outside the door.

D.L.: Outside their door?

T.B.: I didn't have it in my hand.

D.L.: You, you hadn't planned to use it on the other girl.

T.B.: No . . . and . . . this is very hard, . . . having conversations not, not, like this, in, in that, Dr. Lewis, you're more interested in me in, in, in what was going on in my head and how this developed. Certainly far more than the police are.

D.L.: I hope so.

T.B.: But it's, it's, it's, this particular point, the actual point that, of course, we have been focusing on for the past few days, and nothing tightens up my head and makes me feel nauseous more than having to talk about it.

D.L.: Is it because you are afraid that it will harm you further?

T.B.: No, it's just very unpleasant, awakening the very worst memories and, of bringing back it all.

D.L.: What state do you think you were in?

T.B.: What state?

D.L.: Yes. What do you think you were feeling? Because, apparently, whatever it was went on for at least two people. And you left there, so that whatever the state was, it's, let's say, not just an orgasm and it's through. Can you describe it?

Ted laid his head on his hands and I laid my hands on his head.

D.L.: So you were saying that you had, by that time, become a threat.

T.B.: Well, yeah, I mean, that whole kind of consciousness was just totally dominant. I mean, the need, the thought, the feeling, the excitement of harming, of getting some sort of sexual gratification at harming someone, was absolutely paramount. Driving me. I mean, that was coming from some source within me, and yet it was not me. And it was very powerful, very strong, very erratic, and when people comment, "Well, gee, this [the Chi Omega murders] is really out of character, this is really different," well, in some ways it was. Yet they really didn't know the whole history of what I've done, so they don't know that it's . . . I had gone through a frenzy episode or two before, so this . . .

D.L.: Do we know about it?

T.B.: We haven't talked about it, I mean, yet. Well, there's just so much to talk about, where do we begin?

D.L.: Do police know about it? About these frenzy episodes?

T.B.: Not really, they don't know what happened.

D.L.: But they know you did it?

T.B.: The . . . they think they do, yeah. Well, anyway.

D.L.: And in this state, what was it like? Can you describe it?

T.B.: It was just a . . . how can you describe it, there's no describing it, nothing can do it justice, it's just a hyper . . .

D.L.: It the woman conscious while you're doing it?

T.B.: No.

D.L.: So you, what, hit her on the head, or what?

T.B.: Yeah, yes.

D.L.: You did . . . So this is all you, with a feeling like she's dead?

T.B.: Right.

D.L.: Maybe even dead.

T.B.: But you see the difference here is I'd never, this is what I'd never done before. I'd never bitten anyone before, and this is an indication, you know, how . . . I don't know . . . supercharged or whatever, bestial, even, I was at that time.

D.L.: If there had been a police officer there, could you have stopped?

T.B.: Where? Somewhere in the neighborhood, you mean, or outside?

D.L.: No, once you had started, could you have stopped, do you think?

T.B.: Well, I would have . . . yes . . . and I would equate that to a predator having pulled down the prey, is approached by a bigger predator, and runs off. For its own survival. I don't know if that makes sense?

D.L.: It does.

T.B.: The predatory instincts and the survival instincts are still intact. You're not totally oblivious—I wasn't totally oblivious to my survival.

D.L.: I guess you must have had that intact to have gotten away from there without leaving any signs or anything or taken anything with you. Part of you was still observant of what was going on.

T.B.: Right. It's that kind of consciousness. Again, it's a consciousness which is comparable to that of a predator. On a very basic level of existence, not a lot of intellectual, moral, obvious considerations involved there. Just . . . a . . . I'd be just thinking of, like, there she is, and knocking her unconscious and going back to cover up, step by step, just . . .

D.L.: Were there times different from this, when you kept the person conscious, with there being pleasure in her being scared?

T.B.: No. Well, yes, there were many times the girls were conscious, but—and I'm quite serious about this—I never got off, never was aroused or excited in any way by the women being scared.

D.L.: You weren't?

T.B.: That was never a facet of what, what I got off on. It was, in fact, more often than not, I think, what was a driving force was, I would have to restrain myself sometimes, not to . . . to keep the victim alive a little longer.

D.L.: Why?

T.B.: It would seem that . . . because there would be times that I would kill the victim really quickly, and then later on I'd feel badly, and I'd say to myself, Why didn't you keep her alive a little longer, etc., etc.

D.L.: Why would you have kept her alive a little longer?

T.B.: For some sort of sexual gratification, but . . .

D.L.: Well, you could still have sexual gratification if she were dead.

T.B.: Yes, but it's different. Obviously, it's different.

D.L.: Less responsive.

T.B.: Well, even that. But it's just different. But it seemed like there was this driving need to have everything happen in a flash, like first the taking possession or control, and then stripping the victim, and then some sort of sexual activity, and then it would happen so quickly; beating, oftentimes.

D.L.: What about the time Michaud wrote about when—I don't know if it's true or not—but he implies that there were two people in the same place being with each other. Is that true?

T.B.: Two people . . .

D.L.: Yeah, that you had abducted one, then another on the same day, and that they were both in the same place, and you implied to him that one saw what you did to the other. Is that true?

T.B.: No, that's not true.

D.L.: It's not true?

T.B.: I may have implied . . .

D.L.: It's very important. I wish I had the book here . . . You never had one girl watch while you harmed another girl?

T.B.: No.

D.L.: So where the hell did he—you read that book—get that for his book. Where the hell did he get that idea?

T.B.: Well, okay, I can tell you why he has that idea. Again, we were, in order for him to write this book, at the time I was steadfastly denying any guilt and saying that I was entirely innocent.

D.L.: And you were steadfastly hedging.

T.B.: I was hedging and that was the understanding—that we would see how close we could go, we'd be flirting around, and try to keep the editors happy. And so when he came down to that point and he wanted to talk about Lake Sam . . . Here was our premise: that I would *speculate* based upon—you've heard this—based upon my knowledge of what I'd read in the newspapers, and my experience in the law, on what happened. But I'd also, and when I speculated, I would make sure to alter significant facts so the police couldn't say that I was saying things that only someone who'd been there would know, so I altered significant facts, so if anything they'd say, "Well, obviously if he believes what he said, he couldn't have done it." So I thought it was, in the case of Lake Sam, where there were two in five-hour stretch or so, it was . . . I just thought it was . . . I could say, and I did, that they both were abducted by somebody and taken to some place.

D.L.: But Michaud asked, could one have seen the other, and you said yes.

T.B.: Yes—why not?

D.L.: So you made yourself look far more callous and cruel. It didn't occur to you?

T.B.: No, that did not occur to me. Because I knew the police would know, in all likelihood, that there was no such place that I could have done that.

D.L.: Ted, what else do you feel may have contributed to this state that you haven't told anyone? That you have felt deeply, either ashamed of or that you felt you would hurt someone else.

T.B.: There is so much . . . I don't know where to begin.

D.L.: I think that's what we should really talk about now.

T.B.: Oh yes. Yeah. I'm going to need to take a bit of a break.

Ted sat up and looked around outside the glass booth. No one was paying particular attention to us, but there were more correctional personnel milling around than usual, more comings and goings from the superintendent's office. Lots of preparations had to be made for the next day. He turned and looked wordlessly into my eyes, that person deep inside him peering out at me, communicating with me. We were sharing an understanding of his death. I was there for Ted that day. I was pure of heart.

"Go ahead," he said.

D.L.: What do you feel you have not talked about with anyone, but that you know affected your behavior?

Ted paused for a while.

T.B.: I'm thinking. It's a good question, but one that covers a lot of ground. Just don't know where to begin. I don't know where to begin, but I'll try.

He sighed deeply, said nothing for a few moments.

T.B.: What have I not told anyone that has had an influence and effect? . . . I know that I've a tendency to . . . I mean, I've gotten sort of, become fond of describing it in a certain way, even though I know I've learned a lot about how this all developed over the years. I sort of got a set scenario, and I have a feeling I've tended to rule out some things that I should probably talk about. For instance, I keep coming back to—I've talked a lot about how different life events and stress in combination, and pornography and all of that . . . But I've talked about that so much, so much it seems to overshadow things that are more subtle, that are more . . . important. What do you—help me out a little bit here.

D.L.: You said you felt very, very embarrassed and guilty about some things you told me about before, things in your youth, things which, by the way, I don't think you need to feel terribly embarrassed or guilty about. But my guess is that there are other events in your life that you either feel embarrassed for yourself, or maybe for someone else, that you feel are terrible. And yet, that might shed light on what could create such feeling—such sexual feelings and such angry feelings.

T.B.: Of course, we're right down to it. I've pieced together an explanation of sorts which makes sense, and yet I don't know. I wish I did know. I mean, why do, why are some of us affected by the same thing one way and some of us the other. The vast majority of people can view the kind of so-called pornography I've been talking about and not be moved this way. Why? I mean, it's a combination of factors, is obviously unique in many ways. Why did you become the kind of person you are? Why did you become a psychologist and not a ballerina or tightrope walker? I'm not . . . that's what I'd like to understand, why. I think for me sometimes it's, sadly, just because. Forgive me for digressing a little, maybe this will help. You asked me why I never sought help. At first I didn't think I needed it. Then I suffered from delusions that I could handle it myself. Then it was too late because I knew if I sought help, that was—I didn't trust anybody.

D.L.: They'd turn you in.

T.B.: Yeah. Yeah.

D.L.: Why don't you try very hard to relax, feel very, very, very relaxed, so relaxed you can't even lift up your head. Feel very, very relaxed, you're almost asleep. I mean, so relaxed that your head is free of worrying about anything now, and think way, way back. What else is it that you are reminded of to tell me about your childhood and your family that you're pretty sure you haven't told me before.

Ted had laid his head down on his hands, but his handcuffs cut him and he was unable to concentrate. I cupped his head in my hands. I had never been this way with Ted before, touching him, comforting him. But today was different. Today was very, very different. Today I was a human being and he was a human being, and in some way we were the last two people on Earth—on his Earth, at least; in his lifetime, at least. Finally, Ted spoke, for a moment reaching deeper than he'd ever gone before, touching the very essence of his tragedy.

T.B.: Well, looking back now I couldn't, I couldn't, certainly didn't, see it or understand it. I can only say that . . . as a young adult engaged in this kind of behavior, what I lacked and didn't understand and express was love. Now I know that sounds—it's very broad territory there, but . . . And there's a lot of people, I think, who are handicapped in one degree or another in their ability to sense and express true loving, compassionate, feelings truthfully and honestly. And yet I just feel that . . .

By love, I mean the ability to sense someone else's feelings and when to comfort them and to protect them and do good things for them. And in turn have that same kind of feeling, be the focus of that same kind of feeling. I feel that wasn't there in me—I mean, how else? There's no way a person can hurt someone, physically, kill someone, if you're a loving person. I mean, truly loving.

D.L.: You feel that you didn't have an empathy for these people, and that it had something to do with early on.

T.B.: Well, yeah. I know that . . . sure . . . had one thing been different, my whole life would have been different. I mean, you could pick a million and one moments along the way.

D.L.: Which one? Which thing would you name? Something in your childhood?

T.B.: The connections, to me, with what we're talking about in terms of violent behavior are just more evident in later life. Even though I can see they set the stage. But even up to the time I was twenty years old, I mean, I had not gone down the path. I was still essentially okay, hadn't harmed anyone.

D.L.: You thought about it, but you hadn't. You know, you can wonder whether the onset of the bipolar mood disorder was the straw that broke the camel's back. Because you seem to date the first terrible depression to being around '67, '68.

T.B.: Right. That's a good point.

D.L.: So that I would guess that, even in my experience you see, even if people have been horribly battered, not just unloved, but horribly battered, that alone doesn't create that kind of thing. And also just having a kind of manic-depressive kind of illness, that usually doesn't create that kind of thing, but sometimes when there's some kind of physiological vulnerability factor . . .

T.B.: Right. Some predisposition which, you know, I think, I don't know that science, or social science, had reached the point, to identify this predisposition, whatever it is.

D.L.: But, you know, in manic-depressive illness, the limbic system is also very much involved, because that has to do with feelings—joy, sex, rage, whatever. So that we do know a little bit about it, and it seems very likely, to me, that the vulnerability may have made it possible for you to step over the line between fantasy and act.

T.B.: Yeah. That's, that makes sense to me. In that vulnerability, a sense of somehow being receptive to that kind of negative stimulation, that kind of powerful stimuli.

D.L.: You know, we do know that Richard Speck, I think that it was he that shot out of the Texas tower, that he had a tumor—I believe that it was of the temporal lobe, and the temporal lobe is part of the limbic system. I believe that he had a tumor; unlike most people who have tumors—they don't go and shoot somebody, or the like—he shot up a town, and my guess is that there are experiential things that are important. But I'd put money on the fact that that tumor also created the vulnerability to be explosive. It's very possible the mood disorder did that for you. If you wanted, if you lost [your appeal], let us find out if there's anything in the brain. Because you seem to suspect that there's something that just keeps going, and it isn't explained by whether your mother loved you or not. And I agree with you.

T.B.: No, here again, conventional routes just doesn't seem to explain it.

D.L.: No.

T.B.: Well, I . . .

D.L.: You know, Ted, even if we win in this, and even if, please God, we win and they spare your life, you should consider donating your brain—thirty years from now, or now, say whenever—in order to understand this thing. I think, first of all, less morbidly, to make such a decision, that you should. None of us will ever know when they do autopsies what people find. It's something that you should think about even if you win, to make a contribution to humanity, because you don't want other people to just . . .

Dorothy put her pad on the table and drew a representation of a brain, circling a small area. Ted leaned forward; he was very interested. He'd been searching for some understanding of why this had all happened to him. No one factor seemed sufficient to him, and the explanation of it being a combination of factors was unsatisfying; it still seemed nothing more than a moral weakness. But what if there had been physical cause; something physically obstructing that part of his brain that would have felt empathy for others, from others. The love spot. Ted said he would like to do it, to donate his brain after his death, but he didn't want to commit to anything before talking to Diana Weiner. He said he didn't want to make this any harder for her to bear than it already was.

D.L.: Do you have any other questions you want to ask me?

T.B.: Well, I think that I've asked you just a couple minutes ago about, the big question is, you know . . . even with all that you see in my chart, how does it explain the unique behavior that I was involved in?

D.L.: I don't think it does. I think it just gives you a hint. And I think that these other contributions are far more important, or certainly more justified. I mean, why should you lose it when other people don't? And, then, I do suspect that there are things you don't remember that were more intensely negative.

T.B.: Yes.

D.L.: And, just without telling me, do you remember things now that you're not telling?

T.B.: Honest to God, honestly, if, part of it is, you know, again we can go step by step, incident by incident, but we don't have time. I'm sure we'd come up with new stuff. But if I'm not telling you something now, it's not because I don't want to tell you, it's just because I don't remember it.

D.L.: All right.

T.B.: And might remember under different circumstances, not right now.

D.L.: Well, let's hope that in a few moments we can arrange those different circumstances, and then see if we can't help you to remember or jog the memory. We probably should stop now.

T.B.: What time is it?

It was one o'clock when we shut off the tape recorder. I went to get the warden's secretary to take Ted's last requests. She was startled that I expected her to talk to him directly, and she was afraid to enter the room. She stood at the door with her steno pad like a waitress, "*And what would you like with your execution?*" Ted had no extraordinary requests, no special meals. He wanted three things: to have his attorney and nonattorney visiting times combined to one four-hour visiting time that night; to have Dorothy added to the list for the final visit; and, for the one "contact" visit he was allowed at the very end of the night, he wanted to see Diana Weiner.

It was time to leave, even though there was still much unsaid. Our time was up, and Ted had a busy afternoon ahead. He had more meetings with law enforcement, and his video interview with radio evangelist The Reverend Doctor James Dobson. At the door, I put my arms around Ted and held him for a moment—for the first and last time.

On our way out of the prison, Dorothy and I spied the state's three psychiatrists in the lobby waiting on standby to contradict our expected claim that Ted was incompetent to be executed.

CHAPTER 17

On the way back from the prison, Dorothy and I stopped for lunch in Gainesville. I was on a safe spot on the game board, in a cool, empty café on a quiet, sunny street with an animated Dorothy Lewis. She so rarely took time out to lunch that she considered it a rare treat, and I was not inclined to deny her. We chatted there peacefully for over an hour, as if time had stopped. It hadn't. Jim and Mike Ollen had dropped off a stay motion in Lake City on their way from Tallahassee to Gainesville that morning—crisscrossing middle and northern Florida like bees in clover. Jim already had had a telephone hearing with Judge Peach in Lake City on our new claim about Judge Jopling copying Judge Cowart's opinion. We'd already lost, and Jim was feverishly preparing an appeal brief for the Florida Supreme Court, which was out of town and out of session and would require extraordinary measures to get the brief to.

When we got back to the hotel I found Jim glued to the phone. Down to the wire, exhausted, and losing his voice, Jim had started to cling to his outside sources, the death penalty experts. As he spent these last hours talking with Mike Mello and others, I felt shut out and useless. I declined Dorothy's offer of a brandy.

When she and I returned to the prison that night at eight o'clock we learned that the warden had denied all three of Ted's last requests.

Maybe it was to tighten control at the approach of such a public event; maybe it was to prevent us from coming up with any tricks, such as Dorothy suddenly declaring Ted incompetent; maybe it was just to show who was boss. Or maybe it was to give the loathsome Ted Bundy a little extra punishment, a little extra turn of the screw. Whatever it was, it shook me. It seemed so unnecessarily cruel. I had expected that by eight we'd only be one hour into Ted's four-hour combined visit. But now it turned out that his final legal visit had started at seven and was ending at nine—sharp. I had only an hour left. Also, Dorothy was not allowed to come in with me. After much negotiation, the guards at the newly-erected checkpoint at the entrance to the prison grounds finally let me bring her in, so she wouldn't have to wait outside in the cold—which had been their original suggestion—but I had to leave her in the lobby. Undaunted, the ever busy Dr. Lewis, never one to waste time, whipped out her notebook and began drafting a research proposal on some other matter. I went through the inner gates and was ushered into the visiting room by Sergeant Cronauer, Ted's death-watch guard. It seemed to be his specialty. He was a round-faced, affable man, warmly smiling and empathetic. It was clear by the familiarity with which he addressed me as "Polly" that he had come to know me through Ted, sitting and talking to him in his isolated death-watch cell, keeping him calm and keeping an eye out for signs of trouble. His job was easing everyone's way toward the execution, preventing unpleasant scenes, doing his part to make the end go smoothly. Like a solicitous funeral director. Tonight he was host for the final viewing.

The mortal blow to my heart came when I was led into the visiting room and saw that no one was there but Diana. Somehow I had thought that there would be a group of people, somehow I had always imagined Ted having a lot of people in his life, a lot of people who would come to say good-bye to him. Maybe it was all the publicity that made me think that, that gave him an aura of importance. Maybe he was, publicly; but personally he was important to almost no one. Carole wasn't there, and she didn't want a final phone call from him, either. She was hurt by his relationship with Diana and devastated by his sudden wholesale confessions in his last days. And Carole's son, Jamey, did not visit Ted that final day, although he had done so dozens of times over the years. The week before he had begged Ted to spare Carole and not go public; but Ted had trampled on her heart.

So it was just Ted and Diana, alone at the far end of the room, at the last booth. The guards stayed a respectful distance back, at the other end. Diana gave up her chair for me. The three of us huddled around the glass barrier, looking at each other, sharing that space in time as fully as we possibly could. I told Ted about the progress of his legal case. We were waiting on two different appeals, one in the Florida Supreme Court, the other in the U.S. Supreme Court. I told them how sorry I was that Diana was not allowed at the personal visit. I truly was sorry. If nothing else, Diana was Ted's best friend and I wanted him to have her comfort.

Ted pushed a piece of paper up against the glass. It was the waiver that Dr. Lewis had drafted for permission to use his brain for research. He looked back and forth between Diana and me, saying, "We should discuss this." I knew Diana's view—she was totally opposed to some part of Ted being removed from his body and denied a final resting place. I knew that Ted was interested in the possibility that research would show whether he had some physical brain defect that explained his inability to feel normal emotions, to feel love. But I wasn't his lawyer anymore. I was a human being with a dying friend. I did not want to get into a tug-of-war over Ted's brain.

Ted told me that he had gotten a lot out of our interview with Dr. Lewis that morning and wished that we could have had time to explore those issues further. He asked that I use our interviews to help explain him to others, to explain that he was not a monster. He stared into my eyes and finally asked a question that was obviously very important to him:

"I need to know. Did you and Jim like me?" My heart dropped.

"Of course, Ted, of course." I tried to push those words into Ted's heart and allow him to believe it, as he apparently did not. I didn't care what the truth was.

I was called out for a phone call. There were two messages to return calls. One was from *Nightline*. We had frantic messages from the press everywhere we went now. I couldn't believe their persistence. I couldn't believe the prison gave me the message as if it were urgent. Why would I waste this time with them? The other was from Jim back at the hotel in Gainesville. In searching for a phone to use, I came upon the superintendent, who was waiting out the night with other law enforcement officials, and was introduced to Bill Haigmeier, the FBI agent who had been visiting Ted for the last few years. He expressed his sympathy for what I was going through. "I know Ted was always real grateful for the work you were doing for him," he said. Why hadn't he tried to *help* then? How could he have just gone along for the ride, meeting with Ted, forming a relationship with him, all the time accepting that it was going to terminate in Ted's execution?

When I got through to Jim on the phone I learned that the Florida Supreme Court had ruled against us. We were still waiting for the U.S. Supreme Court, which seemed to be having an internal debate about granting the stay. That was encouraging. I told Jim to leave for the prison right away, because the legal visit would be ending in thirty minutes.

When I returned to Ted, he held a letter against the glass that he had written to me and Jim, thanking us for our representation. "I hope you likcd me," it said. "I hope this wasn't just an unpleasant legal chore for you." His note ended with, "I feel close to you now." Because he was not permitted to pass anything to us at the time, the letter eventually went to Diana—along with his remains.

At nine o'clock I rose to leave. To my amazement, I was propelled against the glass to kiss and hug Ted, as best we could. I didn't know how I got there; it was a force from within, beyond my control. I left him alone with Diana for a final good-bye and walked out the door. I burst into tears and was surrounded by the waiting arms of Sergeant Cronauer. I hadn't cried in years. Ted's aloneness, the final cruelty of not allowing him a personal visit with Diana, his closest friend, and the utter finality of our meeting welled up in me like a fireball and burst. I sobbed like never, ever before. When Diana came out, we cried together.

Outside, Dr. Lewis and I ran into John and Marcia Tanner, who were on their way inside the prison. They were to be Ted's only contact visitors. Born-again Christians who had been counseling Ted over the last few years, they glowed with satisfaction at sending him on his way.

"You two will be the last to see Ted," I said.

"No, we won't. The last will be Our Lord, Jesus Christ."

They cast their eyes skyward, their faces beaming.

Jim had been stopped at the prison checkpoint. Legal visitation was over. I tried to convince the superintendent over the phone to let Jim see Ted. No go. It didn't matter that he was late because they had changed the rules without telling us. It didn't matter that Jim was late because he was still communicating with the courts to try to save Ted's life. The warden had decided. We drove in the pitch blackness to the convenience store down the road. Standing in the dark, in the cold January night air, we used the pay phone to call the governor's and the attorney general's officers. They were sympathetic but could not help. The warden had complete control now. Jim, who had been arguing the case for nearly a week straight, with little sleep and no rest, was so hoarse that he could barely speak. We drove away in defeat.

Back at the hotel, the news was in. By the time we got there it was midnight and the U.S. Supreme Court had voted 5–4 against granting Ted a stay of execution. It was all over. The horrible capriciousness of it was that 5–4 would have been enough for the Court to take his case, to order a full briefing over the following months, to hear oral argument, to issue a long, considered written opinion some months or even years later. But it wasn't enough to postpone the execution in order to hear that appeal. The Supreme Court would never hear Ted Bundy's appeal, only because the governor of Florida had scheduled him to be killed first. Those four votes to grant a stay also mocked the Eleventh Circuit's expeditious determination denying a certificate of probable cause to appeal, the ruling that no reasonable jurist would find merit to our claims.

I called Ted at the prison; it was like calling into a series of locked rooms.

"Flar'da State Prison."

"Mr. Turner, please."

"Turner, here."

"Mr. Turner, this is Polly Nelson. I need to speak to Ted. We have a decision."

"Just a minute. I'll put you through."

"Hello? Ms. Nelson? Hold on, please."

"Hello? Polly?"

It was Ted. He sounded as he had the very first time we spoke. His voice was deep and gravelly. His speech was hesitant. There were long silences that neither of us knew how to fill. But it didn't feel like the first time. I knew him now. For three years I had held his life in my hands as best I could, and now I had to let him go. He would go the rest of the way alone.

I told him about the decision. He recognized the irony immediately.

"Five to four? Doesn't that mean? . . ."

"Right. It was enough to grant cert., but not enough for a stay."

We both fell silent.

"I'm sorry," I finally said, although it did not seem appropriate. Nothing seemed appropriate. I could think of nothing to say.

I knew he didn't expect me to apologize for the outcome. He knew that I didn't expect him to tell me that it wasn't our fault, that we had done all we could. We both knew all that. Our silence transmitted our thoughts, our mental clasping of hands, our repressed sighs. I wanted to comfort him, to protect him, to give him hope, but no words came. I couldn't think of any precedent, any analogous situation in real life. He was going to be killed in the morning, and there was no longer any possibility that he would be spared. He wasn't dying, but he was going to be dead.

Finally, when what could not be put into words no longer needed to be put into words, when time had turned the page, I spoke, so that my voice would be with him. He was already gone, though, into a place so private, so unknowable by me, that I was afraid to intrude.

"Are the Tanners still there?" I asked.

"Uh . . . yes," he said, without interest.

"Did you talk to your mother yet?"

"Uh . . . no." He tried to pull himself back to the present, back to the role of a prisoner closely monitoring his remaining rights. But his voice was soft, cracked. "I'm calling her at one. I talked to them earlier, and that's the best time for me to call."

"Are you going to talk to Carole?"

"That's up to her. I don't know if she's going to call or not. I don't think so."

My eyes were filled with tears. Actually, it felt like one big tear pressing against the back of my eyes and dripping around the sides. I was sitting in the middle of one of the double beds in Jim's hotel room, my stocking-footed feet tucked underneath me, my suit feeling like a straitjacket, surrounded by carryout bags from the Taco Bell and file folders filled with papers that once burst with vital potential and now lay limp, useless, superfluous. Jim sat on the other bed, his eyes hidden by the glint of his eyeglasses, looking down at his legal pad, reflexively making marks, jotting a word once in a while, then underlining it, then drawing a line back up to a previous word, back and forth, back and forth, gradually coming to a stop. I handed the phone to him. Except for everything, it was like we were parents talking to our son at school; it was like I was the mom and now Dad would repeat everything

I'd said, as if we weren't sitting together, as if he hadn't been listening the whole time. *Here, Dear, say good-bye to our Ted.*

After the phone call, Jim and I stayed frozen in place. Speechless. Helpless. Motionless. Finally, I pulled myself to the desk, picked up the phone and dialed, number-by-number, breathing like a bellows to keep my tightening chest from squeezing all of the air out of me, the phone number of a place I had called so often but would never call again.

"Flar'da State Prison."

Another deep breath.

"Mr. Turner, please."

"Just a minute."

"Turner."

"Mr. Turner, this is Polly Nelson."

He started to protest, to say that I had already spoken to Ted after the final decision and I was no longer entitled to speak to him. I knew that. I kept on talking right over him—I hadn't called to talk to Ted.

"Mr. Turner, Jim Coleman is going to attend the execution tomorrow. Can you tell me what time he should be there in the morning?"

Until this moment, I hadn't accepted that there would an execution and hadn't made any arrangements with the prison. Turner sounded surprised, ready to object again since it was rather late to be adding to the list of visitors allowed through the gate the next morning. He chose an intermediate position, not committing himself to giving permission in case that was the wrong thing to do, in case he would be the one to jinx Bundy's execution, now that it was a go.

"Uhmm, five-thirty."

"Where should he go?"

Now my chest was heaving.

The superintendent's voice softened.

"Oh, they'll be meeting in the administration building, Polly." He'd never called me by my first name before.

"Thank you. He'll be there."

PART VI

CHAPTER 18

I had planned to sleep through. It was over for me. I had finished my job. I had had my cry. It was over. Nothing left to do but get us all back home. So I hadn't set the alarm. For a full week, I'd been leaping out of bed after only a few hours' rest for another hearing, another brief, another crisis. Now that all that was over I had planned to sleep until ten, order room service, and relax.

It didn't work out that way.

My eyes opened at the exact moment of the execution, at 7:06 on the morning of Tuesday, January 24, 1989. I pulled them shut. I was going to sleep through. They snapped back open. They stared at the clock. The hands on the clock never seemed to move. Time would not move forward. My body was immobile, too. I felt drugged, paralyzed, as if I had a terrible, terrible hangover. It was not over. I was still a prisoner. Trapped, confined, condemned. I didn't feel anything. Not relief, not anger, not sadness, not grief, not pity, not hunger, not thirst. I didn't think anything, either. I was completely in the grasp of the buzzing prison radar, so strong that morning that it reached past Starke, all the way to Gainesville, all the way to my bed in the hotel where I was registered under a false name. It held me in suspension.

Eons later, after the ice age, after the stone age, it was ten o'clock.

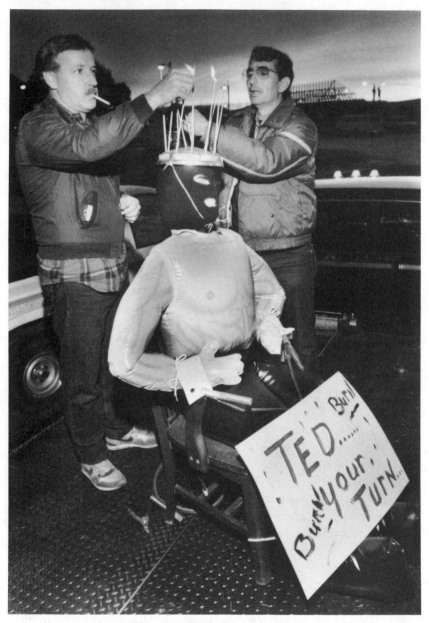

Butch Pearce, left, of Starke, and Bob Reeves, of Gainesville, light up a Bundy effigy at the prison shortly after 7 A.M., when Ted was scheduled to die. PHIL SEARS

Media converge on prison spokesperson Bob Macmaster at Starke after Ted's execution Tuesday morning. PHIL SEARS

Television crews gather equipment in anticipation of Ted's execution. AP/WIDE WORLD PHOTOS

Demonstrators rejoice as Ted is executed. AP/WIDE WORLD PHOTOS

I pulled the phone over and laboriously, painfully, like an invalid, made travel arrangements for us all. I got out of bed and met Dr. Lewis. We had breakfast across the highway at a pancake house that featured free refills of Florida orange juice. Dorothy kept looking at me, prodding me, trying to nose under the veil of my paralysis. Since I wasn't saying anything, Dororthy had the floor to herself, and she brought up a subject that was on her mind.

"Last night I offered you a drink and you said you didn't drink. Why's that?"

"I'm an alcoholic," I said.

"How do you know?"

"Because when I drank I couldn't stop. I'd drink ten, twelve drinks and it still wouldn't be enough."

"You know," she said, "several of my private patients, when they first came to see me, told me they were alcoholics, but every one of them turned out to be clinically depressed. Without knowing it, they had been trying to treat their depression with alcohol. And it sounds like that's what you were doing."

Then Dorothy took a napkin and drew a diagram of synaptic connections in the brain.

Demonstrators celebrating with fireworks on hearing the news of Ted's execution
JOHN MORAN

"Antidepressants are the one clear contribution psychiatry has made to humankind. It may be the only real good we've ever done."

She showed on the napkin how the serotonin flow between the synapses, disrupted in depression, is righted with medication. Then she wrote down a name.

"Here's the name of a doctor in Washington I trust very much," she said. "Call him. Tell him I told you to call. Ask him to refer you to someone very good. Not just anybody—someone who's a real expert at this."

I took the diagram and referral, but I resisted the suggestion that I needed "drugs." It seemed like it would be a betrayal of the trust I'd placed in my support groups.

Anyway, I thought I'd be feeling better soon, now that my terrible responsibility was over. But it would be nearly a year before I would begin to recover, and only then was I able to admit I needed help.

When we got back to the hotel, Dorothy marched right up and knocked on Jim's door as I peeked out from mine. I did not want her

Youths wearing TGIFryday shirts JOHN MORAN

to do that. I did not want to see him. I did not want to see his face. I did not want him to have to face me. He had been there. He had watched Ted be killed. I did not want his face to tell me what had happened. I did not want mine to say, *Our Ted is dead.*

Jim did not answer his door. He and Mike Ollen did not make our flight. Dr. Lewis and I flew out of Gainesville on a noisy propeller plane that eventually made conversation impossible. But before Dorothy gave up trying to maintain her verbal lifeline to me, she speculated about what really had been wrong with Ted.

"It's funny," she said. "I always tell my graduate students that if they find me a real, true psychopath, I'll buy them dinner. I never thought they existed, I thought psychopathology was just covering some other disorder, the real cause. But I think Ted may have been one, a true psychopath, without any remorse or empathy at all. Isn't that interesting?"

We parted at the airport in Atlanta. Dr. Lewis asked if I had time to walk her to her plane to New York—she was reluctant to leave me.

The crowd applauds as officials announce Ted's death. COURTESY OF THE
SUN-SENTINEL

For once, I bypassed the opportunity to spend a few more minutes
with her. I could not speak or hear another word. I was compelled to
fold back inward, a walking cocoon. Back in Washington I stumbled
into my apartment, dropped my bags on the floor, piled all the quilts
and blankets I could find on top of my bed, peeled off my clothes, and
climbed inside. It was still mid afternoon. The phone rang; it was a
reporter from the *Philadelphia Inquirer* wanting to know whether what
Dr. Norman was reported to have said that day was true—that Ted
had killed more than one hundred women. I started shaking under the
covers. Reporters had never called me at home before. I had thought
it was my sanctuary, and now it had been violated. I felt exposed,
vulnerable. I told her I hadn't heard the report and hung up. I pulled
a quilt over my head. It's over, I thought. Don't they know it's over?

The reporter's editor called back. Maybe, he said, I had misunder-
stood. The question wasn't whether I had heard the report of what Art
Norman had said, but whether it was true. I sighed and surrendered.

One thing was over, I realized. I didn't have to pretend any longer that Ted was not a murderer. That was over. And I didn't have to put a spin on everything I said to make sure that it didn't harm Ted's case. That was over, too, the play. The curtain had fallen on the last act at 7:06 that morning. I was no longer Bundy's Lawyer. I was something more human size.

"Okay, let me explain what was going on when Art Norman was interviewing Ted, and where that estimate of over a hundred came from . . ."

Sleep would not come to me that afternoon either, and I finally dragged myself in my blankets to the couch to stare at the television. I was trying to pull time along, away from the execution. I was trying to break the roaring silence in the apartment, to color the grey that surrounded me. But every channel carried news of Ted's execution, with films of the white hearse bearing his body past the jeering crowds waiting outside the Florida State Prison. I would change the channel at the first mention of "Florida" or "Ted Bundy"—words that now assaulted me like rightist death squads bursting through the door—but I still saw it all, my final view of Ted.

Two weeks after the execution Jim forced me to take a vacation: "Just do it. Treat it like an assignment." I had no energy and no imagination, but guessed that something like Club Med probably had a memorable phone number, something like 1-800-Club-Med. It did. I left the next day. On Paradise Island, I ate and ate and slept and slept, regaining the weight I'd lost litigating during the last week of Ted's life and, thus, undoing the only good that had come of it. A club employee looked exactly like a young Ted. I kept staring at him and imagining how much Ted would have wished to be him—free, alive, a job among the beautiful people, no black marks against him. I thought of the *Weekly World News* printing pictures of his dead body, mutilated by the autopsy. I yearned for things to have been different for him.

After the managing partner told me to start thinking about leaving the firm, I tried to get back to work on my one remaining case and to plan my future. I interviewed with some companies, but my heart was not in it. I still wanted to be under the covers. So I sorted and packed the roomful of Bundy files and left the firm. I received an order from Judge Zloch at that time entitled "Suggestion of Death," canceling his

pending proceeding in the Chi Omega case, "it having been represented to the Court that the petitioner has been executed." On my last
day, Bill Haigmeier, the FBI agent who had interviewed Ted behind
my back, sat with me amid the boxes of briefs and news clippings and
notes and letters and asked me more questions. He did not want to let
go. I finally gave him the FBI questionnaire for serial murderers that
Ted had completed and enhanced for him but that I had confiscated.
There was no reason to withhold it now, except that it was another
piece of evidence of how Ted was the very definition of heartless evil.
And I still did not want to know that, to have to face it by others
knowing it.

When I finally could, I watched the videotape of Ted's interview
with the Reverend Doctor James Dobson, which had occurred on Ted's
last afternoon. My meeting with him that same day came flooding back
to me. It was the same Ted, the same hesitant voice and furtive eye
contact, the same self-conscious face, the same washed-out yellow
T-shirt. He was sincere in wanting to get his message across about the
dangers of violent pornography: He had always wanted to do something
about it, to make people realize the part it played in creating him and
other violent offenders. He had tried to encourage the FBI to stake out
adult movie houses and follow the patrons as they left. He was certain—from what he had felt and done, and from what other men on
death row had told him about their own behavior—that the men who
preyed on women were there.

Ted had been bound and determined to make that tape with Dobson. Even though it was to be broadcast only after his death, I had
asked Ted to do me one favor, as his lawyer, and to not discuss the
Florida crimes, just in case we got a stay of execution at the very last
minute. On the tape, Dobson asks him about the murder of Kimberly
Leach. Ted hesitates and glances around, deciding what to do. I love
that moment. I'm sorry, that sounds chirpy, like being "very happy"
about a stay of execution for the murderer of innocent victims. But I
love to see Ted struggling with my instructions, deciding whether to
restrain himself or do as he pleases, assert control. He finally chokes
out that he can't talk about it, though he'd like to.

That few seconds of film is Ted's gift to me. The Reverend Dobson
interprets his hesitation as overwhelming remorse.

That was my gift to Ted.

STATE OF FLORIDA

OFFICE of VITAL STATISTICS

AMENDED
2-1-89

CERTIFICATE OF DEATH
FLORIDA

LOCAL FILE NO. 4

1. DECEDENT'S NAME (First, Middle, Last)			2. SEX
THEODORE	ROBERT	BUNDY	Male

3. DATE OF DEATH (Month, Day, Year)	4. SOCIAL SECURITY NUMBER	5a. AGE-Last Birthday (years)	5b. UNDER 1 YEAR		5c. UNDER 1 Day
January 24, 1989	533-44-4655	42	Months	Days	Hours	Minutes

6. DATE OF BIRTH (Month, Day, Year)	7. BIRTHPLACE (City and State or Foreign Country)	8. WAS DECEDENT EVER IN US ARMED FORCES? (Yes or No)
November 24, 1946	Burlington, Vermont	No

9a. PLACE OF DEATH (Check only one; see instructions on other side)

HOSPITAL: [ ] Inpatient [ ] ER/Outpatient [ ] DOA OTHER: [ ] Nursing Home [ ] Residence [X] Other (Specify) Inmate	9b. INSIDE CITY LIMITS? (Yes or No) No

9c. FACILITY NAME (If not institution, give street and number)	9d. CITY, TOWN, OR LOCATION OF DEATH	9e. COUNTY OF DEATH
Florida State Prison	Starke	Bradford

10a. DECEDENT'S USUAL OCCUPATION	10b. KIND OF BUSINESS/INDUSTRY	11. MARITAL STATUS - Married, Never Married, Widowed, Divorced (Specify)	12. SURVIVING SPOUSE (If wife, give maiden name)
Student	College	Married	Carol Boone

13a. RESIDENCE - STATE	13b. COUNTY	13c. CITY, TOWN, OR LOCATION	13d. STREET AND NUMBER
Florida	Bradford	Starke	Florida State Prison - HW.16

13e. INSIDE CITY LIMITS? (Yes or No)	13f. ZIP CODE	14. WAS DECEDENT OF HISPANIC OR HAITIAN ORIGIN? (Specify No or Yes - If yes, specify Haitian, Cuban, Mexican, Puerto Rican, etc.)	15. RACE — American Indian, Black, White, etc. Specify.	16. DECEDENT'S EDUCATION (Specify only highest grade completed) Elementary-Secondary (0 - 12)	College (1 - 5)
No	32091	[X] No	White		5

17. FATHER'S NAME (First, Middle, Last)	18. MOTHER'S NAME (First, Middle, Maiden Surname)
John C. Bundy	Louise Cowell

19a. INFORMANT'S NAME (Type/Print)	19b. MAILING ADDRESS (Street and Number or Rural Route Number, City or Town, State, Zip Code)
Paul Decker	P.O. Box 747, Starke, Florida 32091

20a. METHOD OF DISPOSITION	20b. PLACE OF DISPOSITION (Name of cemetery, crematory, or other place)	20c. LOCATION — City or Town, State
[ ] Burial [X] Cremation [ ] Removal from State [ ] Donation [ ] Other (Specify)	Colonial Crematory	Gainesville, Florida

21a. SIGNATURE OF FUNERAL SERVICE LICENSEE OR PERSON ACTING AS SUCH	21b. LICENSE NUMBER (of Licensee)	21c. NAME AND ADDRESS OF FACILITY
Richard E. Williams	1681	Williams-Thomas Funeral Home, 404 N. Main Street, Gainesville, Florida 32601

22a. To the best of my knowledge, death occurred at the time, date and place and due to the cause(s) as stated. (Signature and Title) ▶	23a. On the basis of examination and/or investigation, in my opinion death occurred at the time, date and place and due to the cause(s) and manner as stated. (Signature and Title)

22b. DATE SIGNED (Mo., Day, Yr.)	22c. HOUR OF DEATH	23b. DATE SIGNED (Mo., Day, Yr.) NOVEMBER 24, 1989	23c. HOUR OF DEATH 7:16
	M		

22d. NAME OF ATTENDING PHYSICIAN IF OTHER THAN CERTIFIER (Type or Print)	23d. PRONOUNCED DEAD (Mo., Day, Yr.) NOVEMBER 24, 1989	23e. PRONOUNCED DEAD AT (Hour) 7:16

24. NAME AND ADDRESS OF CERTIFIER (PHYSICIAN, MEDICAL EXAMINER) (Type or Print)
WILLIAM F. HAMILTON, M.D. 274 SW 5 Street Office of the Medical Examiner Gainesville, Florida 32601

25a. SUBREGISTRAR - SIGNATURE AND DATE	25b. LOCAL REGISTRAR - SIGNATURE	25c. DATE REGISTERED
Sharon D. Covington, 1-24-89	Connie H. Werges Chief Deputy	1-24-89

26. PART I. Enter the diseases, injuries, or complications that caused the death. Do not enter the mode of dying, such as cardiac or respiratory arrest, shock, or heart failure. List only one cause on each line.

IMMEDIATE CAUSE (Final disease or condition resulting in death) ➔

a. ELECTROCUTION
DUE TO (OR AS A CONSEQUENCE OF):

Sequentially list conditions, if any, leading to immediate cause (Disease or injury that initiated events resulting in death) LAST.

b.
DUE TO (OR AS A CONSEQUENCE OF):

c.
DUE TO (OR AS A CONSEQUENCE OF):

PART II. Other significant conditions contributing to death but not resulting in the underlying cause given in Part I.	27a. WAS AN AUTOPSY PERFORMED? (Yes or No) YES	27b. WERE AUTOPSY FINDINGS AVAILABLE PRIOR TO COMPLETION OF CAUSE OF DEATH? (Yes or No) YES	28. CASE REFERRED TO MEDICAL EXAMINER? (Yes or No) YES

29. IF FEMALE, WAS THERE A PREGNANCY IN THE PAST 3 MONTHS? [ ] YES [ ] NO	30a. IF SURGERY IS MENTIONED IN PART I or II ENTER CONDITION FOR WHICH IT WAS PERFORMED	30b. DATE OF SURGERY (Mo., Day, Yr.)

31. PROBABLE MANNER OF DEATH [ ] (Specify) Accident, suicide or homicide; or undetermined. HOMICIDE	32a. DATE OF INJURY (Month, Day, Year) JAN. 24, 1989	32b. TIME OF INJURY 7:07 A M	32c. INJURY AT WORK? (Yes or No) NO	33. DESCRIBE HOW INJURY OCCURRED EXECUTION OF DEATH SENTENCE
	32d. PLACE OF INJURY - At home, farm, street, factory, etc (Specify) DEATH HOUSE	32f. LOCATION (Street and Number or Rural Route Number, City or Town, State) HIGHWAY 16 FLORIDA STATE PRISON PO BOX 747, Starke, Fl.		

HRS Form 512, 89 (Obsoletes Previous Editions)

THIS IS A CERTIFIED TRUE AND CORRECT COPY OF THE OFFICIAL RECORD ON FILE IN THIS OFFICE

BY: Connie H. Werges

OLIVER H. BOORDE
State Registrar

HRS FORM 1564A (8-88)

CERTIFICATION OF VITAL RECORD

EPILOGUE

The day before Ted was executed, George Bush took office as president, touching a chord within the public's consciousness with his promise of a "kinder, gentler America." The death penalty—reinstituted in the United States in 1976, yet outlawed in most other Westernized nations—is part of the crueler, harsher America it seems we have become. It is not a tragedy that Ted Bundy is dead—we all die some day. It is not a tragedy that Ted died for his crimes—he was not falsely accused. But it is a tragedy that the state of Florida killed him. The deliberate taking of life with forethought is the crime for which society reserves its harshest punishment, its most complete condemnation. Yet that describes capital punishment exactly. Ted's death certificate accurately lists the cause of his death as "HOMICIDE." It was my responsibility to stop Ted's execution. But the entire time I had the case I felt a sick feeling of blasphemy for even participating in the discussion. Death is different. It is not just another punishment on the continuum, it is not merely one step harsher than life in prison without parole. It is trampling on God's territory, just as Ted did.

Halfway through this case the state of Florida claimed that attempting to execute Ted Bundy had already cost the state six million dollars. Life in prison—which the state had agreed to in the plea bargain and which the Chi Omega trial jury almost recommended even after finding him guilty—would have cost less than one million dollars. For the happenstance of Ted blowing his own plea bargain while on drugs secretly provided by the jail's physican, and Judge

327

Cowart erroneously instructing the Chi Omega jury that it had to break its 6–6 deadlock for life, more than five million dollars more of taxpayer money was spent. That's five million dollars that could otherwise have gone for schools, or roads, or effective law enforcement. The execution of Ted Bundy did not make the streets safer. He was not deterred by the death penalty and neither will other psychopathic killers like him be deterred.

And it wasn't only the state that paid. By the time Ted Bundy was executed, the less than one hundred partners of Wilmer, Cutler & Pickering had—reluctantly, but unsparingly—spent $1.5 million on his case. That's $1.5 million the firm otherwise would have allocated to providing other types of legal services free of charge.

What did we the public get for all that money and lost opportunity? A sense of revenge, an illusion of justice, entertainment of the lowest order. The opportunity to bring children to the grounds of Florida State Prison, hang frying pans around their necks, and teach them to chant "Fry, Ted, Fry." The opportunity for local taverns to celebrate with a "Bundy Barbecue." The opportunity for otherwise decent and circumspect people to wave and smile with glee at a passing hearse without feeling embarrassed or ashamed.

Author and attorney Polly Nelson

INDEX